18TH-CENTURY
GERMAN PORCELAIN

Portrait of Augustus III. Modelled by J. J. Kändler.
Meissen. *c.* 1740.

[*Frontispiece*

18TH-CENTURY
GERMAN PORCELAIN

by George Savage

*Macht doch den zweiten Fensterladen auch auf,
damit mehr Licht hereinkomme*

GOETHE

SPRING BOOKS · LONDON

FOR DIANA

Originally published 1958 by
Barrie and Rockliff Ltd.
© Copyright George Savage 1958
This edition published 1967 by Spring Books
Drury House · Russell Street · London WC2

Printed in Great Britain by
Fletcher & Son Ltd, Norwich
and bound by
Richard Clay (The Chaucer Press) Ltd, Bungay, Suffolk

PREFACE

DESPITE the interest which collectors and students in both England and the United States have always taken in the porcelain of Germany, information in English has been singularly scarce. Particularly does this apply to the smaller factories, about which little is available, although their work is often seen and frequently collected.

In some ways the body of information which exists in German is larger and more precise than in the case of comparable English factories. I cannot pretend that the present work is as comprehensive as I should have liked to make it, but space and time are both finite,[1] and to bring this book within reasonable compass, I have had to select from a vast amount of source material what I consider to be the most useful and necessary information.

I have recounted the history of each factory, when sufficient records exist, at some length. Not only does this help to infuse life into what might otherwise have degenerated into a tedious description of objects which, however fascinating in themselves, would have been unrelated to their historical background, but the material thus provided often helps to resolve difficult problems of attribution.

[1] *vide* the late Professor Albert Einstein.

vii

The collector of such things possesses much more than a mere assemblage of porcelain. He is also heir to the joys, the sorrows and the struggles of the men who made it. He can enter vicariously into their lives, and hold in his hand the veritable record of triumphs over odds, of successes and failures, of painstaking research and astounding luck, of frauds, larcenies and subornation. This is the history ignored by the historian who thinks in terms of battlefields and council chambers.

Few people can be sufficiently detached to see Germany in perspective, and the colourful pageant of its history is too little known outside the country itself. It has been truly said that in human affairs there are no rewards and punishments, only consequences, and the tragedies of the last few decades ought not to be allowed to obscure the value of the German contribution to European culture.

Porcelain is not only an art, it is also a series of social documents of the first importance, and this is no less true of the porcelain of Germany than of other countries. The pages which follow will, I hope, provide for the general reader a picture of life in the eighteenth century a little more viable than the pages of the average historical treatise.

I should like to take this opportunity of recording my indebtedness to such mentors as Friedrich H. Hofmann, Gustav Pazaurek, Robert Schmidt, and many other writers from whose pages I have profited, and whose works have been consulted frequently in the preparation of this book. Their work has been done with typical German thoroughness, and often the greatest difficulty has been to decide what to select from the vast amount of material which their researches have made available. To them I must refer my reader who wishes to pursue the subject in greater detail. It is unfortunate that, except for a single volume by Robert Schmidt, no translations are available, but the titles are listed in the Bibliography.

I owe a particular and lasting debt of gratitude to Diana Imber

for her assistance in preparing this volume for the press. Not only
has she spent many hours helping me with the necessary research,
and in collating the information gained, but she has reinforced my
serious linguistic deficiencies with a fluent command of the
language which was never at a loss for the exact turn of phrase in
translating a difficult passage. She has also made many suggestions
of the utmost value, and whatever merit this book may have it
owes largely to her untiring assistance.

I should also like to thank the Librarian and staff of Eastbourne
Public Library, and the various German libraries who went to
endless trouble to find scarce and out-of-print works for me,
which helped in no small measure to remedy the deficiencies of
my own library.

For valuable assistance with illustrations, and in other ways, my
thanks are especially due to the Earl of Shrewsbury and Waterford,
Lady Patricia Lennox-Boyd, Mr. and Mrs. Henry Stern, Mrs.
C. B. Stout, Señor José M. Mayorga, Mr. and Mrs. K. A. L.
Rhodes, W. R. B. Young Esq. and Dr. F. S. Lacks. To Mr. H.
Weinberg and the Antique Porcelain Company I am indebted,
not only for photographs, but for many opportunities to study
examples in their magnificent collection of German porcelain.
My gratitude is due to Mr. William A. Coolidge for the trouble
he took to get me a colour transparency of his superb portrait of
Augustus III which is the frontispiece to this volume, and to Mr.
Weinberg for arranging this for me.

My thanks are also due to the following museums for their
assistance in providing material for illustrations: the British
Museum, the Victoria and Albert Museum, the Museum of Fine
Arts, Boston, the Metropolitan Museum of Art, New York, the
Museum für Kunsthandwerk, Frankfurt-am-Main, the Bayerisches Nationalmuseum, the Staatliche Kunstsammlungen, Cassel,
the Hastings Museum and Art Gallery, the Hove Museum and
Art Gallery, and the Wellington Museum, Apsley House. I am
especially grateful to Miss M. Greenshields and the Trustees of the

Cecil Higgins Museum, Bedford, for the many photographs provided from this superb collection.

It has not been possible to acknowledge the source of each object on the various plates, but a list showing the whereabouts of the items illustrated is to be found on p. xi.

GUESTLING,
  SUSSEX   JULY, 1957

ACKNOWLEDGEMENTS

Antique Porcelain Co. Ltd.: 10, 18, 19 (*a* and *b*), 29, 38 (*a* and *b*),
   39 (*a*), 50, 75, 103 (*a*)
Bayerisches Nationalmuseum: 78
Boston Museum of Fine Arts: 2 (*a*, *b*, *c* and *d*), 4 (*b* and *c*), 6 (*a* and
   b), 7 (*a*, *b* and *c*), 9 (*a*), 12, 22 (*d*), 30 (*b*), 31, 57, 60 (*a*),
   63 (*a*), 84 (*a*, *b* and *c*), 97 (*b*), 99 (*a*), 103 (*b*), 114 (*c* and *d*),
   115 (*c*), 128 (*a* and *b*)
British Museum: 6 (*c*), 8 (*a*), 9 (*b*) 15 (*b*), 25 (*a* and *b*), 41 (*a*), 49
   (*a*, *b* and *c*), 53 54, (*b*), 63 (*c*), 64 (*b*), 66 (*b*), 67 (*a*), 70, 71,
   72 (*a* and *b*), 76, 81, 92 (*a*), 97 (*d*), 98, 99 (*b*), 100, 117 (*a*),
   120 (*b*), 127 (*b*), 129, 130 (*a* and *b*), 133, 135 (*a*), 136 (*c*),
   137, 138, 142 (*a* and *b*), 144 (*a*, *c* and *d*), 145, 147 (*a* and *b*),
   150 (*a*)
Cecil Higgins Museum, Bedford: 16 (*c*), 22 (*a*), 23, 26 (*b*), 28 (*a*),
   30 (*a*), 35 (*a*), 37 (*b* and *c*), 39 (*b*), 40 (*a* and *b*), 41 (*b* and *c*),
   45, 46 (*b*), 47, 48 (*a*, *b*, *c* and *d*), 52 (*a* and *c*), 55, 56, 58 (*a*),
   59 (*b*), 65, 66 (*a*), 69 (*a* and *b*), 73 (*d*), 79, 80, 87 (*a* and *b*),
   89 (*a*), 91, 101 (*a*), 102 (*c*), 110 (*a*), 116 (*b*), 119, 121 (*a* and
   b), 122, 124, 131 (*a* and *b*), 134 (*a*), 140, 141 (*a*)
William A. Coolidge, Esq.: *Frontispiece*, 24
Hastings Museum: 4 (*a*), 63 (*b*), 83 (*a*), 16 (*b*), 104 (*a*), 109,
   126 (*b*)

Historisches Museum, Frankfurt-am-Main: 96

Hove Museum and Art Gallery: 32 (*a* and *b*)

Mr. and Mrs. Sigmund J. Katz: 149 (*a* and *b*), 150 (*b*)

Dr. and Mrs. F. S. Lacks: 22 (*b*), 141 (*b*), 146 (*a* and *b*)

Lady Patricia Lennox-Boyd: 11 (*a* and *c*)

Señor José M. Mayorga: 62 (*c*), 64 (*a*), 82 (*a* and *b*), 84 (*d*), 85, 110
      (*c*), 111 (*a*), 118

Metropolitan Museum of Art, New York: 5, 13 (*c*), 15 (*a*), 67 (*b*),
      68 (*a* and *b*), 77 (*a* and *b*), 90, 101 (*c*), 110 (*b*), 120 (*a*),
      123 (*a*, *b* and *c*), 125, 135 (*b*), 136 (*b*), 139 (*b*), 141 (*c*)

Museum für Kunsthandwerk, Frankfurt-am-Main: 3, 17, 34, 61

K. A. L. Rhodes, Esq., M.A., LL.B.: 52 (*b* and *d*), 58 (*b*), 59 (*a*), 60
      (*b*), 62 (*a*), 83 (*b*), 92 (*c*), 97 (*a* and *c*), 106, 114 (*a* and *b*),
      115 (*a* and *b*), 116 (*a*), 128 (*c*), 134 (*b*)

The Earl of Shrewsbury and Waterford: 59 (*c*), 87 (*c*), 92 (*b*),
      101 (*d*), 105 (*b*), 113 (*c*)

Staatliche Kunstsammlungen, Cassel: 127 (*a*)

Mr. and Mrs. Henry Stern: 4 (*d*), 113 (*a* and *b*), 117 (*b*), 127 (*c* and *d*)

Mrs. C. B. Stout: 8 (*b*), 11 (*b* and *d*), 13 (*a*, *b* and *d*), 14, 26 (*a*),
      35 (*b*), 42, 43 (*a*, *b* and *c*), 44, 54 (*a*), 73 (*c*), 89 (*b*), 94 (*a* and
      c), 95 (*b*), 101 (*b*), 112 (*b*), 136 (*a*)

Victoria and Albert Museum: 1, 20, 27, 33, 36, 73 (*a* and *b*), 74, 86
      (*a*), 88, 95 (*c*), 102 (*a*), 107, 112 (*a*), 132, 139 (*a*), 143, 144
      (*b*), 148, 151, 152 (*a*) and (*b*)

Wellington Museum, Apsley House: 108

W. R. B. Young, Esq.: 46 (*a*), 51 (*a* and *c*), 62 (*b* and *d*), 77 (*c*),
      93 (*a* and *b*), 94 (*b*), 95 (*a*), 117 (*c*), 126 (*a*)

CONTENTS

ILLUSTRATIONS

INTRODUCTION

THE subject of this book is German porcelain, not the porcelain of Germany. In the eighteenth century, Germany as a political entity did not exist. It is essential, therefore, to preface this work with some brief remarks about the area which is to be discussed.

The Holy Roman Empire, despite Voltaire's gibe that it was neither Holy, nor Roman, nor an Empire, acted as a cement that, for centuries, held together the German states against assaults from outside. It began to decay finally with the Reformation and the Counter-Reformation. By the time of the Peace of Augsburg in 1555 Protestantism and Catholicism were given equality with each other, and this led directly to the Thirty Years' War in which the Empire was a battle-ground. When the Peace of Westphalia was concluded in 1648, most of the Empire was no more than a collection of impoverished small states and oligarchies ruled by dukes, electors, prince-bishops, and the like. These were approximately equivalent to the great land-owning peers of England, and, until 1701, none of them had so much as the title of King.

The Thirty Years' War was one of the most destructive which Europe had known until that time. Conducted largely by armies of professional soldiers, whose pay, more often than not, was in arrear, towns and villages were pillaged and the armies became little more than casually-disciplined bands of brigands. Germany was completely devastated, and the armies were followed by large bands of starving camp-followers who quarrelled and fought over the loot for bare survival.

It was almost a century before the destruction let loose on the German people by these religious wars was finally repaired, and the concentration of power gradually fell into the hands of Prussia and Austria. Between 1740 and 1763 there were the Wars of Succession between Frederick the Great of Prussia and Maria Theresa, Empress of Austria. These culminated in the Seven Years' War, started in 1756 by Frederick's invasion of Saxony. Prussia (assisted, at first, by England) became the principal German state after many vicissitudes, and its victory and subsequent hegemony drew the other German states together.

A period of relative prosperity followed until the French Revolution, which caused consternation among the Princes of Germany. Frederick William II of Prussia decided to support the French King. This disastrous step led to a fresh series of wars in which the campaigns of Napoleon Bonaparte once more made Germany a battlefield, and the various states and duchies were manipulated to suit his personal ambitions and political necessities.

The unity of Germany was not assured until the uprising of 1848 when a series of liberal measures were forced on to the governments of the smaller states. This was followed by the accession to the Prussian throne in 1861 of William I, and the subsequent appointment of Bismarck to the premiership. By 1867 only Bavaria, Baden and Württemberg, the Catholic states of the south, were outside the union, and these entered the Confederation during the surge of patriotic feeling which followed the successes of the Franco-Prussian War of 1870.

The factories discussed in this book are situated in an area represented, today, by East and West Germany and Austria, and their work forms a coherent classification linked by a common culture, and derived, for the most part, from a common source— the original factory of Meissen, in Saxony.

To study the art of the eighteenth century without considering the part played by porcelain would be to miss an important factor, and the porcelain of Germany is, without doubt, the most influential of any.

The German factories were fortunate because, for the most part, they had royal patrons who absorbed often spectacular losses for no better reason than the prestige attached to the possession of a porcelain factory. This enabled those responsible for their direction to spend time and money on projects which were not expected to be a commercial success—an enviable position which none of the English factories enjoyed.

If we assess the artistic value of surviving specimens of English porcelain honestly and without prejudice, we are compelled to admit that, in most cases, whatever the merits of the soft porcelain body, the primary inspiration was German, and specifically from the Meissen factory. From 1750 to 1760 hardly a single English figure was unaffected by the work of such modellers as Johann Joachim Kändler. Some of this copying seems to have been completely without understanding. My attention was recently attracted to a photograph of a dog in Staffordshire salt-glazed ware which bore on its collar the initials *MPM*. Of course this was copied from a Meissen model, and the letters proclaim its origin, unrecognized by the Staffordshire potter, since they mean *Meissner Porzellan Manufaktur*.

The porcelain of Meissen in particular has had a peculiar fascination for the English under the misnomer of "Dresden China". Good, indifferently bad, or just plain rubbish—*gut, mittel und auschuss*—the English market has always absorbed it in large quantities. In the 1750's we find Nicholas Sprimont, the proprietor of the Chelsea factory, petitioning against the importing of Meissen porcelain, and at the same time asking Sir Charles Hanbury Williams, Ambassador to the Court of Dresden, to buy some for him to copy. Sir Charles was thrifty, and gave Sprimont permission to copy from his existing collection in England, most of which had probably been given to him by the Count von Brühl, the Minister of Augustus III,[1] so that the German factory was not even paid for the porcelain which supplied Sprimont's modellers with inspiration. During the nineteenth century Meissen was sending porcelain to England by the ton to embellish middle-class china-cabinets—porcelain, for the most part, in such poor taste that it was only outdone by the Victorian complacency of Staffordshire. But, at a time when porcelain had, in every country, fallen from its once high estate, ought we to blame the Germans for showing the same bad taste as that which prevailed throughout Europe? At least, here and there, were some small echoes of former glories.

It would be unfair to the English manufacturer to give the impression that these influences were entirely one-way traffic. Wedgwood's creamware and, to a lesser extent, his jasper-ware, were both extremely popular on the Continent, and influenced a number of German factories. Creamware in particular, by providing a clean, inexpensive earthenware for the rising *bourgeois* class, gave to porcelain as an art an effective death-blow by forcing it into purely commercial channels. Meissen did not recover entirely from this until after the war of 1914-18, when there was some revival of its old artistry and skill under the director, Adolf Pfeiffer, who was aided by such modellers as Paul Scheurich and Max Esser.

Any work dealing with German porcelain must, of necessity, devote a great deal of space to a consideration of the Meissen factory, because it was here that the art of porcelain in Europe was born. In some ways this is a pity, since information in English on the work of Meissen is comparatively easy to come by. It is in information about the other factories—Höchst, Nymphenburg, Frankenthal, Ludwigsburg, and so forth—that English and American students of porcelain are so badly served. Undoubtedly these factories owed much to Meissen. Often they were founded by men who had derived their knowledge and experience from employment at Meissen. Frequently they copied Meissen styles and models without much variation, and with still less

---

[1] Gifts to ambassadors were frequently made.

acknowledgement. But here and there they did original work of importance. One has only to instance the work of Vienna which, to some extent, lies a little outside the main stream; the superb modelling of Franz Anton Bustelli at Nymphenburg who, in his own vein, has never been surpassed; and some of the work of Berlin who took the lead from Meissen at the close of the Seven Years' War in 1763.

The style of work in the eighteenth century falls into three well-defined categories—the baroque, the rococo and the neo-classical. To describe the features of each style so that they will be instantly recognizable is not easy, but examples will be found on Plate 35 (baroque), Plate 61 (rococo), and Plate 107 (neo-classical).

It is usual to say that baroque more or less began with Bernini who designed St. Peter's in Rome, but, fundamentally, the development of the style is symptomatic of the prevailing spirit of the age. It was a swing away from the formal classicism of the earlier period, using the term in its wider sense, towards something more dramatic. El Greco was a baroque artist, and his work not only reveals accentuated and sometimes distorted rhythms, but the whole concept is theatrical, and full of movement and violent contrasts. In the field of ceramics generally this influence was somewhat modified and sometimes overlaid by the adulation of Chinese porcelain, but the figures of Kändler's predecessor, Johann Gottlob Kirchner, show the principal baroque mannerisms far more acutely than those of anyone else. Kändler was a baroque artist, but his work was coloured by a strong sense of naturalism.

The rococo style grew from the baroque. It had its origin in France. The word from which the term is derived, *rocaille*, rock-work or grotto-work, is some indication of its affiliations. A *rocailleur* is a grotto-maker, and some of the earliest English figures in this style had rock-work bases encrusted with shells. Water was a fashionable theme in the early days of rococo which we can see equally in the Swan Service from Meissen and the crayfish salts of Chelsea. The latter are derived from silver originals, and an important part in the origin of the rococo style is sometimes awarded to Juste-Aurèle Meissonier, an architect and *ornemaniste* who was also a master of the Paris Guild of Goldsmiths.

The essential difference between baroque and rococo is that the ornament of the latter lacks symmetry. The baroque *Laub- und Bandelwerk*, a leaf-and strap-work ornament much used on early Meissen and Vienna porcelain (Plate 68), was elaborate but symmetrical. The point is well illustrated by the use of the acanthus leaf. At first sight this classical ornament seems uncompromising enough, and as applied to early Meissen porcelain it is perfectly symmetrical, but a French architectural example of the same leaf during the rococo period has the tip twisted to one side.

Perhaps the distinction may be made clearer by saying that the rococo artist preferred ornament to shape. Baroque figures, despite occasional distorted poses, always have a definite coherent form, to which ornament is completely subsidiary. Rococo figures, on the other hand, although they started somewhat timidly with the addition of a few scrolls to the bases, came eventually to the point where elaborately trellised and curving arbours reduced the figures themselves to subsidiary proportions (Plate 79).

Rococo is often said to be " playful", and I think this describes it well. The Saxon court was fruitful soil for the implantation of a playful rococo. The Prince under whom the Meissen factory was founded—Augustus the Strong—was a spendthrift with an enormous appetite for life. He died in 1733 before the rococo period began. His successor, Augustus III, was indolent, and entirely in the hands of his favourite Minister, the Count von Brühl, who was perhaps incompetent as a statesman although his directorship of Meissen raised the art of porcelain to new heights. Whilst his extravagance with money was hardly calculated to aid the prosperity of Saxony, von Brühl added fresh lustre to the royal factory.

In 1748 the town of Pompeii was discovered beneath some vineyards, and the neighbouring town of Herculaneum had been found a little while before. Both were situated on the shores of the Bay of Naples, and had been completely buried in an eruption of Vesuvius in A.D. 79. Systematic investigation of the sites, however, was not begun until 1755. As the old streets and roofless houses were brought to light, enthusiasm grew. The volcanic ashes had helped to preserve the remains of the town, and even of some of the inhabitants, by encasing them in a kind of plaster. This interest in the ancient world received additional impetus from the publication of books dealing with classical antiquities, notably those by the Comte de Caylus and by Sir William Hamilton, husband of Nelson's mistress. From Germany Johann Joachim Winckelmann, the historian of ancient art, visited both Pompeii and Herculaneum in 1758, and again in 1762, and published the result of his studies. He had, in 1755, been given a pension by Augustus III to enable him to prosecute his studies in Italy.

Winckelmann's work was eagerly read by Goethe who was greatly influenced by it, but the fashion for classical art was presently joined to a sentimental vein brought to the surface by Goethe himself. In 1774 he wrote *Die Leiden des jungen Werthers* (*The Sorrows of Young Werther*), a narrative suggested by the suicide of a fellow-student at Leipzig University who shot himself whilst possessed by a hopeless passion for the wife of another man. This novel became such an instantaneous success throughout Europe that it obviously merely crystallized existing ideas. It was, in fact, an eighteenth-century equivalent to the twentieth-century best seller, and the comparison is apt because its intellectual content was on a similar plane, although this was disguised to some extent by the author's particular genius. Its effect was electric. Young men and women gave way to imaginary sorrows in imitation of Werther, and men committed suicide with a copy of *Werther* in hand. The book opened floodgates of sentimentality which can well be seen in later figures and groups from Meissen by Michel-Victor Acier, whilst Werther and Lotte were used as subjects for porcelain painting.[1] This perverted the essential

[1] See Plate 33.

simplicity of the neo-classical style by complicating it with false emotions. It led, in one way or another, to the excesses of the German Romantic school, and to the degeneration of the arts in Victorian England from which we are at last beginning to emerge.

The neo-classical style was unsatisfactory when translated into terms of porcelain. It led to attempts to make porcelain figures which would be small imitations of marble statues. To do this, two of the greatest charms of porcelain were deliberately discarded—its glaze and its colouring. But the idea was based on a false assumption. The artists who favoured "biscuit" (or unglazed) porcelain did not realize that the statues of classical antiquity had been coloured. Owing to the effect of burial these were always recovered in an uncoloured state, and it was thought that this was how they had appeared originally. But both the Greeks and the Romans coloured their statuary, such things as eyes being frequently inlaid in addition, and it was the custom to do so until Renaissance times. The white and uninteresting marble surface existed as a quality of ancient statuary only in the mind of the eighteenth-century neo-classicist.

In this sense, then, either baroque or rococo are more satisfactory as styles for the manufacture of porcelain than neo-classicism. The introduction of the latter effectively killed in Europe both the art of porcelain and the fashion for it. These were effectively interred by Josiah Wedgwood. Both his creamware and the jasper-ware translated well into the new style, and they were an instantaneous success on the Continent as well as in England. Despite attempts to revive the art of porcelain by resuscitating the eighteenth-century rococo style, it has never since come to life with the same vigour. At the present time taste prefers the fine stonewares of the Chinese Sung dynasty when the emphasis was on form and the colour of the glaze. Porcelain, to a considerable extent, depends on the quality of the painted decoration, and it is hardly likely that work of this kind could become a commercial possibility today. The craftsmen no longer exist, and the cost would be prohibitive.

The characteristics of these styles in porcelain are fairly easy to recognize. The baroque style is limited to the earlier work of Meissen and Vienna, since the other factories were founded after the fashion for rococo had become established.

Figures of the baroque period can often be recognized by their bases. Some, such as the early seated figures of Chinamen (the so-called " Pagoda " figures) from Meissen, do not have a base at all. Others have a square base, and some, of which the figure of St. Nepomuk by Kirchner is an example, have an architectural base for moulded or painted ornament (Plates 3 and 34).

Later, when the transition to rococo first becomes evident, bases were flat with rounded corners and small applied flowers, although the architectural base was still used, as may be seen from a figure of a Freemason modelled by Kändler about 1740 (Plate 48c). The year 1745 saw the first tentative ornament of the base in a form which was a recognizable forerunner of the rococo scroll. The scrolls, however, were slight, and can only be seen in rare instances at this time. The first employment of well-defined scrolls appears about 1750. Whilst the use of these scrolls was kept within bounds at Meissen, Nymphenburg— influenced by Bustelli—allowed them to go beyond the base to become an elaborate arbour which was often trellised and which frequently dwarfed the figures. Much the same thing happened at Frankenthal under the two modellers by the name of Lück (Plates 79 and 100).

The neo-classical style was preceded by the transitional style of Louis-Seize (Plate 63c). This inclined to the neo-classical severity, whilst retaining elements of the rococo. But the tendency to severity increased gradually, and the bases later became oval or circular in shape, often with a border of impressed classical or formal ornament. Also to be noticed is a " natural " representation of the ground, appropriately coloured, as with some figures from Höchst by Melchior of the early 1770's (Plate 92a). The use of floral and leafy swags, and masks of classical derivation, can

EGP—C

also be seen. Truncated columns, and similar architectural ornament, were used as points about which figures were grouped.

The baroque style in service-ware can best be seen in the early work of Meissen, and of Vienna during the du Paquier period (Plate 6c). Both porcelain and stoneware of the first period at Meissen, from 1712 to 1720, show the style very effectively when the derivation is not oriental. At a slightly later date such things as the *bouillon* or cream-pots on three paw feet are typically baroque (Plate 22b), although they were eventually adapted to the rococo style by the addition of a knop of applied flowers and twig ornament instead of the earlier formal knop. The tall slender cup is also baroque, as well as the coffee-pot with the handle in the shape of the letter " S " or of a script " T ". Slightly more elaborate handles, and a bird's head spout, belong to the same period, and many of the tea-pots have a squat and flattened shape (Plate 23). The baroque style is not so frequently seen in service-ware because of the many derivations from oriental porcelain of one kind or another.

The development of the rococo style shows itself in the adoption of the floral knop, and handles based on twigs and stems. These knops were often fragile and delicate, and can sometimes be seen in the form of fruit with leaves. European flowers of all kinds became more popular as decoration as the years advanced, more or less replacing oriental derivations, and plates in the form of leaves were not uncommon, as well as tureens modelled as animals, fruits and vegetables. Moulded ornament became popular, even, as with the Swan Service from Meissen, spreading across the surface of the plate in a way which left little or no room for painted decoration. Occasionally painted decoration became an integral part of a piece, plates of leaf form, for instance, being decorated with the ribs and veining, although a few small and scattered sprays of flowers usually appear between the veins.

Vases, too, became much more elaborately encrusted with ornament. This reached its height at Meissen in the *Schneeballen-vasen*, the surface of which is literally covered with applied

guelder roses. These vases were first made for Louis XV, and
bear his portrait in relief in addition to the sun immediately above.
A set of vases by Eberlein—later copied at Chelsea—symbolized
the seasons, and have *putti* in various places, some at the base and
some at the shoulders, as well as the attributes of the seasons
liberally applied.

The neo-classical style is characterized by much severity of line.
Coffee-pots become straight-sided, and the handles are an affair of
straight lines and angles. Eventually, even the scattered flowers
disappear, leaving the surface a plain white with a central painting
of topographical landscape, or a piece of book illustration (*Werther*
is an example) surrounded by a formal symmetrical border. Such
grounds as gold stripes on white or blue are not uncommon.

Whilst service-ware of all kinds was made in great variety,
articles in porcelain were not limited to the more conventional
kinds, especially during the rococo period, but invaded realms
which had hitherto been the province of other materials. Small
items of jewellery, such as ear-pendants, are an example. Inkstands and writing sets are not an uncommon survival, although
they are rarely complete. They had ink-bottles, sand-boxes, quill-
holders, and, quite often, a hand-bell.

Among the smaller items which were often elaborately painted
were boxes of all kinds—needle-cases, *étuis*,[1] tooth-pick cases,
patch-boxes, scent-bottles, snuff-boxes and so forth. Sometimes
these were made in the form of such things as asparagus sticks,
little *putti*, and in many other ways. The smoker was catered for
by tobacco boxes, pipe-bowls and tobacco stoppers. Tobacco
boxes were made in three different sizes, and were often expensive
because of the quality of the painting. They were frequently used
as royal gifts, and bear portraits of the ruler. Others have coats of
arms, scenes of gallantry, landscapes, bouquets and so forth. Many
boxes were mounted in copper, silver, silver-gilt and, finest of all,
in gold. Fashion decreed, too, that walking canes should have a

---

[1] The *étui* was a case containing a number of small implements, such as folding scissors,
knives, etc. They were made during the eighteenth century in a variety of materials.

porcelain handle, and these were often of extremely high quality. Modellers of the calibre of Franz Anton Bustelli did not despise modelling for such purposes.

Clock-cases and watch-stands were common and often freely ornamented with rococo scrolls, figures and applied ornament of this kind. The fashion for *ormolu* mounting was joined to that for porcelain, and delicately modelled porcelain flowers were added to metal stalks and foliage. These flowers were a particular speciality of the Frankenthal factory.

The bedchamber was furnished with wash-basins and ewers, soap-dishes, toilet boxes, and the *veilleuse*, or *réchaud*, intended for heating food during the night, an example of which appears on Plate 85. Such necessary conveniences as the chamber-pot and the *bourdaloue* were sometimes decorated with care and skill sufficient to make them cabinet specimens today.

Table-services had everything which could possibly be required, including handles for knives and forks, as well as elaborate centre-pieces and things which were more purely decorative. Sweetmeat stands and condiment sets were frequently elaborately modelled and painted. Tea-kettles with spirit lamps and bronze handles were a new ceramic departure.

It seems that it was the fashion at the German courts during the period of the rococo style to take dessert at a separate table which was laid beforehand. For this reason large centre-pieces, with additional figures scattered among the other table appointments, could be set out elaborately. When the rococo period ended, the new styles did not lend themselves to the making of dessert services of this kind.

The centre-pieces were often enormous. A Meissen *Temple of Honour* was in 264 pieces, with no less than seventy-four figures, and it included a representation of Mount Parnassus. A relatively small version of this exists in the Kunstgewerbemuseum at Frankfurt-am-Main (Plate 61).

How elaborate these table decorations became may be deduced from an inventory of 1753 of Count von Brühl's *Konditorei*. This included churches, Italian towers, town houses, peasants' houses, gondolas, basins and bowls for fountains, pedestals, columns, capitals and so forth. Figures were especially designed to fit into the centre-piece, as well as to stand individually. They were also combined with articles for use: a woman seated beside a covered sweetmeat bowl, or a gallant and his lady beside a pierced flower-holder. Figures combined with candle-holders were commonly made, for table use or for the bedchamber.

Sèvres made plaques for ornamenting furniture and sedan chairs, but the fashion was followed to a lesser extent in Germany. Porcelain was, however, used architecturally and for furniture, as at Meissen and Vienna, and such things as porcelain tables and mirror-frames were made, as well as chandeliers. These are now very rare, although nineteenth-century reproductions are to be seen from time to time (Plate 24).

Vases of all kinds were made. They were often in sets of three or five, or in pairs, and were intended for a variety of purposes; for example, those with pierced covers were used for *pot-pourri*—fragrant leaves and herbs to scent the air.

For something like fifty years European porcelain styles were derived almost entirely from Meissen, and almost every Meissen innovation was copied faithfully elsewhere (Plate 111a and b). Much of the earlier Meissen porcelain owes its inspiration to the Orient, and it is not often realized that the porcelain of Japan was at least as influential as that of China. This came mostly from Hizen Province, and was brought to Europe by the Dutch, one of the ports of shipment being Imari, later to give its name to a particular style of decoration.

Because information on this aspect of the import of porcelain is not easy to find, I give the following brief summary of the events of the seventeenth century which led to this position.

The first specimens of oriental porcelain reached Europe by way of Spain and Portugal, and in 1596 the *Itinerario van Jan Huygen van Linschoten* was published, of which the following is an extract: "How they [the Chinese] make porcelain more exquisite than crystal. To tell of the porcelains made there is not to be believed, and those that are exported yearly to India, Portugal, and Nova Hispania, and elsewhere! But the finest are not allowed outside the country on penalty of corporal punishment, but serve solely for the Lords and Governors of the country and are so exquisite that no crystalline glass is to be compared with them. These porcelains are made inland of a certain earth which is very hard which is pounded to pieces or ground, and they leave it to soak in troughs cut out of stone, and when it is well soaked and frequently stirred as milk is churned to make butter they make of that which floats on top the finest work, and after that somewhat lower the coarser, and so on, and they paint them and make of them those figures and likenesses they want, and then they are dried and baked in the kiln.''[1]

Volker refers to the Portuguese carrack, *San Jago*, captured by the Dutch off St. Helena, which was brought as a prize to Middelburg in 1602 and which contained much porcelain. Another, captured in 1604, contained vast quantities of porcelain, of which a dinner service was sold to Henri IV of France. James I of England was also a purchaser. This porcelain was blue and white of the period of the Emperor Wan-li, and, in some measure, events of this kind account for the relatively large quantity of porcelain from this reign which still exists in Europe.

By about 1600 the Portuguese had begun to order from China porcelain made to special designs for European use, and Chinese export porcelain can be said to date from this period.

The first porcelain to arrive in Holland, otherwise than by capture, appears to have come in 1610, with the arrival of the *Roode Leeuw met Pijlen*. This carried almost 10,000 pieces, but by 1614 the *Gelderland* was on its way with 70,000.

The Dutch East India Company arrived in Japan in 1600, and established a trading station at Hirado in 1609. By 1641 they had been granted a monopoly of such trading to the exclusion of other European nations. The maritime enterprise of the Dutch

---

[1] T. Volker, *Porcelain and the Dutch East India Company* (Leiden, E. J. Brill, 1954).

can be judged from the fact that, by 1634, they were importing Chinese porcelain into Japan!

The year 1658 saw what must have been the first export of Japanese porcelain. This was a coarse ware, and was shipped to other far eastern markets in competition with the coarser varieties of Chinese porcelain. The pigments used for decoration were carried from China to Japan in Dutch ships. About the same time we notice the mechanism of trade going into reverse with the dispatch of some models to Cologne and Siegburg on behalf of a Japanese nobleman who apparently liked German stoneware.

Japanese porcelain appears to have arrived in Holland for the first time about 1660, the shipment amounting to 5,500 pieces, and there is a note to the effect that, in the same year, there was an order in hand for 40,000 pieces which were to be made in Hizen, probably at Arita, and by 1662 it was possible to write in a letter from Batavia that " Japanese porcelain is now in better demand in Holland. . . . "

Most of this Japanese export ware came from the kilns of Hizen Province, the greater part from Arita, although a small amount from Kutani (Kaga Province) was also shipped. How much can be judged from the relative scarcity of the latter in Europe.

The earliest shipments were probably of blue and white, very popular at the time, and Japanese blue and white porcelain of the seventeenth century with shapes based on European stoneware and metalwork is not uncommon, although it is too often confused with Chinese wares of the Ch'ien Lung period.

Japanese porcelain did not arrive in Europe in really appreciable quantities, however, until the end of the seventeenth century, when we see the kind of slight, asymmetrical decoration associated with the Sakaida Kakiemon family. The collection at Hampton Court, made by William and Mary, is of this kind, and is said to have been completed by 1694. William, of course, came from Holland as Prince of Orange. It is probable that the first import of porcelain decorated in overglaze enamel colours occurred during the last quarter of the century, and that it replaced blue and white decoration in popularity very speedily. Nevertheless, blue and white continued in demand, and we shall later see that much attention was devoted at Meissen to the attainment of a successful underglaze blue.

It is probable that, on balance, Japanese porcelain was at all times during the eighteenth century more popular than Chinese as a source of decoration. Surviving examples painted in the Kakiemon style are far greater in number than those painted with Chinese motifs. Porcelain derived from the Chinese is, until the latter half of the century, mostly of the *famille rose*, and specimens are scarcer than those in the Japanese style.

At Meissen the purely oriental styles were superseded by European motifs fairly speedily. Somewhere between the two we have the *chinoiserie*—a curious blend of oriental and European motifs—of which a number of examples are shown in the plates (e.g. Plate 11). For the most part these were confined to Meissen and Vienna among the German factories, the others being established at a time when the fashion was waning, although the influence of later artists such as Boucher and Pillement led to figures and groups in the Chinese style (Plates 50 and 100).

The popularity of the *chinoiserie* as a decorative motif was probably due to France, although the Dutch were the earliest in the field. As early as 1658 Cardinal Mazarin had a collection of Chinese porcelain and embroideries. The presence of Chinese silk in Europe was not particularly new, the Romans having imported it from China during the period of the Emperors, when it was known as Coan silk and famed for its semi-transparency. In 1687 it is recorded that the Dauphin had an apartment at Versailles hung with tapestries with Chinese motifs, and it is probable that these things were imported through Holland because the Compagnie Royale de la Chine, which traded with Canton, was not established until 1705.

Numerous works attest to the interest in Chinese art and culture in France. Bouvet's *Etat Présent de la Chine en Figures* was published in 1697, and the plates of the Emperor and his officials were reasonably authentic as to costume. The *Nouvelle Mémoire sur l'Etat Présent de la Chine* of Le Comte, with engraved plates by Edelinck, are somewhat more in the manner of the true *chinoiserie*, being much less true to life and having a stronger fantasy element. The first true *chinoiseries*, however, in France can probably be found in the work of Watteau done for the château of La Muette about 1708.

Somewhat later we have the characteristic work of Boucher, some of which became the inspiration for porcelain figures and groups. An example, taken from his *Suite de Figures Chinoises* of about 1735, is shown on Plate 50.

Boucher was followed by Pillement whose work was engraved for the most part around 1760. The fantasy element in Pillement's work is particularly strong, and he is the last artist of any standing to devote much time to the *chinoiserie*.

German sources are discussed elsewhere at greater length, but one example of derivation from the Chinese which did not touch the German factories is the curious predilection among English potters for the so-called " Mandarin " style, popular at Canton in the latter part of the eighteenth century. These grossly over-crowded and overdecorated scenes epitomize all that is worst in Chinese decoration, and their adoption can only be attributed to a desire rampant among the smaller English manufacturers to give plenty of colour for the money, regardless of quality.

Except for a minor excursion into soft porcelain at Volkstedt, in Thuringia, all German porcelain is of the hard variety, sometimes called true porcelain because of its resemblance to the Chinese material from which it was derived.

Hard porcelain is primarily the result of a fusion under intense heat of white china clay, or kaolin, and a fusible rock, called, by the Chinese, *petuntse*. This rock is a kind of feldspar,[1] and hence is termed "feldspathic". If fired alone, it yields a translucent mass.

---

[1] Sometimes erroneously spelt " felspar ". The origin is to be found in the German *feld*, a field.

By itself, however, it does not possess the necessary cohesiveness to stand the firing process. Nor is it plastic. The usual method of working is to grind it to a fine powder, and then to mix it with clay. The clay, being plastic, enables an article to be shaped by ordinary methods of pottery formation, and it retains this shape during firing. For these reasons the Chinese refer to clay as the "bones" and the rock as the "flesh" of porcelain.

European porcelain-making took two very different directions in the eighteenth century. When Chinese porcelain was first imported into Europe many attempts were made to reproduce it. No exact methods of chemical analysis were available, and the early experimentalists had to judge from physical appearance. The most obvious one was the quality of translucency, and the only translucent material in common use was glass.

Beginning at the end of the sixteenth century, experiments were made in mixing the ingredients of glass with a plastic clay. This yielded a more or less translucent porcelain which was softer than the Chinese, was fired at a lower temperature, and was extremely difficult and temperamental to handle in the kiln. This type of porcelain breaks with a sugary fracture, whereas Chinese porcelain and its derivatives usually break or chip in a similar manner to glass, the sugary appearance being absent.

A few experimentalists recognized the essential difference between the artificial variety and Chinese porcelain, and the Chinese formula was eagerly sought. It was discovered finally by Ehrenfried Walther, the Graf von Tschirnhaus, a nobleman of the Saxon court, and his discoveries were finally adapted to manufacture on a commercial scale at Meissen in Saxony by Johann Friedrich Böttger.

Böttger's first porcelain, however, whilst resembling that of the Chinese fairly closely, was still not true porcelain because the fusible stone was alabaster, a really close approximation being delayed until the adoption of a feldspathic rock some years later. Nevertheless, as I record later, there is some reason for thinking that von Tschirnhaus knew of the part played by the feldspathic rock, and experimented with it. Whether or not alabaster was a compromise introduced for some reason by Böttger alone it is impossible to determine.

Centuries before the birth of Christ, the Assyrians discovered that the addition of tin oxide to a glass-like glaze yielded an opaque white enamel which could be used to cover earthenware bodies. This discovery eventually reached Europe, and led to the achievements of Italian *maiolica*. A flourishing industry for this kind of earthenware (also termed *faïence*) was well established in Germany by the seventeenth century, and the experience thus gained helped to establish the new porcelain industry when manufacture became possible. In many cases, factories for the manufacture of *faïence* were run side by side with porcelain undertakings, and painters worked on both materials. In some cases, there is confusion in the old records between the two, and even now it is not always possible to be certain in some cases whether the term " porcelain " actually refers to *faïence* or porcelain. The wares of Delft, in Holland, were sometimes referred to as "*Hollandsche porselein*", although they were tin-glazed earthenware.

The term " *faïence* " has been the subject of many misconceptions. It is amusing to see that the usually omniscient Fowler (*Modern English Usage*) regards it as a superfluous word which ought to be cast out of the language. Because it is erroneously regarded in numerous standard works of general reference as synonymous with all kinds of pottery and porcelain, I propose to clarify the meaning for the casual reader.

The word has a limited, regional, meaning. It is correctly used to refer to pottery having a glaze made opaque with tin oxide *when it has been made in Germany or France*. The same kind of pottery made in Italy is termed *maiolica*, and in Holland and England, *delft*. The geographical line of demarcation is a little difficult to draw rigidly. It would, in fact, be better to regard the definitions of *maiolica* and *delft* as fixed, and to refer to tin-glazed pottery made elsewhere as *faïence*.

The factories of Germany owe their origin to the inspiration provided by Meissen. A notable feature of the eighteenth-century scene is the wandering workman who, by devious means, acquired the secret of manufacture, and carried it from factory to factory. Some of these men were genuinely in possession of the secret; some had picked up odd scraps of information and believed they had something to sell; others were charlatans and swindlers who had sufficient knowledge to be plausible, and who moved on when they had milked their credulous patrons of all they could get without making closer acquaintance with the state prison. Sometimes they did not move on sufficiently quickly, and there are records of prison sentences meted out freely to workmen who transgressed the regulations intended to keep factory secrets inviolate.

The more important of these migrants are discussed elsewhere in this volume, but, in passing, the names of Christoph Konrad Hunger, Adam Friedrich von Löwenfinck, Joseph Jakob Ringler, Johannes Benckgraff, Nikolaus Paul, and Christian Daniel Busch deserve mention.

Vienna was an early offshoot of Meissen, the successful production of porcelain being due to the subornation of Meissen workmen, but from the date of its inception in 1719 a long period intervenes, and the other German factories were not started until the middle of the century. Although the work of many of these is important in its own right, they owed much to Meissen, and copying of this factory's styles can be seen everywhere in Germany from 1750 onward.

Other influences on German porcelain came from the craft-workers of Augsburg in Bavaria. Augsburg is an ancient city which, during the eighteenth century, was a great centre for goldsmiths' work, enamelling, engraving, and related crafts of all kinds. Engraving on copper was done on a considerable scale, and prints from Augsburg were used extensively by the factories as inspiration for porcelain decoration.

Porcelain during the eighteenth century reflected faithfully the changes in fashion, and the rise and fall of various sections of the community. In particular, the weakening influence of the courts, and the rise of the merchant class—the *bourgeoisie*—can be seen in the mid-century swing away from the eccentricities of baroque and rococo towards a sentimental and less colourful pandering to middle-class virtues.

As I have said previously, German porcelain is very well documented, and although there remain many minor problems of attribution, these are not particularly serious. Most of them are no more than the identification of possible work by *Hausmaler*, the outside decorators who played an important part during the early years of the century. Most German porcelain is well marked, although the customary caution against forged marks applies here as elsewhere.

A few minor factories, such as Bayreuth, Würzburg, Ulm and elsewhere, present problems in attribution which may be resolved in future, but for the most part no such problems as those presented by some early English porcelain are to be found.

Eighteenth-century German porcelain exists in large quantities in England and the United States, although the work of factories other than Meissen has not always received the attention it undoubtedly deserves. At its best it is the finest ever to be made: at its worst it competes on level terms with most other European factories.

1

THE MEISSEN FACTORY

THE most important porcelain factory in Europe is undoubtedly that situated some twelve miles outside Dresden, in Saxony, in the small town of Meissen. The porcelain made here is frequently referred to erroneously as 'Dresden' and, in France, as 'Saxe'. The proper term for the products of what was formerly the royal factory is 'Meissen porcelain', and anything else is inexact and confusing.

Dresden is the principal city of Saxony, and lies on both banks of the River Elbe, the Altstadt (old town) being on the southern side. On the other bank is the Neustadt (new town), which is not, in fact, particularly new, the term merely differentiating between degrees of age. Until the early years of the present century, the two parts were joined by a bridge across the Elbe called the Augustusbrücke, but this has since been replaced by a series of modern bridges.

Dresden has always been one of the cultural centres of Germany, and at one time supported a large foreign colony. It possessed a magnificent library housed in the Japanische Palais, a notable collection of pictures and engravings in the Zwinger, and an important collection of porcelain in the Johanneum Museum.[1]

[1] But see my remarks on page 29 on the question of the present whereabouts of works of art in Germany. Dresden was seriously damaged during the last war.

Meissen, a picturesque city founded in 928, has been called the Saxon Nürnberg because of its winding streets and alleys and old buildings. The two principal buildings are the Cathedral and the Albrechtsburg, a fortress which adjoins it. The latter was built in the fifteenth century by Arnold of Westphalia, and at one time housed the porcelain factory which was removed to its present site in the Triebischtal in 1863.

It was at Dresden that the first true European porcelain was made. Its inception and the discovery of the Chinese secret were both due to the devoted labours of a member of the Saxon court, Ehrenfried Walther, the Graf von Tschirnhaus, with the assistance of an alchemist of somewhat doubtful reputation, Johann Friedrich Böttger. In their task they had the patronage and the financial support of Friedrich August I, Elector of Saxony, better known, perhaps, as Augustus II, King of Poland. His family of 354 children, one of whom later succeeded him as Augustus III, gained him the name of *August der Starke*—Augustus the Strong—and his amours have been amusingly chronicled by Karl Ludwig von Pöllnitz.[1]

The discovery of the porcelain secret has, in the past, been attributed alike to von Tschirnhaus and to Böttger. This aspect of the history of the Meissen factory has not hitherto been discussed at length in English, and because it is important to the student, I have devoted some space to it before passing on to a survey of the later history of the factory and its wares.

The Graf von Tschirnhaus, member of an old Bohemian family, was born in 1651 in Kieslingswalde. He studied at Leiden University (1668–1674) and subsequently undertook a comprehensive tour of Europe which finished in Paris in 1675. Here he was in touch with the Académie Royale des Sciences, and made the acquaintance of the Freiherr Gottfried Wilhelm Leibniz, the mathematician and philosopher, who communicated with many of the most prominent figures in the scientific world of his time, including Sir Isaac Newton.

[1] *La Saxe galant* [sic] (1734).

Some time between 1675 and the end of 1676 von Tschirnhaus appears to have made preliminary investigations into the secret of porcelain manufacture. The course of these experiments is obscure, but it seems to have included an attempt to fuse kaolin by concentrating radiant heat upon it with a concave iron reflecting mirror. The adoption of such a method shows considerable scientific knowledge, but investigations of this kind were proceeding elsewhere in Europe. For example, at the end of 1676, probably in an effort to reinforce the experience gained during the previous year, von Tschirnhaus visited an Italian, Canon Manfred Settala of Milan, who claimed to have found the secret of porcelain manufacture by this method. Von Tschirnhaus continued his journeying during 1677 and 1678, concluding with a visit to Leibniz at Hanover.

He returned to Saxony in 1679, and began to experiment with a copper mirror, including the discoveries made with this instrument in a thesis later read before the Académie Française in 1682. He journeyed home to Kieslingswalde by way of Holland, and no doubt took the opportunity to study the *faïence* kilns of Delft in operation.

By 1689 he had built an even larger mirror with which he intended to melt a variety of highly refractory substances. This later found its way into the museum at Dresden. But metal mirrors were not entirely satisfactory, and considerable advances had been made in grinding and polishing glass mirrors and lenses. Von Tschirnhaus therefore built a glass-house with water-driven grinding and polishing machinery.

As Hofmann[1] so truly remarks, it is evident from this preoccupation with ever-higher temperatures, and the researches into the melting point of various refractory substances, that von Tschirnhaus not only had a definite end in view, and was working systematically towards it, but that he had more than a glimpse of the principles underlying the manufacture of Chinese porcelain. This impression receives reinforcement from the fact that a

[1] *Das Porzellan der europäischen Manufakturen im 18ten Jahrhundert.*

PLATE 1

Portrait of J. F. Böttger.
Meissen. *c.* 1780.

PLATE 2

(a) Judith with the head of Holofernes. Red stoneware. Meissen. 1710–1715.

(b) Head of Emperor Vitellius. Red stoneware. Meissen. c. 1715.

(c) Spouted bottle. Moulded decoration of Oriental derivation. Red stoneware. Meissen. c. 1715.

(d) Vase thrown and turned on the wheel. Red stoneware. Meissen. c. 1715.

PLATE 3

Harlequin from the Italian Comedy. Red stoneware.
Meissen. *c.* 1715.

PLATE 4

(a) Cylindrical tankard. Ground and polished red stoneware with silver mounts.

Meissen. 1710–15.

(b) Chocolate-pot. Brown glazed red earthenware decorated with *chinoiseries* in silver silhouette.

Bayreuth. *c.* 1730.

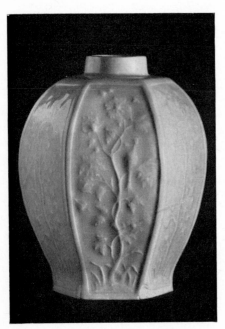

(c) Tea-jar with moulded decoration. Porcelain. Böttger period.

Meissen. *c.* 1715.

(d) Small *chinoiserie* figure. Porcelain.

Meissen. *c.* 1715.

PLATE 5

Pilgrim bottle. Black-glazed stoneware painted with Chinese landscapes.
Meissen. *c.* 1715.

PLATE 6

(a) Pilgrim bottle. Black-glazed
stoneware painted with floral subjects.

Meissen. c. 1715.

(b) Pilgrim bottle. Red stoneware
with applied decoration.

Meissen. c. 1715.

(c) Tea-pot in the form of baroque metal-work. Polished red stoneware.

Meissen. c. 1710.

PLATE 7

(*a*) Cup and saucer decorated with birds in enamel colours.

Meissen. *c.* 1715.

(*b*) Cup and saucer decorated with applied leaves.

Meissen. *c.* 1715.

(*c*) Tea-pot decorated with enamel colours. Porcelain. Böttger period.

Meissen. *c.* 1720.

PLATE 8

(a) Cup and saucer painted with figures and a border of baroque ornament. (Perhaps *Hausmaler* decoration.
Meissen. c. 1720.

(b) Cup and saucer painted with figures after Jacopo Callot.
Meissen. c. 1720.

PLATE 9

(*a*) Bowl decorated with *indianische Blumen* and elements of the banded hedge pattern. Meissen. *c.* 1725.

(*b*) Reverse of two dishes painted in the Kakiemon style, showing incised Johanneum inventory marks. *c.* 1725.

PLATE 10

Service decorated with *chinoiseries* in Höroldt style.
Meissen. *c.* 1730.

PLATE *11*

(*a, left*) Cream-jug decorated with a *chinoiserie*.
Meissen. *c.* 1730.

(*b, above*) Plate painted with a large *chinoiserie* in the
centre, the borders with miniature scenes after
engravings by J. G. Höroldt.
Meissen. *c.* 1730.

(*c, below*) Tea-pot with similar decoration, but
framed with gilt traceries and Böttger's lustre
pigment.
Meissen. *c.* 1730.

(*d, right*) Coffee-pot decorated with *chinoiseries* in
Höroldt style.
Meissen. *c.* 1730.

PLATE 12

Silver-mounted tankard decorated with a *chinoiserie* in Höroldt style.
Meissen. *c.* 1725.

PLATE 13

(*a, left*) Coffee-pot painted with Chinese figures and *indianische Blumen* in the manner of A. F. von Löwenfinck.

Meissen. *c.* 1730–35.

(*b, above*) Tea-pot of *Fond-porzellan* painted with Chinese boys in panels, by A. F. von Löwenfinck.

Meissen. *c.* 1735.

) Plate painted in colours with a fantastic animal nd border of landscape with figures by A. F. von Löwenfinck.

Meissen. *c.* 1735.

(*d*) Plate decorated with a Chinese scene in the manner of Löwenfinck.

Meissen. *c.* 1730.

PLATE 14

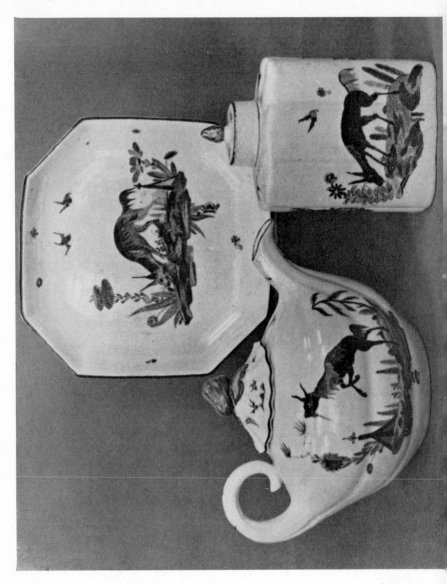

Tea-pot, spoon-tray and tea-jar
decorated with fabulous animals
by A. F. von Löwenfinck.
Meissen. c. 1735.

PLATE 15

(b) Porringer and cover decorated with *chinoiseries*. The handles have the monogram "FA" for Friedrich August—Augustus III. Meissen. 1733.

(a) Tea-jar made for Archbishop-Elector Clemens of Cologne, with coat-of-arms and insignia. C. F. Herold. Meissen. *c.* 1735.

PLATE 16

(a) Cup and saucer decorated with *indianische Blumen*.
Meissen. *c.* 1725.

(b) Cup and saucer decorated with *chinoiseries*.
Meissen. *c.* 1730.

(c) Sugar-box with silver mounts, decorated with *chinoiseries*.
Meissen. *c.* 1725.

considerable part of 1693 and 1694 was spent in chemical researches into the nature of different kinds of earth. Hofmann refers to a letter written by von Tschirnhaus to Leibniz in which he claims to have succeeded, at last, in making porcelain in his laboratory, but it is impossible now to say whether he had, at this time, succeeded in making true porcelain, or whether it was an artificial variety of the kind already being manufactured at St. Cloud.

It is remarkable that, without the guidance of any kind of exact body of chemical knowledge, von Tschirnhaus should have experimented with the melting-point of asbestos, a calcium magnesium silicate, as well as what appears to have been kaolin. It certainly seems possible that he had succeeded in making a passable reproduction of Chinese porcelain, but only with the aid of his burning-mirrors. No kilns had, at that time, been designed in Europe which were capable of reaching the firing temperature of true porcelain—1,450 degrees centigrade—and this aspect was to cause much trouble later. The temperatures attainable by the use of properly adjusted mirrors were so high that in 1694, during the course of experiments in Florence, it is said that a diamond was melted. Certainly this was done during the eighteenth century at the expense of Duke Cosmo of Tuscany !

By 1694 Augustus was taking an interest in the researches, and von Tschirnhaus was given a commission to visit places in Saxony where semi-precious hardstones were to be found. A factory was built in Dresden for the purpose of making artificial agate, and by 1700 Augustus had assisted in the establishment of an improved glass-house which von Tschirnhaus was able to use for the experimental firing of ceramic bodies. Nevertheless, the temperatures essential to fuse true porcelain were much in excess of those needed to manufacture glass, and in 1701 we find him again in Holland, at Delft, doubtless in quest of experience in kiln-design to assist him to provide the necessary degree of heat. About this time, too, von Tschirnhaus appears to have had news of one Herr Preussler of Breslau, who has since been identified with the

Hausmaler Preussler or Preissler, who may have claimed knowledge of porcelain manufacture, and who was certainly painting Chinese porcelain at this time (see chapter 14).

The year 1701 saw von Tschirnhaus in Paris, where he visited the factory at St. Cloud, then making a successful soft porcelain. He was critical of it, saying that none of it was as good as "real porcelain", proving that he was well able to differentiate between the Chinese material and its substitutes. There is also a letter in which the Baron von Canstein describes to a friend a conversation with von Tschirnhaus on the subject of an offer made to Augustus in exchange for help in establishing a porcelain factory. Von Canstein had seen specimens, and was so much impressed by them that he considered seriously offering financial help with the project.

Augustus was much occupied with his war with Sweden, which was going badly, and he does not seem to have been particularly enthusiastic about porcelain manufacture at this time. In 1703, therefore, von Tschirnhaus approached the Stadthalter of Fürstenberg—a place which was later the site of a successful factory—referring to von Canstein's offer, and to another from the *Oberhofmarschall*, von Kettler.

These brief notes of the situation as it stood in 1703, when von Tschirnhaus finally met Böttger, are, I think, sufficient to show that not only had he been engaged for many years in the search for true porcelain, but that he had also met with some measure of success. Moreover, he was conducting his researches on systematic and scientific lines, in the course of which he was taking advantage of the most advanced theories in the realm of physics and chemistry which were then available.

Our knowledge of Böttger shows us a somewhat different picture. Johann Friedrich Böttger (Plate 1) was born in 1682 at Schleiz, in Thuringia, the son of a cashier in the mint, and received preliminary instruction in chemistry before he was finally apprenticed to a Berlin apothecary named Zorn. Far from pursuing his studies in a detached spirit of inquiry, he was almost at once led into the semi-mystical paths of alchemy, and the search for the philosopher's stone—a magical stone reputed to be able to transmute lead into gold. Although the infant science of chemistry had by no means freed itself from the influence of alchemy, it is clear that the systematic investigations of von Tschirnhaus were on an altogether higher plane than those of Böttger, which were more akin to those of the Witches of *Macbeth*.

Nevertheless, the ignorance and cupidity of Frederick I, King of Prussia, led him to finance Böttger in this task. Whether or not Böttger at this time realized the essentially fraudulent nature of 'his claim to be able to make gold from lead, it is quite evident that he did so later, since the Dresden collection contains pieces of silver and gold which he claimed to have produced from copper and lead, but which could only have been used, by means of substitution, to deceive Augustus, who had, by then, become his patron and employer.

By 1700 the suspicions of Frederick had been aroused, and the gold-maker fled from Berlin to Wittenberg. Augustus was in desperate straits for means to finance his Swedish war and seized Böttger, using a military escort to bring him to Dresden.

Now Böttger was in an extremely dangerous position. By 1703 no lead had been transmuted. Augustus, his coffers drained of about 40,000 thalers[1] wasted on a fraudulent project, lost patience and placed him under the supervision of von Tschirnhaus. The year 1705 finds Böttger's reputation so tarnished that he was imprisoned in the Albrechtsburg in a final attempt to sharpen his wits.

Von Tschirnhaus no doubt realized the fraudulent nature of Böttger's pretensions, and that his training would make him a useful laboratory assistant. The suggestion that it would be far more valuable to use his services in pursuing researches into the manufacture of porcelain probably saved Böttger's life.

[1] The *thaler*—whence the American " dollar "—was worth about five shillings in the eighteenth century. Comparably, in these days of inflation, about £1 is a fair equivalent ($2.80 at present exchange rates).

At first Böttger thought his new position undignified: he wrote above his door:

Gott, unser Schöpfer
hat gemacht aus einem Goldmacher einen Töpfer.[1]

In the summer of 1706 the King authorized the construction of a new laboratory, which was opened finally in November 1707, and the philosopher's stone was forgotten. But Augustus was still in need of money, and Böttger's neck was far from secure. For this reason, after a preliminary gesture of defiance, in which he announced pettily that he did not want to be mixed up with porcelain experiments which were the concern of von Tschirnhaus, Böttger worked at his new tasks with industry. No doubt he speedily acquired considerable knowledge of the earlier researches of von Tschirnhaus, since it was possible that, at some future time, his life might easily depend on his usefulness as a porcelain arcanist.[2]

By 1708 von Tschirnhaus was able to show Augustus porcelain of sufficiently good quality to warrant a start being made on the construction of a factory in Dresden-Neustadt. At this point Peter Eggebrecht, perhaps of Dutch extraction, was engaged to help with production. The first intention was to engage in the manufacture of faïence, and this was done to a limited extent. Eggebrecht had been employed previously at Funcke's faïence factory in Berlin.

Von Tschirnhaus and Böttger speedily changed their interest from the manufacture of faïence to that of red stoneware (Jaspisporzellan), and red Dutch floor tiles. The management of the factory was assigned to Böttger, whilst von Tschirnhaus continued his laboratory researches into the secret of porcelain.

In July 1708, von Tschirnhaus was made Geheimrat (Privy Counsellor) and director, although he refused to use the titles until his researches had been successfully concluded. A little more than three months later he died.

[1] " God our creator has turned a gold-maker into a potter."
[2] An arcanist is one who possessed the arcanum or secret of porcelain manufacture.

Hofmann (op. cit.) illustrates several somewhat primitive beakers as the work of von Tschirnhaus, and chemical analysis has shown them to resemble true porcelain; that is to say, they are made of feldspathic rock. Böttger's first porcelain employed alabaster in place of feldspathic rock, which seems to preclude later manufacture of these specimens. Hofmann (op. cit., fig. 44) pictures a covered box, somewhat in the manner of St. Cloud, with applied prunus sprays and painted flowers which, he suggests, may have been the test piece said to have been given to Baron Kettler in 1702. This is in the Landesmuseum at Cassel in company with one of the burning-glasses used by von Tschirnhaus.[1]

The state porcelain collection in Dresden has a box in an unglazed yellowish porcelain, engraved in a manner similar to that used by glass-engravers, with a portrait of Augustus and an allegory of his coronation as King of Poland, both of which were derived from a Dresden medallion of 1697. A box of this kind would almost certainly be made as a commemorative piece, and it is therefore likely to have been contemporary, or nearly so, with the date of the striking of the medallion. Hofmann suggests that this might have been the porcelain shown by von Tschirnhaus to the Baron von Canstein in 1703.

Böttger has for the most part been regarded as the discoverer of the porcelain secret in those works in English which discuss the origins of German porcelain, a notable exception being W. B. Honey, who refers to "Tschirnhausen and his assistant Böttger". The Böttger legend has assumed such proportions, in fact, that some ten years ago one writer actually referred to Böttger as having been given facilities and assistants, *including von Tschirnhaus*. In Germany Böttger's principal supporter is Professor Ernst

[1] In all cases in which I use the present tense in referring to objects in German museums and collections, it is to be understood that this does not necessarily refer to the position at the time when this is being written. It would have been impossible to check the whereabouts of all the items herein mentioned because of the extensive changes which have taken place since 1939. For example, some porcelain which was in the Berlin collections is now in Darmstadt. Little or no reliable information can be obtained about objects which are, or were, in East Germany. A great deal was removed to the Western Zone before the iron curtain rang down. The Dresden collections may be unscathed, but the city was disastrously damaged during the war.

Zimmermann, who wrote at an earlier date than Hofmann, already cited, but whose work is much more copiously annotated.[1] Zimmerman refers to a work of 1837—*Erfinder des sächsischen Porzellans* by Englehardt—in which the claims of von Tschirnhaus are vigorously pressed. It is the more difficult to follow Zimmermann in his criticism of the work of Englehardt because much of the latter's source material is no longer in existence, but he accuses Englehardt of insufficient knowledge of chemistry, and suggests that, for this reason, he was unable to evaluate Böttger's contribution to the problem. Englehardt regarded Böttger as a charlatan because he was an alchemist, and there is a certain amount of substance in the charge; whereas, if we make due allowance for the period, von Tschirnhaus undoubtedly was a chemist and physicist in the modern sense of the words, relying upon experiment and the inferences to be drawn therefrom.

Zimmermann goes on to accuse Englehardt of taking undue notice of the weaker side of Böttger's character, another aspect of which will be discussed later, but it will emerge more clearly as we proceed that, not only was Böttger addicted to the bottle, but he was also heartily disliked by some of his colleagues in the management of the factory. The evidence, therefore, is in favour of Englehardt's judgement.

Von Tschirnhaus is certainly credited by Zimmermann with having made small quantities of porcelain, and it is admitted that certain specimens (illustrated by Hofmann as the work of von Tschirnhaus) contain feldspar. Here Zimmermann draws the conclusion that since alabaster was used in place of feldspar during the Böttger period, and feldspar was not employed until later, it could not have been used by von Tschirnhaus, but to me this seems a *non sequitur*. Von Tschirnhaus may well have known the possibilities of feldspar.

It is unnecessary to go into all the evidence in the present work, since this may be found set out in Zimmermann's book, but, briefly summarized, his conclusions are that von Tschirnhaus and

[1] *Die Erfindung und Frühzeit des Meissner Porzellans* (1908).

Böttger must have worked closely together, that von Tschirnhaus would have proclaimed his discovery had he been in a position to do so, and that, since Böttger was virtually a prisoner, there could have been no question of the credit being mistakenly bestowed. Again, Zimmermann contends that since von Tschirnhaus could not design kilns to reach the high temperatures necessary to fire true porcelain successfully, he could not have been the discoverer of the secret.

To my mind none of the points advanced enables us to come to any kind of definite conclusion. It is not, for example, suggested by Hofmann that von Tschirnhaus made porcelain on a commercial scale, but the report that a diamond was melted with the aid of a burning-glass shows that sufficiently high temperatures could be attained to fire small pieces and experimental lumps of material successfully. Moreover, von Tschirnhaus had visited porcelain factories and studied kiln design at first hand.

It is true that he did not proclaim his discovery of the porcelain secret, but a curious obscurity seems to have shrouded the position in 1708. In July of that year Dr. Jakob Bartelmei was given details of the process under oath, which he then relayed to Augustus. In the same month von Tschirnhaus was made *Geheimrat* and director. The two events seem to have a causal relationship. Hannover[1] says that the secret was so jealously guarded that nothing has been preserved in writing as to the *year* when the discovery was made, and—without citing evidence—says that it was, at the earliest, 1708, and that it is not certain that von Tschirnhaus lived to see it. Böttger, he says, did not feel himself in full possession of the secret until March 1709, and it was not until this date that he informed Augustus of his latest discovery. The lapse of time may, in fact, have been necessary for Böttger to complete investigations into the problem of glazing the material, and of colouring it suitably—researches which were already in being at the time of the death of von Tschirnhaus in October 1708. The date for the announcement of Böttger's completed researches is

[1] *Pottery and Porcelain* (English edition), vol. III, p. 34.

given as 20th March, 1709 (Hofmann) and 29th March, 1709 (Zimmermann). Böttger told Augustus that he had found a good white porcelain as well as a suitable glaze, and could produce this with all the usual painting so as to be at least as good as the Asiatic.[1] A commission appointed by Augustus to report on the discovery seems to have been distinctly unimpressed by Böttger. Despite this, the Royal Saxon Porcelain Manufactory was eventually founded on 23rd January, 1710. The same year saw the new invention exhibited at the Leipzig Fair, and the factory was established in the Albrechtsburg at Meissen. The conversion of this fortress to a porcelain factory was far from the only instance of its kind. Elsewhere castles, barracks and all kinds of disused and derelict buildings were pressed into service, and it was not until much later in the century that buildings began to be erected especially for the purpose.

There were many technical difficulties still to be over-come. The white clay from Kolditz, until then in use, proved unsatisfactory and unpredictable, and at the end of 1710 it was replaced by clay from Aue in Vogtland, which was discovered on the estate of Johann Schnorr von Carolsfeld, and henceforth known as *Schnorr'sche weisse Erde von Aue*. This clay continued in use until well into the nineteenth century.

By 1713 porcelain was being offered for sale at the Leipzig Fair, and it seems certain that by this year it was being produced in considerable quantities.

Augustus was led by the possession of a successful porcelain factory into a number of grandiose projects, and in 1717 he acquired the Holländische Palais in Dresden-Neustadt, which was built in 1715 for Jakob Heinrich, the Graf von Flemming, by the *Landbaumeister* Matthäus Daniel Pöppelman. This Augustus re-named the Japanische Palais, and intended to fill it with oriental porcelain and the products of the new factory, the upper floor being reserved entirely for porcelain from Meissen.

---

[1] " guten weissen Porcellain [*sic*] sammt der allerfeinsten Glazen und behörigen Mahl-werck in solcher Perfektion zu machen wisse, dass solcher dem Ost-Indianischen wo nicht vor, doch wenigstens gleich kommen soll."

By far the most ambitious of the schemes later fostered by Augustus was a project for porcelain animals and birds of life size, which were intended to fill a large central gallery. This experiment was finally abandoned, leaving behind a long trail of kiln-wasters and extensively fire-cracked specimens, although a few of extremely large size were successfully produced.

The Japanische Palais eventually housed nearly 40,000 pieces, which were put finally into storage in 1775, and later formed part of the *Porzellansammlung* (Porcelain Collection) of the Johanneum, the Dresden museum which housed the collection. From time to time specimens from this collection have been sold, the last sale of consequence occurring just after the 1914–18 war. This accounts for the occasional appearance in the market of specimens bearing the Johanneum inventory mark scratched into the glaze with a diamond (Plate 9b).

The hostility of the commission to Böttger did not abate. The *Hofkammerrat* Michael Nehmitz was Böttger's particular enemy, and the former's position as factory director gave him suitable opportunity to express his dislike. The years between 1710 and 1719, when Böttger died, were therefore far from easy. Mutual suspicion was rife, and the secret of manufacture was confided under oath to two persons. One was the brother of Michael Nehmitz, by name Dr. Wilhelm Heinrich Nehmitz, the other Dr. Jakob Bartelmei, who had already communicated the secret of manufacture to Augustus at the instance of von Tschirnhaus. Dr. Nehmitz is said to have been the possessor of the secret of the glaze, and Bartelmei of the body. This was intended to prevent the defection of anyone who was in full possession of the secret, but it did not stop Samuel Stölzel, who was Böttger's kiln-master, from deserting to Vienna in 1719. Another workman, Samuel Kempe, went to Plaue-an-der-Havel to start a factory for the production of red stoneware, and a goldworker, Christoph Konrad Hunger, left for Vienna in 1717.

Whilst the development of the network of European porcelain factories during the eighteenth century was principally due to such absconding workmen, some consideration ought also to be given to the granddaughters of Augustus. Maria Amalia Walpurga, for instance, married Charles IV, who founded the Capo-di-Monte factory at Naples in 1743, and Maria Anna Sophia married the Elector Maximilian III Joseph, who first attempted to found the Nymphenburg factory in 1747.

At Meissen the general atmosphere of chaotic administration persisted. Böttger relapsed slowly into an alcoholic stupor, and died on 13th March, 1719. But the defection of Stölzel was not an unmitigated disaster. Tradition has it that Claudius Innocentius du Paquier, the founder of the Vienna factory, made Stölzel's acquaintance at an inn, and suborned him with an offer of 1,000 thalers to take the secret to Vienna. There Stölzel remained until 1720, but the promised salary was not forthcoming, and he returned to Meissen taking with him a young enameller, Johann Gregor Höroldt,[1] who was to play an important part in the development of the Meissen factory, especially between 1720 and 1735. Höroldt's talents seem to have secured for him instant recognition, and in 1723, at the age of twenty-seven, he was appointed *Hofmaler* (court painter). He was responsible for the development of a new and brilliant palette, as well as several kinds of decoration, of which the most important was the *chinoiserie*, later discussed in detail.

The advent of Höroldt begins what is often called the *malerische Periode*, which lasted from 1720 to *c.* 1735, to be followed by the *plastische Periode* from 1735 to 1763, during which figure modelling superseded painting in importance.

Höroldt's origins are somewhat obscure. Born in Jena in 1696, he was the son of a tailor, and probably a pupil of C. K. Hunger. Whilst he certainly introduced a new and more colourful palette to Meissen, it is debatable whether the development of the enamels was entirely his own work. Indeed, Hunger openly accused Stölzel and Höroldt of stealing them from him, and they were

[1] Also spelled "Herold" in divers places. Höroldt is the form used by Johann Gregor himself.

quite obviously used to buy popularity with the Meissen directorate. Otherwise the ease with which Stölzel resumed his former position after his defection would be difficult to explain.

In the position of *Obermaler* (chief painter), Höroldt was responsible for painting and design, as well as for the training of apprentices. Much the same system was adopted as had become the rule at the Imperial Chinese factory at Ch'ing-te-chên. The work was divided among artists, one doing a particular kind of flower, another gilding, still another landscapes, and so on.

In 1731 Höroldt became manager of all the workers of the factory. Johann Joachim Kändler was engaged as a modeller in that year, and received the support of Heinrich, the Graf von Brühl, who later became factory director. As Kändler's influence grew, quarrels with Höroldt became frequent, and the latter's position increased in difficulty until in 1756—the beginning of the Seven Years' War—he fled to Frankfurt-am-Main, where he remained until 1763. In this latter year he returned to Meissen and worked until 1765, when he was awarded a pension. He died in 1776.

There is little reliable information as to the antecedents of Christoph Konrad Hunger, and most of his life is veiled in obscurity. Born at Weissensee in Thuringia, his friendship with Böttger apparently gave him some insight into the arcanum of porcelain-making. He employed this knowledge without conspicuous success in the service of the Vienna factory. He claimed special knowledge of the application of underglaze blue, and of enamel colours. The suggestion that he was approached by Böttger for information on these matters is his own. There is no other record of it.

Hunger was a gold-worker (*Goldarbeiter*) rather than a gilder (*Vergolder*), and he devised a method of decoration with relief gilding, an example of which is shown on Plate 135b. A signed bowl exists.

When he left Vienna in 1719, Hunger went to Venice and helped to found the Vezzi factory. He appears to have left in

1724, and was re-engaged at Meissen in 1727 for a short while, going thence to Rörstrand in Sweden. Later, he tried his luck at Copenhagen, and ended in St. Petersburg in 1740, after which he disappears from view.

His knowledge of porcelain-making has been questioned on many occasions, and he has been regarded as little more than a charlatan. It is perhaps worth a passing thought that Höroldt, when he came to Meissen, was twenty-four years of age, which would seem to have allowed him little time for experimenting with enamel colours. The suggestion that he was a pupil of Hunger's at Vienna may not be too wide of the mark.

The year of Böttger's death saw Augustus determined to re-organize his factory on a more stable basis, and Michael Nehmitz was relieved of his position. He had carried his enmity towards Böttger to a point where his intrigues had severely damaged the factory. Johann Melchior Steinbrück, who had been inspector of the factory in 1712, was appointed administrator, and Dr. Wilhelm Nehmitz was retained as arcanist, as well as Johann Georg Schubarth and David Köhler. Köhler later devised the first practicable underglaze blue—a colour which, although there were extensive cobalt deposits in Saxony, proved particularly difficult. At this time, perhaps at the suggestion of Höroldt or Stölzel, the alabaster used hitherto was replaced by a feldspathic rock from Sieberlehn (*Sieberlehnstein*), which improved and whitened the body.

The years following saw the continued expansion of the factory. The first factory mark, the initials *KPM*, *KPF* and *MPM*, for *Königliche Porzellan Manufaktur*, *Königliche Porzellan Fabrik* and *Meissner Porzellan Manufaktur* respectively, came into use in 1723, and the crossed swords—from the Electoral Arms of Saxony —followed in 1724. The much-abused monogram of Augustus, "AR" was probably first employed about the same time.

Augustus now became intent on furnishing the Japanische Palais with porcelain. German authorities are somewhat divided on the question of the beginning of the passion for porcelain from which he undoubtedly suffered. Hofmann regards it as a somewhat late development which grew from the establishment of the Meissen factory, whereas Schmidt[1] mentions the spending of 100,000 thalers in the first year of his reign. On this point Schmidt would seem the more reliable, since von Tschirnhaus referred to China as "the bleeding bowl of Saxony", and there is the story of the "Dragoon" vases in its favour. These were a series of forty-eight vases which Augustus acquired by exchange from the King of Prussia, giving, in return, a regiment of dragoons.

Schmidt quotes a significant paragraph in a letter from Augustus to Generalfeldmarschall Graf Jakob Heinrich von Flemming:

Ne scavez vous pas qu'il est des oranges comme des porcelaines, que ceux qui ont une fois la maladie des uns ou des autres ne trouvent jamais qu'ils en ayent assez et que plus ils en veulent avoir.[2]

The quality of production improved steadily during the decade between 1720 and 1730. At the beginning even the secret of preparing enamel colours seemed to have died with Böttger, yet—by 1730—because of Höroldt's knowledge and skill, a magnificent range of colours had become possible, both for painted decoration and for the sumptuous *Fondporzellan*—the coloured grounds with decoration in panels reserved in white. Höroldt's palette consisted of strong bright colours of a purity which had not been attainable hitherto. Moreover, outlines did not become blurred in firing. The colours themselves included a brilliant iron-red, a strong rose-purple, turquoise or sea-green, and a slightly yellowish leaf-green. An enamel blue was not achieved until 1728. Even then it was not satisfactory, and is not often seen. It is noticeably inclined to flake off the underlying glaze.

The factory also developed large export markets. France and Holland were particularly profitable customers, and Rudolph

---

[1] *Das Porzellan als Kuntswerk und Kulturspiegel.*

[2] " It is the same with porcelain as with oranges; if you have a longing for the one or the other, you will never have enough."

Lemaire, a Paris dealer, was supplied with porcelain to his own design. At this time and later a considerable trade was done with Turkey. In 1734, for instance, the factory had an order in hand for 3,000 dozen coffee cups, known as *Türkenköpgen*, for Manasses Athanas of Istanbul. These cups lacked handles, and were made especially for the Turkish market. The finished products from Meissen, and from other factories engaged in the same trade, were shipped down the Danube. At Meissen seventy-three different patterns were used for these cups, and the *caduceus* was adopted for Turkish export wares instead of the crossed swords at the request of Athanas, the latter mark being erroneously regarded by the buyers as a Christian symbol.

For some time after its inception Meissen paid little attention to figure modelling. This was general in the early years of the century, and the same course of events may be traced at Vienna. Indeed, it is only within recent years that Vienna figures made before 1745 have been recognized and attributed.

The plastic work of the Böttger period was principally derivative, and no truly original style emerged. The only modeller known at this time to whom anything has been attributed is Georg Fritzsche, who seems to have been responsible for some grotesque and exaggerated figures somewhat similar to the example shown on Plate 4d which may be by his hand. These, however, are not often seen. Fritzsche was at the factory from 1712 to about 1730, but only tentative attributions are possible.

By 1727 greater interest was being taken in figure modelling, and a young sculptor, Johann Gottlob Kirchner, was engaged to take charge of this aspect. He entered into his new position on the 29th April, 1727, when he was twenty-one years old. Apparently the work did not appeal to him. He was a stone-carver and disliked modelling in clay. In 1728 he was discharged, but the factory had no better fortune with its next modeller, Johann Christoph Ludwig von Lücke (self-styled), and on 30th January, 1730 Kirchner was reinstated at higher pay. In 1731 he was awarded the title of *Modellmeister*.

Kirchner was principally occupied with work for the Japanische Palais, for which he did various animal figures.

His work was vigorous, and of great importance. He contributed extensively to the development of the porcelain figure in Europe, and originated the Meissen " model book " in which the styles, shapes and so forth were listed and described.

His relations with Kändler were never good, and frequent quarrels punctuated the time they spent working together. But these quarrels were finally resolved in favour of Kändler, and Kirchner left the factory in 1733.

Von Lücke, who took Kirchner's place in 1728, was also unsatisfactory. His date of birth is unknown, but he was the son of a Dresden ivory-carver, and was himself a sculptor and an ivory-carver. Engaged by the factory in 1728, he was soon in trouble. This may have been due in part to his personal character, and in part to defects in his knowledge; he was discharged in 1729. From this date until 1750, when von Lücke arrived in Vienna, we lose sight of him, but Hofmann states (op. cit.) that his signature is " fairly frequent " on Vienna figures. He was engaged by the Vienna factory on 18th April, 1750 as a modeller and "repairer " at a yearly salary of 1,000 florins and free accommodation. Subsequently he offered his services to the Fürstenberg factory as an arcanist, and was later at Copenhagen and Schleswig. He visited England about 1760, and died at Danzig in 1780 in poverty. The two modellers, Johann Friedrich Lück and Karl Gottlieb Lück, whose work is discussed in later chapters, are both assumed to have been related to him, although the exact degree of relationship has not been established.

In 1733 Augustus died. He was succeeded by his only legitimate son, who became Augustus III. His title to the Kingdom of Poland was immediately disputed by Stanislas Leczinski, who had previously deposed Augustus the Strong for a short period just after 1704, and the War of the Polish Succession broke out. Augustus III sought help from Russia, and Stanislas was driven out once more in 1734. Until the War of the Austrian Succession in 1740, during which Augustus alternately supported and opposed Maria Theresa, the years were comparatively peaceful, and the factory continued to flourish.

In 1733, Heinrich, the Graf von Brühl, was appointed factory director, and remained so until his death. He lent his encouragement to the plastic work of the factory, and in particular to Johann Joachim Kändler, who was appointed *Modellmeister* in this year. There seems to have been a close relationship between the two men to the detriment of Höroldt.

Von Brühl was born in 1700 and, when Augustus III appointed him to the position of administrator of the factory in 1733, he had already taken considerable interest in its working. In his official position he was able to bring much influence to bear to assist the factory both culturally and commercially, and he fostered the growth of figure modelling which, as I have recorded, had been struggling along hitherto in the wake of the painting shop. His life and activities were commemorated by a garden he laid out on a rampart fronting and overlooking the River Elbe, known as the Brühlsche Terrasse, which has since been destroyed.

In 1742 he bought water-colours from the Marquis de Martijon in Paris. These were of some importance because they assisted in the development of the rococo style which had made some tentative beginnings shortly after 1730. This style can be seen in 1737 in the great Swan Service which was made for presentation to von Brühl at the instance of Augustus III. The *Schwanengeschirr* was devised for at least 100 people, and comprised over 1,000 pieces of every conceivable use—vegetable tureens, mustard pots, oil and vinegar bottles, and so on in profusion. The plates were modelled in relief with swans, and the tureens and similar items were ornamented in addition with figures of nymphs, sirens, nereids, tritons and other classical figures. Each piece bore the arms of von Brühl, and most of it was in the possession of his descendants at Pföten Castle until recently, although it is impossible to say whether or not this is still so. A few specimens are in

PLATE 17

Tureen with the Arms of the Kurfürst Phillip Karl von Mainz.
Meissen. *c.* 1735.

PLATE 18

Dish from the Swan Service.
Meissen. *c.* 1737.

PLATE 19

(*a*) Cup and saucer from the Swan Service.
Meissen. *c.* 1737.

(*b*) Figures of swans from the Swan Service.
Meissen. *c.* 1737.

PLATE 20

Ice-pail decorated with *indianische Blumen* in underglaze-blue.
Meissen. *c.* 1735.

PLATE 21

Trumpet-shaped vase.
Meissen. *c.* 1740.

PLATE 22

(c) Sugar-box with yellow ground and landscapes in purple monochrome in panels.
Meissen. c. 1730.

(b) Cream-pot decorated with harbour scenes.
Meissen. c. 1730.

(d, right) Peach-shaped covered bowl of Fond-porzellan.
Meissen. c. 1745.

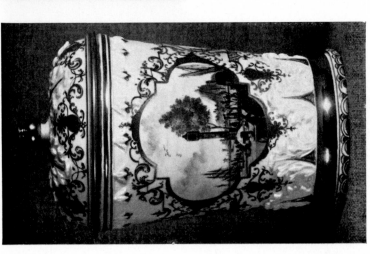

(a) Covered jar, decorated with harbour scenes in a framework of baroque scrolls.
Meissen. c. 1725.

PLATE 23

Tea-pot of early form decorated with harbour scenes in *Schwarzlot*.

Meissen. *c.* 1725.

PLATE 24

Chandelier of Meissen porcelain. *c.* 1750.

PLATE 25

(*a*) Cup and saucer decorated with river scenes and landscapes. Perhaps by J. G. Heintze.
Meissen. 1743.

(*b*) Cup and saucer decorated with harbour scenes.
Meissen. 1741.

PLATE 26

(a) Chocolate-pot and cover painted by C. F. Herold.

Meissen. c. 1735.

(b) Box and cover decorated with landscapes and equestrian figures.

Meissen. c. 1745.

PLATE 27

Dish with a view of Amsterdam.
Meissen. 1763.

PLATE 28

(b) Leaf-shaped dish.
Meissen. c. 1765.

(d) Dish painted with birds.
Meissen. c. 1760.

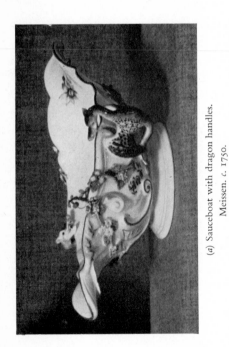

(a) Sauceboat with dragon handles.
Meissen. c. 1750.

(c) Tea-pot in rococo style.

PLATE 29

Tureen and stand with
Watteau scenes.
Meissen. Dated 1754.

PLATE 30

(b) Painting on reverse of tea-pot on Plate 31. Meissen. 1765.

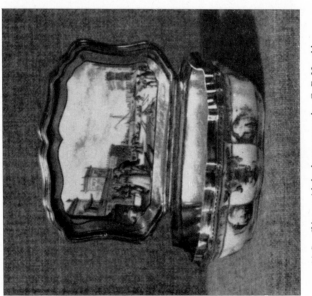

(a) Snuff-box with harbour scenes by C. F. Herold. Meissen. c. 1740.

PLATE 31

Déjeuner set with pastoral
scenes in the manner of
Sèvres.

Meissen. *c.* 1765.

PLATE 32

(a) Cup and saucer in Wedgwood style.
Meissen. c. 1790.

(b) Cup and saucer painted with a child holding a birdcage.
Vienna. c. 1790.

museums, and others are sometimes offered for sale on the art market.

This service was the work of Kändler, helped by Johann Friedrich Eberlein, with Louis Desplaces as designer. Eberlein became Kändler's assistant in 1735.

Johann Joachim Kändler was undoubtedly the greatest of the Meissen modellers, and he disputes with Franz Anton Bustelli of Nymphenburg the title of the greatest modeller of porcelain of all time.

Born at Fischbach, near Dresden, in 1706, the son of a minister, he was apprenticed in 1723 to Benjamin Thomae, the court sculptor. Seven years later he came under the eye of Augustus the Strong, who conferred upon him the title of sculptor to the court of Saxony. In 1731 he was appointed to assist Kirchner, who then had the title of *Modellmeister*, but the quality of his work was such that he speedily overtook his nominal master, and there ensued a series of jealous quarrels between the two men, as well as between Kändler and Höroldt. It says much for the personality of Kändler, as well as for the influence exerted on his behalf by von Brühl, that he was the obvious victor in these exchanges, even in his quarrel with the *Hofmaler*, and in 1733 he was given Kirchner's title of *Modellmeister* which he retained for more than forty years.

Modellmeister were people of importance in the hierarchy of the early German factories. They were often highly paid, much more so in fact than the arcanists and directors. The position was independent of the administration to a remarkable degree, and it is said of Johann Peter Melchior, the Höchst *Modellmeister*, that when he was negotiating with Frankenthal he refused to work "under officials, but only under the court".[1]

Kändler sometimes had as many as 100 workers directly under his control, and the modellers among them borrowed freely from his ideas. Various estimates have been given of the number of different models which Kändler created, but it is undoubtedly

[1] Hofmann (op. cit.).

upwards of 900—Schmidt says in excess of 1,000. Most of these were made for reproduction in moulds, and many became sources of inspiration for the later work of the factory, even to the present day.

In 1764 Michel-Victor Acier was brought from France and installed alongside the ageing Kändler as joint *Modellmeister*. The latter died in 1775 at the age of sixty-nine whilst still at work. His failure to complete the *Reiterdenkmal*, a gigantic equestrian statue of Augustus III, which he undertook in 1751, seems to have affected his spirits, and his work after this project miscarried was neither so great in quantity nor so important artistically.

Among his creations must be numbered the Sulkowski Service[1] and the Swan Service, and his growing influence at the factory is noticeable during the 1730's in the increasing application of moulded decoration to service-ware, culminating in the rich and elaborate mouldings of the services mentioned, which, although a little misguided by modern standards, have never been surpassed as a technical achievement.

Kändler, reporting to a factory commission in 1739, said: " . . . anything can be made in porcelain; if it is too big, make it in two pieces . . . so that everything, even the impossible, can be done in its own way."[2] That he had faith in his opinion may be seen from his attempt to make the over life-size statue of Augustus on horseback mentioned above. A special building had to be constructed in the Albrechtsburg to contain the plaster moulds, but the project was later abandoned. A bust of the King was finished, and is in the Dresden collections.

Apart from a number of portraits of Augustus, Kändler also modelled the Kurfürstin (Electress) Maria Josepha of Saxony, the Tsarina of Russia, and Frederick the Great on horseback. The latter is well known from later reissues which are not uncommon.

In 1749 Kändler delivered personally, in Paris, a mirror-frame

[1] A tureen from this service is an identical copy of one in Augsburg silver in the Dresden collections made by Johannes Biller.
[2] Quoted by Hofmann (op. cit.).

ordered by the Dauphin of France, and took the opportunity to inspect the French porcelain industry, a journey which influenced his future work.

The only known signed example of his work is in the Kunstgewerbemuseum in Dresden. This is the *Triumph of Galatea*, modelled in 1773.

The most important of Kändler's assistants was Johann Friedrich Eberlein, who was born in 1696, came to Meissen in 1735, and died in 1749. Although most of his work was done in collaboration with Kändler, it is possible to see in some of his own work (a series of Chinese figures done in 1743, for example) that his reputation would have been much enhanced had he not been overshadowed by the greater genius of the *Modellmeister*. He helped to create the Swan Service, and his other work with Kändler includes some vases symbolic of the Elements, the *Affenkapelle* (Monkey Orchestra) in 1750, and a series of figures after Bouchardon later discussed.

In 1743 Kändler received additional assistance in the person of Peter Reinicke, whose work is, for the most part, even more difficult to separate, and he and Kändler modelled several sets of figures in close association. It is indisputable that Kändler created a plastic style for the factory, and the lesser modellers were required to keep in line.

The arrival of Peter Reinicke was followed, in 1746, by Friedrich Elias Meyer, later to become *Modellmeister* at Berlin. He remained at Meissen until 1760, and is noted for figures which, it is said, quite frequently have heads smaller than is justified by the proportions of the figure. This is a generalization about which I have always felt a little uncertain. If this was, in fact, one of the idiosyncrasies of Meyer's style, he ought to have taken it with him to Berlin, but he did not, as the figure illustrated on Plate 106 will testify. Meyer worked more purely in the rococo style, whereas Kändler invariably retained some flavour of the earlier baroque. Meyer was born at Erfurt, in Thuringia, and was at first court sculptor at Weimar. Without approaching the importance of Kändler's own work, his modelling is distinctive and often elegant in style.

The year 1744 saw the beginning of the Second Silesian War, during which the Prussians under Frederick the Great occupied Dresden. The kilns were destroyed to prevent Frederick from gaining any useful information about their design, but, this apart, no very serious damage was done.

This war ended in 1748, but it led directly to the Seven Years' War (1756–1763) which was an attempt by a confederation of nations to assist Maria Theresa, Empress of Austria, to dispose of Frederick. For a time, things went so badly for Prussia that Frederick carried poison with which to commit suicide if events took a fatal turn, but the accession of Peter III to the Russian throne improved his fortunes, and the war was finally concluded victoriously in 1763.

Dresden itself suffered severely. Famine and disease were rife in the city, and upwards of 500 houses, as well as five churches, were destroyed by fire. In 1760 the old Kreuz Church was completely destroyed by a bombardment which lasted from 14th July to the 30th.

The effect on the factory was serious. Frederick, in the time he could spare from the prosecution of the war, took more than a passing interest in porcelain. He had previously been a customer of the factory, ordering—among other things—a series of figures of the Muses which were executed by Kändler between 1741 and 1744. Wilhelm Kaspar Wegely, a merchant, had already started a factory in Berlin in 1752 with the assistance of Johann Benck-graff, an arcanist from Vienna.

Meissen was occupied in 1756, and the troops proceeded to loot the stock. The kilns had been destroyed and, wisely, the arcanists fled to Frankfurt.

Frederick formed the intention of removing what remained to Berlin, and to this end sold the factory to Karl Heinrich Schimmelmann, or, what is more probable, forced him to take it in part repayment for money advanced. The factory was subsequently leased to a Dresden merchant named Helbig who contrived to start production once more. Suspicion of working for the enemy seems to have been dispersed later because Helbig was given an official position temporarily when the factory was reorganized after the war. He pleaded that his action was necessary to keep it in operation.

Frederick, not content with removing porcelain valued at 100,000 thalers, set the factory to work for his personal benefit, and ordered vast quantities of porcelain including six large table services. General Zieten " ordered " a service valued at 1,800 thalers for which no payment was received, and set an example followed by others in Frederick's high command, in particular by General Möllendorff, for whom a service was ordered by Frederick himself.

Whilst the factory was engaged in the unduly hazardous business of surviving Frederick and the Seven Years' War, others more fortunate had been making inroads into Meissen's former markets. Sèvres had been particularly active in this way. Therefore, in 1763, von Brühl and the King set to work to reorganize the Meissen undertaking. A new commission was set up in March, barely two weeks after the declaration of peace, and only one of the old names survived, *Geheime Kammerrat* von Nimptsch. The *Kommerzienrat* Helbig already mentioned was made manager of production, and given control of commercial matters in addition. Helbig was a merchant whose skill and experience was of some value in putting affairs on a sounder basis.

The new plans, however, received an almost immediate check from the death of Augustus on 5th October, 1763. This month removed both the King and the able and experienced administrator of the factory, von Brühl, who had guided it through what was to prove its most important and influential phase. He died on 28th October.

Augustus was succeeded by his invalid son, Friedrich Christian, who died after a reign of two months in December 1763, and Prince Xaver became Regent for Friedrich August, who was then a minor. Xaver was interested in porcelain manufacture, and had leanings towards the neo-classical style which was then taking the place of the rococo in France. To this end he founded a school of art in Dresden which was financed in part by the factory, and the court painter and Professor of the Dresden Academy, Christian Wilhelm Ernst Dietrich, was placed in charge of the project. Thus began the *Akademische Periode*, sometimes known as *die Punktzeit* (the " Dot " Period) from the dot which was placed between the hilts of the swords in the mark.

So great was Xaver's enthusiasm for the " beauty of classical art " that even Höroldt and Kändler were placed under Dietrich— Kändler because he was still bitter over the failure of his cherished project, the *Reiterdenkmal*, and Höroldt because, at sixty-eight, he was just about ready to retire, which he did in the following year. Von Nimptsch (d. 1773) was made a life director, and the commission dispensed with the services of Helbig.

Tremendous efforts were made to improve the factory's output both in quantity and in quality, and information was sought from elsewhere. This was carried to the length of appointing a permanent commission to sit in Paris to report on new developments of style evolved at the French factories. In 1766 Fletscher, a member of the commission, went to Paris with two painters, Grossman[1] and Wiedner, both of whom worked at Sèvres, apparently in the capacity of industrial spies. They were particularly charged to find the secret of the enamel blue known at Sèvres as *bleu de Roi*. This apart, attempts were made to gain information from countries other than France. Spain, Portugal, Italy, Switzerland, Russia, Denmark and England were all visited in turn by one Otto, perhaps to be identified with the animal painter, Johann Heinrich Otto. It seems that on these journeys he also solicited orders for the factory.

On the plastic side Kändler approached the neo-classical style even more reluctantly than he had adopted the rococo, and

---

[1] Christoph Gotthelf Grossman; at Meissen from 1750 onwards, and at Sèvres and Ludwigsburg *c.* 1766–*c.* 1774.

Michel-Victor Acier was offered a high salary and a pension to tempt him from Paris. Born at Versailles in 1736, Acier came to Meissen in 1764. He was at once made joint *Modellmeister* with Kändler, and had under him both Peter Reinicke and Carl Christoph Punct. The latter was a modeller at the factory from 1761 to 1765, and became the court sculptor in 1763. Punct died in 1765 and Reinicke in 1768, the factory thus losing two extremely competent workmen.

Acier's installation as joint *Modellmeister* was principally to supply the demand for new fashions in Germany. The work of Kändler was still much in demand abroad.

The prevailing emotional climate of Acier's work—its sentimentality which frequently verges on the maudlin—was, as I have said, influenced by the effect of Goethe's *Die Leiden des jungen Werthers* on the current neo-classical style. That Goethe was a member of the *bourgeoisie* accounts not only for the sensational success of his book, but also for the popularity of the work of Acier which was done primarily to satisfy *bourgeois* aspirations.

Melchior, the Höchst *Modellmeister*, was Goethe's friend, and executed a portrait of him inscribed *The poet of the Sorrows of Young Werther by his friend Melchior done from life.*[1] In chapter 13 I refer to Goethe's own connection with the Thuringian porcelain factories.

Johann Joachim Winckelmann, one-time librarian to the Graf von Bünau at Dresden, advocated the decadent remnants of Greek naturalism, and Roman *bourgeois* derivations from it, instead of the vigorous archaic work which is the finest product of the ancient world, and the combination of these influences on someone like Acier, who had none of Kändler's background of work in the baroque tradition, produced sentimental idealizations of domestic and pastoral scenes, and figures of children which are numerous and often undistinguished. Apart from this saccharin quality, Acier had none of the vigour and earthiness which make Kändler's work timeless in its appeal. Kändler's own attempts at

[1] Schmidt (op. cit.), and Röder and Oppenheim, *Das Höchster Porzellan u.s.w.* (1925).

neo-classicism were half-hearted, with his earlier leanings ill-suppressed. His style, dominant during the finest period of the factory's work, was replaced by derivations from a period which was hardly understood, and Kändler's sense of reality was replaced by a synthetic and contrived emotion.

Acier had for an assistant Johann Karl Schönheit, who had been a " repairer " (*Bossierer*) at the factory since 1745, and later became a modeller, in which capacity he continued until 1805. A less satisfactory acquisition was Jean Troy of Lunéville, who was engaged in 1768 and discharged in 1770 for " inefficiency and frivolity". Perhaps he had been upsetting the worthy Meissen Fräulein! A more important accession was Christoph Gottfried Jüchtzer, who was apprenticed to Kändler in 1769, and who became art director to the factory.

Acier did a certain amount of work from the drawings of a painter and engraver named Johann Elias Zeissig, who called himself Schönau (or Schenau) after his birthplace. Zeissig had been a pupil of Louis Silvestre, a Dresden painter, and was with him in Paris during the Seven Years' War, where he had close contact with Greuze. In 1769 he was invited to come to Dresden, and, in 1773, was given the task of improving the School of Drawing there. Zeissig was under contract to go to Meissen two or three times a year, and to stay there and provide new designs for the painters to copy. He remained art adviser until 1796, and his influence was particularly potent during the period of Count Marcolini's directorate from 1774 onwards. He was responsible for the adoption of many styles current in France.

Christian Daniel Busch returned to Meissen in 1765, principally as an arcanist, and what would now be described as a research chemist. The son of a factory official, Johann Gottfried Busch, he had a varied career. Until 1745 he was at Meissen, and arrived in Vienna in that year. Here, he became a Protestant, and married in 1747. He was at Nymphenburg in 1748 in company with Jakob Helkis, the Vienna painter, and left almost immediately. He then travelled to Bayreuth, and was engaged at the *faïence* factory of

Skt. Georg-am-See. Later he went to Kelsterbach (q.v.) and turned up at Sèvres in company with one Stadelmeyer, who may have been the arcanist at Pfalz-Zweibrücken (see chapter 12).

Whilst his knowledge of the porcelain secret was probably somewhat deficient, Busch discovered an acceptable substitute for the *bleu de Roi* of Sèvres, and improved the glaze used with underglaze blue, as well as designing new and improved kilns which reduced wastage.

A sculptor and woodcarver named Berger introduced the use of charcoal into the firing of the muffle (or enamelling) kilns.

Towards the end of the Academic Period Meissen experienced considerable difficulty in keeping and extending its export markets. This position was worsened by the Sèvres factory's discovery of the true porcelain secret in 1768, since they were then in a position to compete on level terms. Another serious source of competition came from the Potteries in the form of Josiah Wedgwood's newly-invented creamware, which was then beginning its extraordinarily successful career on the Continent.

This, then, was the situation when Count Camillo Marcolini succeeded to the Meissen directorship on the 20th August, 1774. Marcolini was born in 1739, and had been one of the favourites of Augustus III. He was astute and practical, and took great interest in the working of the factory. His immediate reforms included reductions in wages, the discharge of redundant workmen, and the introduction of a system of incentives to hard and conscientious work in the form of bonuses. Sales improved almost at once, and the restrictions were relaxed soon afterwards.

In 1777 a new warehouse was built at Bad Spa, and the same year saw a decree forbidding the sale of Thuringian porcelain in Saxony, which testifies to the commercial acumen of such factories as Volkstedt. This factory in particular made use of a mark ostensibly intended to represent crossed hayforks, but which were so drawn that they had close resemblance to the crossed swords. Certainly to mark the period of his directorship, and perhaps to make life more difficult for these unscrupulous copyists, Marcolini added an asterisk between the hilts of the swords which should not be confused with a much earlier workman's mark used by a painter in underglaze blue. The difficulty was finally resolved by a discussion with the Volkstedt director, Christian Nonne, at Leipzig in 1787.

The decree prohibiting Thuringian porcelain was later stiffened to include the sale of all porcelain not bearing the Meissen mark, but this law was not enforced stringently, probably because to do so would have been to invite reprisals and counter-measures from some of Meissen's export markets. Early in the 1750's Nicholas Sprimont, the owner of the English porcelain factory at Chelsea, had appealed for discrimination against Meissen porcelain, although there is no evidence that serious action was ever taken.[1]

Kändler and Acier were quarrelling, and the quarrels involved the modeller, Eloässer. The latter was eventually instructed to put down all orders in a book which he was to give first to Kändler who could choose half of them, whilst Acier had what remained—sufficient proof of Kändler's pre-eminence. But Kändler died in 1775 at the age of sixty-nine after forty-four years in the service of the factory.

Kändler's work has already been discussed to some extent, and it receives consideration in more detail in the following section of this book, but there is little doubt that his reputation was as high at the time of his death as it is today. This is a singularly unusual example of time confirming contemporary judgements. He left many debts which had been incurred, for the most part, because of the *Reiterdenkmal*. It was suggested at the time that this might be completed as a *Kändlerdenkmal*, but the technical difficulties were too great, and the partially completed work was eventually ordered to be destroyed. All that was left was the small model for the monument, and an unglazed head of the King.

By 1780 the vogue for porcelain as an exotic material was waning. It had, in fact, begun to die with the ending of the fashion for the rococo, and by now the neo-classical style was in

[1] Savage, *18th-Century English Porcelain* (Rockliff, 1952), pp. 91 et seq.

full tide. The simple functional shapes of Wedgwood's cheap creamware set an example followed rapidly by other factories. The new earthenwares were pleasant to handle, and were cheaper and easier to make. Decoration became less elaborate and luxurious.

In 1781 Acier was retired with a pension. His eyesight was failing, and he had lost touch with the artistic movements of the day. His place was taken by Christoph Gottfried Jüchtzer who did much work in biscuit, that is to say, in unglazed porcelain. Biscuit figures had been in vogue at Sèvres since the 1750's, but the Meissen body had never been particularly suitable for work of this kind, and it was not used for the purpose until the period of Marcolini's directorate. Jüchtzer was sent to study a collection of plaster casts which had been purchased by the Elector from Anton Mengs, and many of his models were adapted from this source.

Johann Carl Schönheit and Johann Gottlieb Matthäi were prominent as modellers. Schönheit worked mainly in the style of Acier. Matthäi had been employed since 1773, with a short interval in 1776 at Copenhagen. Originally apprenticed as a painter, he later changed to modelling. He was also keeper of the Mengs collection of casts at Dresden.

But the difficulties multiplied, and nothing Marcolini could do made any lasting improvement. Frequently the workers had to wait for payment of their wages, and, in 1789, the French Revolution, by creating a climate of opinion opposed to luxury in any form, increased the difficulties. By 1790 strenuous efforts were being made to open larger markets in the east—Russia, Poland and Turkey; and lotteries in which porcelain was offered as prizes were tried as a desperate expedient to raise money. But these newly-revived markets were spoiled by the second Russo-Turkish War (1787-1792) and in 1794 by the Polish Revolution.

By 1799 the debts of the factory had risen to such proportions that Marcolini asked permission to resign, but was cajoled into staying since there was no one who could conceivably have taken his place.

Finally, the Napoleonic Wars almost gave the factory its *coup de grâce*. Meissen and Dresden were both heavily bombarded in 1813, and work came to a standstill. A commission was set up in October 1813 by the Russian, Count Repnin, to consider ways and means of reviving it, and Marcolini was dismissed at the beginning of 1814. He died in Prague in the same year.

At this point it is proper to bring to a close this brief historical outline of the fortunes of the first century of porcelain manufacture at Meissen, because, in the present work, we are considering only the eighteenth century. Since that time Meissen has known foreign occupation on one other occasion. In 1945 the Russian armies entered the city, and it is now in East Germany. Nevertheless, it is still working, and it is to be hoped that its products will eventually find their way westward in greater quantities than at present. Whether or not Meissen can regain its old pre-eminence in the manufacture of porcelain in Europe remains to be seen, but for much of the eighteenth century its products were unmatched and unmatchable. Perhaps, even now, the old tradition can eventually be revived.

Böttger's Red Stoneware (Böttgersteinzeug)[1]

The red stoneware developed by von Tschirnhaus and Böttger in 1708 was made in large quantities during the first years of the factory's life, and despite numerous technical difficulties at first attending manufacture, it can be seen in considerable diversity of form and decoration.

The body is extremely hard, harder, in fact, than that of any other contemporary derivation from Yi Hsing ware. An exception is the black glazed variety, which is softer, probably because it was more lightly fired.

This stoneware can be separated into several categories by its surface appearance. The greater number of surviving specimens are a dark brownish-red in colour. Less often, a yellowish cast is

---

[1] *Steinzeug*=stoneware. *Steingut* is a much softer material.

to be seen, and a blackish-grey (*Eisenporzellan*) may have been due to variations in firing conditions. A marbled variety is seldom found. It has been thought that this effect was largely due to an accidental deviation, but Zimmermann[1] illustrates a covered mug decorated with a landscape which may point to its deliberate use. The black glazed ware already mentioned appears to have developed from an attempt to utilize kiln-wasters. Böttger devised the glaze from manganese and cobalt to cover surface faults of colour, and it was frequently decorated with oil-gilding and " cold " lacquer pigments. Martin Schnell, a lacquerer, was responsible for much work of this kind (Plate 5).

This variety apart, when the surface colour varies from the more usual red, the variation is on the surface only, the body being approximately the same in the interior as the more characteristically coloured specimens. This can clearly be seen in examples with engraved decoration which has cut through the surface to the body beneath.

Decoration falls naturally into several divisions. Designs incised with the glass-engraver's wheel are the more important. They are frequently elaborate, and appear to have been an especial favourite with Böttger himself. Probably the most usual design is a kind of *Laub- und Bandelwerk* (leaf- and strap-work), later used in painted form on white porcelain. The black-grey *Eisenporzellan*, and the black glazed ware were both treated in the same way, the incised work revealing the red body beneath the surface. The patterns formed by grinding into facets and depressions were referred to as *Muscheln*, and this was mostly done on a machine called the *Schleif- und Poliermühle* (grinding and polishing mill).[2] Bohemian glass engravers were also employed by the factory on this work (Plate 4b).

The material was so highly regarded that, apart from the care lavished on grinding and cutting, the goldsmiths of Munich and

---

[1] op. cit., illustration 29.
[2] A blue-print of this machine is illustrated by Berling, *Festschrift der Königlichen sächsischen Porzellanmanufaktur Meissen*. The *Inspektor* was the notorious Johann Georg Mehlhorn, discussed at somewhat greater length in the chapter on *Hausmalerei*.

Augsburg were employed to mount it in gold and silver. Setting with such semi-precious stones as the garnet and turquoise was done occasionally, and this practice was used—although very infrequently—for white porcelain at a later date (Plate 4b).

Applied plastic work in the form of leaves of the acanthus and laurel, flowers, vine leaves and things of this kind appears quite frequently, and they were sharply and delicately moulded. Pierced work, in imitation of the *ling-lung* (devil's work) of the late Ming dynasty, was undertaken occasionally, but surviving specimens are rare. Much red stoneware was highly polished, glass-workers' polishing techniques being employed for the purpose.

Whilst specimens decorated with lacquer colours on a black glaze are rarely to be seen, those decorated with enamels are even scarcer. The use of unfired gilding is to be noted, and this may have inspired a group of brownish-black glazed wares with meticulously rendered designs in gold and silver made at Bayreuth shortly after 1730 (Plate 4a).

The forms for which this body was employed were very numerous. Responsibility for this aspect rested principally on Peter Eggebrecht, the thrower, and Johann Jakob Irminger, goldsmith to the Saxon court. Many of the early specimens were close copies of Chinese originals and in some cases were cast from moulds taken directly from them. For the most part prototypes of this kind of reproduction seem to have been provided by Yi Hsing ware, although, in the case of figures, both soapstone carvings and *blanc de Chine* from Tê Hua (Fukien Province) were employed for the purpose.

The influence of Irminger is especially to be seen in the number of forms owing their primary inspiration to metalwork, an interesting variation on this theme being a coffee-pot based on a Turkish form, and having a turban-shaped cover. This kind of derivation is usually easy enough to see because the forms are more appropriate to the shears and hammer than to the potter's wheel. Thrown wares must necessarily have a circular section. Then, certain kinds of ornament are obviously more appropriate to metal. The beaded edge is an example. Repoussé ornament, such as gadrooning, can, in silver, only be fashioned with a pitch-block and hammer—purely a metalwork technique. These designs were transferred into stoneware by moulding, perhaps in some instances by means of moulds taken from an original silver vessel.

The form taken by cups is usually quite characteristic, with small bases curving outwards to a much greater diameter at the lip, and frequently with severe handles made with straight lines rather than curves. At other times the handles are scroll-shaped; sometimes elaborately so (Plate 6c).

Vases especially are repeatedly decorated with masks surrounded by formal ornament based, for the most part, on foliage. The stoneware version of the pilgrim-flask, which is also to be seen in silver, and in glass mounted in Augsburg copper-gilt, has masks of this kind on the shoulders. Knops to covers of vessels and vases are always formal and severe in shape.

I have mentioned the figures cast directly from Chinese prototypes; those in purely European styles were taken from varying sources. Giovanni Lorenzo Bernini was an unacknowledged contributor, and German ivory carvings were frequently copied, as witness a relief showing Judith with the head of Holofernes (Plate 2a). Honey suggests the ivory-carvers, Wilhelm Krüger and Johann Christoph Köhler, as sources.[1] Ivory carvings and Renaissance bronzes were perhaps the principal inspiration for early Meissen figure-work. The *commedia dell' arte* was particularly popular as a subject for figure models, which were brilliantly executed in a somewhat exaggerated baroque style (Plate 3). A few owe something to Jacques Callot (1593–1635)—a painter and engraver of Nancy to whom reference will be made again.

A number of models appear both in red stoneware and porcelain. Of these, a squatting Chinaman with grinning face is probably the most frequent and the most grotesque. The head and shoulders of a child in stoneware is pictured by Zimmermann[2]

[1] *Dresden China.*   [2] op. cit., illustration 54.

and the very rare porcelain version by Zimmermann[1] and by myself.[2]

Many objects were made in this material, ranging from table-wares to such purely decorative things as vases. The latter were often of considerable size, proving that when the initial difficulties had been surmounted, the material gave very little trouble during the process of forming and firing.

The actual date on which the factory ceased manufacture of this stoneware cannot be ascertained. Whilst it still appeared in the lists of 1731, it seems certain that its manufacture was progressively discontinued after the death of Böttger in 1719.

Böttger's White Porcelain (Böttgerporzellan)

In 1710 Böttger showed to Augustus two beaker-like cups, one glazed and the other unglazed, both of which were decorated with flowers in primitive enamel colours. These are now in the Dresden collection, and are pictured by Zimmermann.[3] But the manufacture of white porcelain on a truly commercial scale was not started until 1713, and the body used contained alabaster instead of feldspathic rock, as well as the newly-discovered white clay from Aue. Porcelain made in this way had a slightly yellowish tinge which is at variance with the purer white of the production under Höroldt. The body was fired to biscuit and later glazed, and this may account to some extent for the thickness of the glaze, and the vast number of minute bubbles which are often present in it.

Much of the production was left in white, although some of what is now white porcelain may have been decorated at the time with " cold " or lacquer colours which have since disappeared.

The enamels used were always somewhat primitive and not completely successful, but they were sufficiently distinctive in appearance. They comprised a yellow, blue, green, a rose-pink

---

[1] ibid., illustration 108.   [2] *Porcelain through the Ages*, Plate 20a.
[3] op. cit., illustration 70.

PLATE 33

Part of a *déjeuner* set
with scenes from
Werther.

Meissen. *c.* 1780.

PLATE 34

St. Nepomuk, by Kirchner.
Meissen. *c.* 1731.

PLATE 35

(a) Tea-pot of baroque form. Meissen. c. 1725.

b) Liqueur barrel with *chinoiseries*, by Kirchner. Meissen. c. 1730.

PLATE 36

Ram by Kändler.
Meissen. c. 1732.

PLATE 37

(*a*) Lion by Kändler.
Meissen. *c.* 1740.

(*b*) Bolognese dog by Kändler.
Meissen. *c.* 1740.

(*c*) Tea-pot in the form of a
monkey and young.
Meissen. *c.* 1735.

PLATE *38*

(*a*) A dove.
Meissen. *c.* 1733.

(*b*) Duck and drake tureens by Kändler.
Meissen. *c.* 1733.

PLATE 39

(a) A pair of parrots.
Meissen. c. 1733.

(b) A pair of woodpeckers.
Meissen. c. 1735.

PLATE 40

(*a*) A pair of jays.
Meissen. *c.* 1735.

(*b*) Cock and hen.
Meissen. *c.* 1740.

PLATE 41

(a) *Hofnarr* Fröhlich.
Meissen. *c.* 1740.

(b) Tureen in the form of a goose.
Meissen. *c.* 1737.

(c) Bird on a tree stump.
Meissen. *c.* 1740.

PLATE 42

Figure of St. John the Evangelist by Kändler.
Meissen. *c.* 1737.

PLATE 43

(a) A Bishop by Kändler.
Meissen. c. 1740.

(b) A Nun by Kändler.
Meissen. c. 1740.

(c) Bust of the Apostle Thomas by Kändler.
Meissen. c. 1740.

PLATE 44

Bust of Albert II by Kändler and Reinicke.
Meissen. *c.* 1744.

PLATE 45

Harlequin family by Kändler.
Meissen. *c.* 1741.

PLATE 46

(a) *Harlequin as a bird-seller*, by Kändler.
Meissen. *c.* 1745.

(b) *Harlequin playing bagpipes*, by Kändler.
Meissen. *c.* 1745.

PLATE 47

The Lawyer, from the Italian Comedy, by Kändler.
Meissen. *c.* 1745.

PLATE 48

(a) *Turk with lute*, by Kändler.
Meissen. *c.* 1745.

(b) Figure of a Miner by Kändler.
Meissen. *c.* 1745.

(c) Freemason by Kändler.
Meissen. *c.* 1740.

(d) Gallant as a Mason by Kändler.
Meissen. *c.* 1755.

(*Rosa*), an iron-red and a violet. The rose-pink is characteristic. A " mother of pearl " lustre of a purplish colour was discovered about 1715, and was occasionally used as a ground colour (*Fond-porzellan*), although true *Fondporzellan* was not introduced until the following decade. Honey suggests[1] the possibility of this lustre having been discovered in course of attempts to reproduce the Chinese underglaze copper-red, but gold used as a lustre pigment invariably yields a reddish-purple, and it had been known to have this property for about 150 years. Especially when we consider how rare specimens of underglaze copper-red must have been in Europe at the time, it seems at least as likely that Böttger discovered it in the course of researches into the production of gilding which could be fired in the enamelling kiln. Gold and silver were later both fired on to the glaze successfully, and rare examples of decoration in relief gilding which have been noted may be attributable to Christoph Konrad Hunger (Plate 135b). The earliest attempts at decoration of this kind were no more than oil-gilding.

The porcelain factory was established by royal decree on 23rd January, 1710, and housed in the Albrechtsburg at Meissen in March of the same year. The first productions were mainly replicas of the red stoneware, and applied and moulded decoration was much used from the beginning. This included flowers and foliage, and the acanthus, rose, vine and oak can all be identified. Some of this decoration was formal, probably influenced by oriental patterns and by baroque silver-work. Some was much less formal, and naturalistic flowers and foliage in high relief can be noticed (Plate 7c).

A veritable *tour de force* was the manufacture of porcelain with reticulated walls, reminiscent of the Chinese "devil's work". In some cases vessels thus made had double walls, the pierced design affecting only the outer wall. The twig handle was introduced during this period, although knops and handles are usually severe and formal. Masks, surrounded by formal foliage, were taken

[1] op. cit., p. 45.

over from the red stoneware. An exceptionally satisfying group of wares is quite plain in form, and the best of them are wheel-thrown.

Enamel colouring is not infrequent. Perhaps, at first, it was limited to heightening applied flowers with colour, but it was soon employed much more widely. Formal baroque ornament—" lacework " designs and the forerunner of the *Laub- und Bandel-werk*—is quite often seen. Some primitive landscapes and build-ings in iron-red are amusing, and landscapes and flowers in rose-pink are an example of the use of monochrome which appears to belong to the latter part of the period under discussion.

Gold is used in several forms, quite often alone, and occasionally to excess. Gold was used as a ground, and complete covering in matt gold with chased and burnished patterns appears to fore-shadow a technique used much later in the century. In this latter case, however, I cannot remember having seen a specimen, and would not, therefore, exclude the possibility of those which exist being the work of a decorator outside the factory at a later date.

Silver was used, and has nearly always oxidized to black. It is probably for this reason that its use was eventually discontinued.

The lustre colour mentioned is not at all unusual, and it was employed, also, in the following decade. It can, in fact, be seen as late as 1730.

Many attempts were made to use underglaze cobalt blue, but none was successful, probably because the temperature necessary to fire the body was too high to develop the colour properly. A few specimens thus decorated survive but are both primitive and defective.

Uncharacteristic decorations on undoubted Böttger porcelain are usually the work of outside decorators. Much Böttger porce-lain still in stock in white was sold in 1735 to the *Hausmaler*[1] and subsequently painted. In certain cases the artist responsible can be identified.

---

[1] *Hausmaler*: lit. " home painter". *Hausmalerei* forms a distinct and important group of German wares which were painted by independent artists in their own homes (see chapter 14).

Figures in Böttger porcelain are not often to be seen. Some were made from moulds taken directly from Chinese originals. Others are obvious translations of Chinese subjects into the European idiom. The example shown on Plate 4d is an unusual miniature version. Zimmermann[1] depicts one seated in a shrine which is decorated in a purely European manner with baroque ornament in relief, including the ubiquitous masks. Some of these Chinese figures were made as pastille-burners, the smoke emerging through the mouth.

Naturally, statuettes of Augustus were made. It was necessary to flatter the vanity of a patron so highly placed, but it is also possible to detect in the mock-heroic attitude a certain flavour of irony.

Figures of dwarfs after Jacques Callot—somewhat misshapen caricatures—are often attributed to the modeller Georg Fritzsche. In 1712 Fritzsche is listed as an apprentice at a salary of 1.12 thalers a month, and is the only apprentice mentioned, with the exception of Johann Samuel Grünlich, who was awarded 1 thaler a month.

The same list shows Johann Georg Heinze [sic] as a member of the laboratory staff. He can probably be identified with Johann Georg Heintze, the landscape painter, who did some notable work between 1720 and 1749.

Meissen Service-ware to 1800

The advent of Johann Gregor Höroldt brought some speedy changes for the better in the quality and style of the painted decoration. The enamel colours he introduced gave a new and more brilliant palette, with a greater diversity of colouring than had been possible hitherto. But in addition, research was continued towards the conquest of some of the outstanding technical difficulties. For instance, the use of feldspathic rock in place of alabaster gave a whiter and more tractable body, and the problem

[1] op. cit., illustration 99.

of using cobalt blue underglaze was solved. This eluded the Meissen colour chemists until 1720, although many attempts had been made to use it. The blue and white porcelains of the Chinese Emperors, Wan Li (1573–1619) and K'ang Hsi (1662–1722), were being imported into Europe in large quantities, and were regarded as especially desirable. Augustus offered a reward of 1,000 thalers for the discovery of an effective method of attaining this colour, but it was not until a year after Böttger's death that David Köhler, an arcanist and *Obermeister* at the factory, with the assistance of Johann Georg Mehlhorn and his son, Johann Gottfried, succeeded in evolving a practicable underglaze blue of reasonably good quality. When Köhler died in 1725 he confided the secret to Höroldt, but in 1727 more trouble was experienced, and blue of good quality was not made again until 1732. Johann David Kretschmar then became responsible for this kind of decoration, and added the initial " K " to his work, which appears either in conjunction with the mark of the crossed swords, or on the footring. Other painters added various identifying marks. The letter " E " probably signifies Christian Friedrich Engelmann who worked as a painter in blue, and another addition of the kind was an asterisk which should not be confused with the much later mark of the Marcolini period (1784–1812). Specimens I have noticed have had the asterisk between the *points* of the swords instead of between the *hilts* as in the later pieces.

The earliest examples of blue painting during this period vary from a blackish-blue to a fairly pure blue of a lightish shade. Cobalt frequently takes on this blackish tinge if it is fired at too high a temperature. A much paler colour having a washed-out and " misty " appearance can sometimes be seen on specimens sold as wasters, and some of these were overpainted and overgilded by the *Hausmaler*, F. J. Ferner.

A number of early vases of large size, based on Chinese prototypes, were painted in a blackish-blue, whereas smaller pieces often exhibit blue of a much purer colour, and this variation may have been due to differences in the composition of the body, and the consequent differences in firing temperature required. In fact experiments were addressed towards finding the most suitable body and glaze for this colour, but something may have been due, too, to the impurities in the materials used. This was an extremely common source of trouble during the eighteenth century, no exact methods of refinement then being available.

After the advent of Kretschmar underglaze blue was no longer regarded as particularly fashionable for the more important services, although it was used fairly extensively. The so-called " onion " pattern (*Zwiebelmuster*) of Chinese derivation and the *Strohblumenmuster* of formalized plum-blossom from Japanese sources were popular. The latter eventually was copied at Copenhagen and elsewhere. These patterns were manufactured extensively at the time, and eighteenth-century specimens are not uncommon today. The *Zwiebelmuster* is still employed by the factory. Another pattern in this category, the *Blaublümchenmuster* (blue flower pattern), was derived from the " aster " pattern of the late Ming period.

A few other standard blue and white patterns are the *Chrysanthemummuster*, an elaborate floral pattern with diaper borders, the *Weidenmuster* (willow pattern), a design of Chinese flowers with a drooping willow in the background, the *Festonenmuster* which has formal European foliage in festoons, and the *Blätterkantenmuster*, a border pattern of interlaced leaves. The use of underglaze blue for *deutsche Blumen* and figure painting is rare, but can be seen occasionally.

Underglaze blue was also used in conjunction with enamel colours, principally on porcelain painted in the Japanese *Imari* style. This decoration, based on native brocades, was not particularly popular with the factory, and specimens (nearly always plates) are not common.

Meissen did not at any time achieve much success with underglaze blue, and, apart from the patterns mentioned specifically, relatively little use was made of the colour.

When we turn to the polychrome decorations, we find that the

most important single category is that comprising the little
pseudo-Chinese figures, either alone or set amidst exotic oriental
landscapes. These *chinoiseries* are derived only indirectly from
oriental sources, and are in the nature of imaginative delineations
of the Chinese scene by artists whose enthusiasm outran their
knowledge.

Most *chinoiseries* are drawn in an amusing and exaggerated
fashion. Their popularity as a decorative theme on European
pottery and porcelain was widespread, and lasted for a considerable period. At Meissen the fashion had just about run its course
by the middle of the 1730's, although it lingered on elsewhere.
In porcelain, they owe their inception to Meissen, where the first
to appear were in gold and silver silhouette. Two jugs decorated
in silver silhouette—much the rarer of the two varieties—are in
the Kunstgewerbemuseum at Cologne, and I have recently
observed a double-handled cup of Böttger porcelain thus decorated. The silver, naturally, had oxidized to black.

The attribution of this type to the factory is a somewhat
controversial point, since W. B. Honey[1] expressed the opinion
that this kind of *chinoiserie* ought more properly to be attributed
to later *Hausmalerei*. Whilst some examples, characterized by the
appearance of C-shaped scrolls in the border ornament, should, no
doubt, be given to Barthomäus Seuter as suggested by Honey, in
my opinion to suppose that the whole group should be taken
from the factory in consequence is strictly analogous to throwing
out the baby with the bath water. Honey cited in evidence a cup
and saucer with the " C " scrolls signed *A. Seite 1736 Augusta*,
explaining the appearance of this kind of decoration on much
earlier porcelain by assuming that Seuter had been able to purchase
supplies of earlier ware in white for decoration. This, in fact, he
did—in 1735. There is also record of a tankard with a *Kapuzinerbraun* glaze (see p. 74) decorated with gold *chinoiseries*, signed by
Christian Friedrich Herold, and dated 1732. Whilst the signature

---

[1] op. cit., p. 53, and *Augsburger Goldchinesen und Watteau-Bilder auf fruhem Meissener
Porzellan* (Pantheon, 1938).

and the date suggests that Herold did this in his capacity as *Hausmaler*, he was also a factory artist, and likely to have used factory styles. Examples of glazed red stoneware thus decorated have been recorded, and the Bayreuth use of gold and silver *chinoiseries* in silhouette on imitations of the red stoneware may have been derived from this practice (see Plate 4a). While the latter was still being manufactured in 1720, and for perhaps a decade afterwards, I do not think the *Hausmaler* would have purchased a then outmoded ware which was also such unpromising material for attentions of this kind. Since Honey himself referred (p. 66, op. cit.) to gilt *chinoiseries* as being among the earliest factory work, I do not think he was wholly serious in his suggestion.

Leaving all this to one side, however, it is my opinion that the gilt *chinoiserie* was an established factory pattern by 1720 and I suggest that those rare examples one sees in which the gilding is primitive and imperfectly fired on to the glaze can certainly be regarded as factory work. Despite Honey's opinion to the contrary, I think these may have been the work of Cornelius Funke (or Funcke) who worked between *c.* 1713 and *c.* 1726. Plate 34a leaves no doubt that the gold *chinoiserie* was a factory pattern in 1725. The decoration of this tea-pot, which may have been designed by Georg Fritzsche, would certainly not have been left to a *Hausmaler*.[1]

Chinoiseries in polychrome were probably made fashionable by Höroldt, although the earliest were painted in enamels used during the Böttger period. These may have been inspired by the *Hausmaler*, Aufenwerth. Höroldt's *chinoiseries* are frequently in the manner of an engraving in the Graphische Sammlung in Munich which is inscribed *J. G. Höroldt inv. et fecit 1726*, a statement which is an uncompromising claim to authorship on his part. Engravings of this kind, which have been variously illustrated by Schmidt,[2] Hofmann,[3] Honey,[4] and others, are sometimes brought in

---

[1] Since this was written a newly-discovered vase signed by Höroldt has been illustrated, and has Chinese figures in gold silhouette over a powder-blue ground. See footnote on p. 45.
[2] op. cit.   [3] op. cit.   [4] *Dresden China.*

evidence that this type of painting on Meissen porcelain was executed by Höroldt himself, but this, in my opinion, partakes of at least an element of wishful thinking.

The Höroldt engraving is an amusing production and shows many of the elements to be recognized in a distinctive and important group of Meissen *chinoiseries*—the fire-breathing dragon in the sky, the drum-shaped table with medallions in relief, the curious head-dress of the seated Mandarin, and so forth. The lengths to which the fantasy element was carried can well be seen in the cream-jug illustrated, which, in addition to the more usual Chinese figures, has what seems to be a seated American Indian with a negroid skin colour and a fully feathered head-dress (Plate 11a).[1]

A coffee-service of 1735 shows the Archbishop-Elector Clemens August von Köln wearing a Chinese hat, sword and a cross (Plate 15a), and on two vases from the one-time residential castle of Dresden we find Augustus himself portrayed as the Son of Heaven.[2]

Apart from the suggestion of Aufenwerth already put forward, it is difficult to be certain whence Höroldt derived his primary inspiration. Several German publishers issued books of this kind during the seventeenth and eighteenth centuries, Martin Engelbrecht of Augsburg being an example. Höroldt's own designs showed more than a little originality in their execution whilst following the general mode.

At a somewhat later date, Gillot, Watteau and Boucher also provided inspiration for work of this kind which was copied by the porcelain painters, and the influence of the engraver Pillement can be traced not only on the Continent but in England, to which several designs by Robert Hancock will testify.

There are a number of definite categories into which *chinoiseries* may be separated. The most often seen is that already mentioned as being similar to the Höroldt engravings. It is likely that these

[1] A figure of this kind was made at Chelsea about 1755 (Cecil Higgins Collection, Bedford), and was probably taken from a Meissen model. The flesh is enamelled black.

[2] Arno Schönberger, *Meissener Porzellan mit Höroldt-malerei*.

were given to the factory painters to copy, and they were used either on white porcelain (usually), or in conjunction with coloured grounds (more rarely).

They were by no means the earliest in this manner, however, but were preceded by a group in which the figures are much larger and are mostly delineated from slightly below the waist upwards. These have masses of billowing clouds, slightly tinged with orange, and a curious feature is the number of small birds in the sky, indicated by two or three lines drawn with a fine brush in the conventional manner. They are in panels, and the remainder of the white porcelain is decorated with baroque traceries in gilding reminiscent of those to be seen on Böttger porcelain, where these gilt patterns were sometimes used as the sole ornamental theme.

A development of the Höroldt type of *chinoiserie*, which usually has a green foreground based on a brown stripe, is to be found in the use of gold to heighten the painting itself. The *chinoiseries* on white porcelain are either continuous, perhaps two scenes separated only by isolated *indianischen Blumen*,[1] or are surrounded by an elaborate framing of scroll-work in gold, to which violet and iron-red were often added. Until 1730, the occasional use of Böttger's lustre pigment is to be noted. *Chinoiseries* in reserved panels in conjunction with coloured grounds of a fully-developed kind are generally surrounded by a plain gold line, often of quatrefoil shape, and can usually be awarded a date subsequent to 1730, although there was a yellow ground vase with a rather unusual design featuring a long flight of steps which was signed by Höroldt in 1727.[2]

Of the other artists said to have worked in this style, Christian Friedrich Herold and A. F. von Löwenfinck must be singled out for mention.

Probably C. F. Herold introduced a style in which the *chinoiserie* was given a more or less elaborate base of scroll-work, continuous with the remainder of the surrounding ornament, in

[1] " India " flowers.   [2] See footnote on p. 75.

place of the usual rendering of grass and earth by green and brown stripes. A very distinctive type with a Japanese flavour is sometimes attributed to von Löwenfinck, but the attribution has its elements of doubt. The suggestion that he had a precursor who worked in this style has much to commend it when the facts are examined. In the factory's list of painters of 1731 he appears only as a painter of flowers, but this is later discussed in a little more detail.

The painting of *chinoiseries* must have been in a number of hands, most of whom cannot be identified, even tentatively. Two possible names are Johann Cristoph Horn, who worked between 1720 and 1760, and Johann Ehrenfried Stadtler, who was at the factory from 1724 onwards. There is evidence for the latter in the form of a painting of Chinese figures which is initialled " IES ".

In the list of painters for 1731 the following artists are recorded as painting " *Jappanischen Figuren* "—Johann Christoph Horn, Johann Heinrich Wolff, Christian Friedrich Herold, Johann Gottlieb Herrmann, Johann Gottlieb Erbsmehl and Johann Thob. Locke.

It has been suggested that a tankard in Höroldt style at Leipzig, inscribed *Johann Gottlob Schlimpert, Meissen, 10. July 1725*, was painted by this man, but there is no record of him as a factory artist, and it was almost certainly made *for* him, despite occasional assertions to the contrary. The painter was quite possibly Höroldt himself.

Among the earliest of the purely European subjects we must place Meissen landscape and topographical painting which first appears shortly after 1720, and indeed some of the earliest of the *chinoiseries* are set in landscapes which are European. To this class belong river scenes which were inspired by the River Elbe, and views of the countryside around Dresden. These early essays into landscape had much of the quality of a miniature drawing in perspective, and were rather more topographical in flavour than those of a decade or so later. Schönberger suggests Heintze for this kind of work, and as I have remarked earlier, a Johann Georg Heintze appears in the factory list for 1712. Honey[1] records his existence at Meissen only from 1720 to 1749, and in the latter year he was imprisoned for painting porcelain at home, a practice in which C. F. Herold indulged also, but in his case presumably his kinship with the *Hofmaler* saved him from a like fate.[2]

The early topographical painting had, for the most part, been replaced by the *chinoiserie* by 1725; but somewhat similar themes of decoration were carried out in the early period in the *Schwarzlot* technique (Plate 23), sometimes by the factory, and sometimes by *Hausmaler*. *Hausmalerei* is, in fact, rather more common than factory work in this style. *Schwarzlot*, more popular at Vienna than at Meissen, is decoration in black enamel, strongly linear in drawing (which was probably due to the influence of the engravings from which many of these things were taken), with sometimes the addition of a little iron-red, particularly where it was desired to indicate flesh-colour. Gilding was additional, and the monochrome technique was extended by the occasional use of purple for the same purpose, as well as iron-red.

Representations of shipping in harbours and scenes on the quayside—the so-called " harbour scenes "—became popular in the 1730's, although they had first appeared as early as 1724. They can be seen in great variety, but can be divided into two main classes—the "Dutch Harbour Scene", which is the more obviously European in flavour, and another kind which frequently has exotic oriental figures, Turkish and Chinese, mingling with European merchants on the quayside (Plate 22b). Usually barrels and bales of merchandise are to be seen, with ships of one kind or another, and sometimes vertical hoisting spars in the foregound. These were frequently derived from Augsburg engravings of Italian ports by Melchior Kysell after Johann Wilhelm Baur. A service painted by Johann Balthasar Borrmann (1725–1784), subsequently at Berlin, shows Dutch ports and harbours, and was done for the Stadtholder of Holland about 1763 (Plate 27).

[1] *Dictionary of European Ceramic Art.*   [2] See p. 212.

The principal artists engaged on this kind or work were C. F. Herold, J. G. Heintze and Bonaventura Gottlieb Häuer. Occasionally one finds a piece of this period with an " H " in gold on the base, inside the foot-ring. But lest my reader be tempted to identify an initial of this kind with either Höroldt or Herold, it is wise to remember that the factory did not at any time favour the practice of an artist signing his work so that it could be identified by anyone outside its walls. Moreover, as Schönberger[1] so aptly comments, in a situation where there are painters named Höroldt, Herold, Heintze, Häuer, Horn and Herrmann, a single initial of this kind is very slender evidence for an identification.

Christian Friedrich Herold (or Heroldt) was probably a kinsman of J. G. Höroldt. He was born in 1700, and there is evidence that he worked in Berlin for Alex. Fromery as an enameller. He was at Meissen from 1725 until two years before his death in 1779. There is a cup and saucer in the British Museum signed *C. F. Herold invt. et fecit a Meisse 1750, d. 12 Sept.*, and a number of other works, principally enamels, are known signed in other ways (Plate 26a).

Häuer's work so closely resembles that of Heintze that it is almost impossible to separate the two. He joined the factory in 1724 at the age of fourteen, and the list of painters of 1731 records him as having been born at Freiberg in 1710. At this time he was painting " delicate " figures and landscapes—*In feinen Figuren u. Landschaffien* [sic]. His work has been identified by a service discovered in Switzerland and later sold in London. This bore the initials " BGH ".

Heintze was later at Vienna and Berlin, but nothing of his work at these places has been identified. A signed enamel plaque by him is in the Landes Gewerbemuseum at Stuttgart, and I have observed a cup and saucer which I considered to be by his hand which had the initials " JGH " on an inn-sign. Milestones bearing a date, or recording the distance to Dresden, are regarded as being by Heintze (Plate 25a).

[1] op. cit.

Other painters of landscapes—*Landschaften*—in the same list are Herold, Heintze, Johann Benjamin Wentzel, Johann Gottlieb Erbsmehl, Johann Christian Diettrich and Johann Gottlieb Lehmann. Diettrich was also an instructor at Meissen, and it is, perhaps, worth a passing thought that he may have been related to Christian Wilhelm Ernst Dietrich, who was almost the same age, and who became art director at Meissen in 1764. The latter painted and initialled a tankard in 1730 which is in the Victoria and Albert Museum (Plate 143). Karl Wilhelm Böhme painted both landscapes and figures from 1736 to c. 1761. He was later *Obermaler* at Berlin.

A distinct development of the landscape may be noticed in the battle scenes (*Schlachtenszenen*) which come into use in the early 1740's. Some are camp scenes, and others depict actual combat. The artist responsible for the earliest examples cannot be identified with certainty, but the subject was a favourite with Johann Balthasar Borrman who worked at Meissen prior to 1763, and from this year until 1779, at Berlin.

Another painter of battle scenes was Christian Friedrich Kühnel (1719–1792), who was at the factory from about 1740 to 1780. A plate in the Franks Collection (British Museum) is signed by him. Turkish and Polish soldiers in combat are likely to be by his hand. These would have been painted after 1775, the year of the Russo-Turkish War.

Although the Italian Comedy (*italienische Komödie*) was a popular subject for figures, the representation of characters from this source are chiefly to be found in paintings in the manner of Watteau done during the 1750's. Nevertheless, almost the first recorded instance of a Harlequin in European porcelain painting can be seen in a plate of about 1725,[1] and Watteau scenes are to be noted from about 1735 onwards (Plate 29), some in green monochrome.

Armorial services (*Wappengeschirre*) are those painted with the arms of the owner, a typical example being the Swan Service made

[1] Arno Schönberger, op. cit.

for von Brühl, and that made for the Elector of Mainz in which the armorial bearings are carried on a shield supported by a realistically modelled lion standing on its hind legs where ever this could be used appropriately (Plates 17 and 18).

Flower painting at Meissen falls under two distinct headings— the *indianische Blumen* (India flowers), and the *deutsche Blumen* (German flowers). The former were taken from Chinese and Japanese sources, and include formalized Japanese flowers, as well as the more luxuriant derivations from the Chinese *famille rose*. The Chinese source used was the later work of the reign of the Emperors K'ang Hsi (1662–1722) and of Yung Chêng (1723– 1735). The palette was based on that of the Chinese, and frequently exceeds the original in brilliance. These colours were first used in China shortly after 1700, but were not popular until the reign of Yung Chêng. The finest Meissen examples of this kind of painting can be seen on vases made for Augustus which sometimes bear his monogram as a mark.

The *deutsche Blumen* (Plate 21) became fashionable about 1735, and were a revival of an earlier style of *faïence* painting. At Vienna this decoration appears at an earlier date than at Meissen. At first these flowers were stiff and formal, and were copied from such works as the *Phylanthus Iconographia*[1] of Johann Wilhelm Weinmann, a Regensburg apothecary, which was published in Augsburg in 1737, as well as similar works by Schmidhammer and J. D. Preisler, and one mentioned in chapter 14 which was, in part, the work of Bartholomäus Seuter. As time passed the initial stiffness relaxed, and the painting became more naturalistic in style, with flowers tied in bouquets, or thrown across the surface in sprays. A class of flowers which have shadows round them (*ombrirte deutsche Blumen*), and small insects similarly treated, are attributed to the painter Johann Gottfried Klinger on the evidence of a signed tankard dated 1742 in the Berlin Schlossmuseum.

---

[1] In full: *Phylanthus Iconographia, or the real presentation of more than one thousand indigenous and foreign plants, trees and weeds.*

Klinger was at Meissen in 1731 and appears in the list as an apprentice (*Lehrling*). His age is given as twenty years. He was at Meissen until 1746, when he left to work at Vienna where he remained until his death in 1781. There is little doubt that he also functioned as a *Hausmaler*. Honey gives his date of birth as 1701[1] which conflicts with the Meissen list.

Indianische Blumen (Plate 9a) were divided, as I have said, into two distinct kinds. The term " India flowers " stemmed from the fact that imports of far eastern porcelain came to Europe in the ships of the East India Companies, and Japanese porcelain was accorded equal status with the Chinese.

Until recently Japanese porcelain was little known, even among collectors of far eastern ceramics, but Augustus and his contemporaries gave it a high place in their esteem, and it is, in many instances, superior to Chinese productions of the same period. Particularly does this apply to the porcelain of Arita and Kutani. The finest polychrome porcelains from Arita (Hizen Province) were decorated by Sakaida Kakiemon, a member of a family of porcelain enamellers, and porcelain decorated in the Kakiemon style was not only in great demand, but was copied by most of the early European factories. The style, itself, is unmistakable. It is characterized by asymmetricality, and the white porcelain ground is much in evidence. The palette is distinctive—iron-red, turquoise, green, a lilac blue, and yellow. Underglaze blue was employed on the earlier specimens. Often a chocolate brown line was used to define the rim, and less often a little gilding can be seen. The colouring of the European derivatives follows that of the originals more or less closely, sometimes so closely as to be almost indistinguishable on superficial examination.

To this group belongs such patterns as the *Quail*; the *Banded Hedge*, the *Flying Squirrel* (*fliegender Hund*); the *Yellow Tiger* (*gelbe Löwen*), first used on a service made for Augustus about 1728; and the *Red Dragon* (*roter Drache*), a design carried out in

[1] *Dictionary of European Ceramic Art.*

iron-red and gilding about 1730.[1] The *Hob in the Well* pattern, a characteristic Kakiemon design, is illustrated by Zimmermann.[2] This is so called from the name given to it at the English factory of Chelsea. It records the story of the boyhood of the Chinese sage, Ssŭ Ma, who saved a playmate from drowning in a large porcelain fish-bowl by smashing it with a stone. The use of underglaze blue on these Japanese derivations indicates a date about 1725.

Apart from the patterns I have named, there were a number, less well known, which were either copied direct, or used in combination with others, that is to say, a Meissen pattern might contain the elements of several Japanese patterns. The small decorative accessories, such as formal single flowers and flower-sprays, were reasonably faithful copies of the Japanese originals, and were often used to cover small glaze faults. Small insects and flowers in the European style were frequently used for the same purpose, and this was a practice taken over from the earlier decorators of German *faïence*.

The later Japanese style, called the " Imari " from the name of the port of shipment in Hizen Province from which this porcelain was exported, is overcrowded in comparison with the Kakiemon types, and the general aspect is fussy and unpleasing. Apparently the factory was of the same opinion, because it is relatively scarce.

Decoration in the Chinese manner usually consists in conservative copies of existing Chinese porcelain painting. Thus, we have the magnificent vases made for Augustus with peonies and flowers in the *famille rose* palette. The *rose* of Höroldt was rather more inclined to a purple colour, perhaps as the result of firing at a slightly higher temperature than that used in China. If the firing temperature of *rose* enamel is progressively raised, it becomes increasingly purple in tone.

Famille verte is an earlier Chinese style characterized by the

---

[1] The German equivalents of the English names for these Japanese patterns are given in brackets. They are not a translation.

[2] *Meissner Porzellan*, Plate 5.

PLATE 49

(*a*) Chinese figure. Eberlein.
Meissen. *c.* 1735.

(*b*) Chinese figure. Eberlein.
Meissen. *c.* 1735.

(*c*) Chinese Lovers in an arbour. Eberlein.
Meissen. *c.* 1745.

PLATE 50

Group of *chinoiserie* figures.
Meissen. 1740–45.

PLATE 51

(a) Mother and children, by Kändler. Meissen. c. 1750.

(b) *The Good Housekeeper*, by Kändler. Meissen. c. 1750.

(c) Hurdy-gurdy Player and Bagpiper, by Kändler. Meissen. c. 1740.

PLATE 52

(a) *The Drunken Fisherman*, by Kändler.
Meissen. c. 1745.

(b) Fisherman, by Reinicke.
Meissen. c. 1745.

(c) The goat-seller, by Kändler.
Meissen. c. 1740.

(d) Beggar leaning on a staff.
Meissen. c. 1750.

PLATE 53

Alte Liebe. Satirical group by Kändler.
Meissen. *c.* 1765.

PLATE 54

(*a*) *Toilette of the Princess.*
Meissen. *c.* 1750.

(*b*) Woman in a crinoline.
Meissen. *c.* 1741.

PLATE 55

Lady and Gallant, by Kändler.
Meissen. *c.* 1740.

PLATE 56

Lady and Gallant, by Kändler.
Meissen. *c.* 1740.

PLATE 57

River God. Contemporary ormolu mounts.
Meissen. *c.* 1750.

PLATE 58

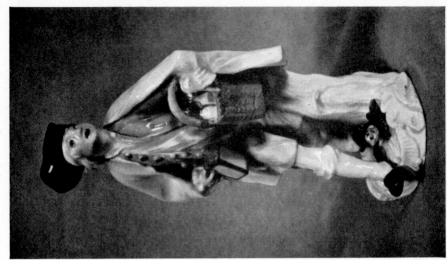

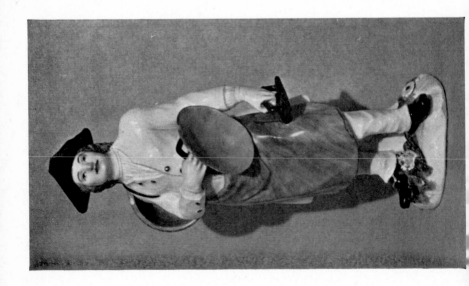

(a, left) Chaudronnier, by Kändler.
Meissen. c. 1745.

(b, right) Nightwatchman, by Kändler
and Reinicke.
Meissen. c. 1753.

PLATE 59

(a) *A Polish Hussar*, by Kändler and Reinicke.
Meissen. *c.* 1750.

(b) Peasant mounted, by Reinicke.
c. 1750.

(c) Peasant with cow, by Reinicke.
c. 1750.

PLATE 60

(a) *Prudentia*.
Meissen. *c.* 1750.

(b) *Vulcan*, by Reinicke.
Meissen. *c.* 1741.

PLATE 61

Temple of Love, by Kändler.
Meissen. *c.* 1750.

PLATE 62

(a) Girl playing a woodwind instrument.
Meissen. c. 1755.

(b) Figure of a child.
Meissen. c. 1755.

(c) *Putto* as a sculptor, by F. E. Meyer.
Meissen. c. 1755.

(d) *Putto* carrying a magic lantern.
Meissen. c. 1755.

PLATE 63

(a) Bacchus group.
Meissen. c. 1770.

(b) Figure of Apollo.
Meissen. c. 1765.

(c) Family group by Acier.
Meissen. c. 1775.

PLATE 64

(*a*) Fluted bowl with baroque ornament.
Vienna. *c.* 1725.

(*b*) Flower holder with underglaze blue and lilac decoration.
Vienna. 1721.

presence of a brilliant green enamel. The palette also contains a red which was obtained from iron oxide. This is quite distinct from *rose*, and approaches a rust-red in shade. These are seen with relative infrequency.

A painter not hitherto accorded more than passing mention is Adam Friedrich von Löwenfinck who was seventeen years of age in 1731. He was born in 1714, and apprenticed at Meissen at the exceptionally early age of thirteen years. He worked as a painter of "flowers in colour", and ended his apprenticeship in 1734. Apparently dissatisfied with his position at the factory, he fled to Bayreuth in October 1736, where he became a flower-painter on *faïence*, and when the factory pursued him there, he went on to the French factory at Chantilly, then making a tin-glazed soft porcelain. He returned to Germany about 1740, and obtained employment as a painter, first at Ansbach, going thence to Fulda. Then he left for Höchst, where he was connected with the earliest attempts to found a factory there, probably in the capacity of arcanist, and, finally, after many vicissitudes, he came to the *faïence* factory of Haguenau, in Alsace, and died there in 1754. His wife, Maria Seraphia, continued to operate this factory after his death.

Adam Friedrich had two brothers, Carl Heinrich von Löwenfinck, who was apprenticed at Meissen in 1730 at the age of twelve years, and who was later at Chantilly, Ansbach and Fulda, after which we lose sight of him, and Christian Wilhelm, who was apprenticed at Meissen in 1734, ended his apprenticeship in 1740, and later worked at Fulda, Höchst and Haguenau. These two brothers were both flower painters.

Adam Friedrich von Löwenfinck is a typical example of the wandering arcanist so common at the time. His work at Meissen includes, perhaps, some *chinoiseries* rather more in the Kakiemon style, and animals with curious trifid tails and often sharply-pointed noses (Plates 13b and 14). The exact identification of his flower painting is difficult. Some signed examples of his later work have been recorded, and it has been suggested that he concealed his initials occasionally in his painting at Meissen. Although I have not, myself, seen a specimen thus signed, the possibility ought to be borne in mind in examining specimens likely to have been painted by him, since he was obviously a dissatisfied workman.

Fondporzellan means, simply, porcelain decorated with ground colours. Usually, panels are left in white—reserved is the correct term—within the confines of which decorative painting is executed. The line of demarcation between ground and reserve is usually covered by a plain band of gold to accent the transition, and to hide any raggedness of the edge of the ground colour. Porcelain with a coloured ground is not a European invention. The Chinese used this kind of decoration during the Ming dynasty (1368–1643) (Plate 13b).

The first use of ground colours at Meissen can be found in the early 1720's. The *Kapuzinerbraun* (sometimes called *Kaffeebraun*) may have been the invention of Samuel Stölzel. The term probably refers to the colour of the habit of the Capuchin monks, of whom one was modelled by Kändler at a later date. The alternative, coffee-brown, is self-explanatory.

Six dishes of this kind were delivered in 1722, and thus we can date the introduction of *Kapuzinerbraun* with some accuracy. Ludwig Danckert[1] refers to *Schnittdekor* (cut decoration) in connection with this glaze. The meaning is a little obscure, but I think he is referring to a development of the Böttger technique in which the design was cut through the glaze to reveal the white porcelain beneath. *Schnitt* can mean equally cut or incised. I have been successful in locating one specimen corresponding to this reading of *Schnittdekor*, and it is confirmed to some extent by the fact that Dutch glass-workers amused themselves by cutting birds and flowers on cups of "dead-leaf brown", which may have been Chinese, or of Meissen porcelain with the *Kapuzinerbraun* glaze.

[1] *Handbuch des europäischen Porzellans* (Munich, 1954).

Underglaze blue itself was adapted for use in powder form. This was done commonly in China, where the colour was blown on to the porcelain through a bamboo tube which had a silk screen at one end.

By about 1727 many important ground colours had been devised. A vase in the Dresden Collection[1] had a yellow ground and was signed *Johann Gregorius Höroldt inv. Meissen den 22. Jann. Anno 1727*. Honey's suggestion that the inscription refers to the yellow ground can hardly be contested. This was the only specimen of porcelain known signed by Höroldt, and since Augustus was especially eager for a yellow ground, it would appear to have marked a special occasion.[2] This colour was speedily available in shades which ranged from pale biscuit to a deep yellow, and about the same time the factory were able to use three distinct shades of green, including a sea-green which inclines to turquoise and a light apple green. Pale grey, lilac blue and lavender were all available, as well as a *clair-de-lune*, which is a pale greyish-blue made in imitation of the colour of certain eighteenth-century Chinese wares which, in their turn, copied the *Ko* ware of the Sung dynasty. A rich crimson-purple, somewhat resembling the raspberry in shade, is a particularly sumptuous colour.

A celadon glaze was known, but rarely used. "Celadon" refers to a coloured glaze developed by the Chinese as early as the T'ang period (618–906). It is usually green in colour, and the term is probably derived from the fact that Salāh-ed-dīn, Sultan of Egypt, sent forty pieces of this ware to Nūr-ed-dīn, Sultan of Damascus, in 1171—a time at which it was of the greatest rarity outside the country of its origin. The Meissen version of this glaze is represented in the British Museum (Franks Collection) by a very rare model of an elephant. No other factory could use this colour during the eighteenth century.

[1] Illustrated by Zimmermann, *Meissner Porzellan*, Plate 11.
[2] This vase was destroyed during the war, but a vase signed "J. G. Höroldt fec. Meissen 17 Augusti 1726" was discovered in 1952. This is painted with *chinoiseries* and *indianische Blumen* in conjunction with a powder-blue ground and gold silhouettes. See Handt and Rakebrand, *Meissner Porzellan des Achtzehnten Jahrhunderts, 1710-1750* (Dresden, 1957), p. 23 and Plates 36 and 37.

These ground colours later fell into disuse, to be replaced by the *Mosaikrand*, or *Mosaik* border, in which small areas of ground colour were overpainted with diaper patterns and scale designs somewhat similar to those to be seen on contemporary Worcester porcelain in England.

About 1730 experiments were conducted with coloured pastes —pale blue, brown, green and grey—which were decorated with white reliefs and glazed.[1] These may have been Wedgwood's inspiration when, later in the century, he developed his blue jasper-ware which was similarly decorated, but unglazed. The principle is the same. If this is so, we can see an amusing example of back-copying in the Marcolini period towards the end of the century, when Meissen did a certain amount of *Wedgwood-arbeiten* in the form of portraits and classical medallions in a body imitating the jasper, with relief work in white, as well as service-ware (Plate 32a).

Many experiments were made with porcelain bodies, and a number of different variations may be distinguished by careful observation. The earliest examples have, mostly, a creamy tone, and occasional divergences towards a smoky colour which probably arose from variations in the carbon monoxide content of the kiln atmosphere. Considerable differences in the " colour " of white porcelain can always be observed, the principal variations being between bluish-white and yellowish-white. The " whitest " porcelain is the one which preserves a balance between these two extremes, with, perhaps, a trifling bias in favour of blue. One cause of the differences in Meissen pastes is that the standard body would not take underglaze blue painting easily, and special mixtures had to be made for this purpose.

Meissen porcelain also varies in translucency, but in my experience, there is little or nothing to be inferred from this which could help to fix the date of a specimen. Occasionally specimens will exhibit the " moons " more familiar in the soft-paste porcelains. These are small circular patches and flecks of greater

[1] A specimen in the Zwinger is illustrated by Handt and Rakebrand, op. cit., Plate 24.

translucency, and are probably caused by air-bubbles trapped in the body. In my experience they are only to be seen in such wares as saucers, plates and dishes, which have either been thrown by hand, or formed by some such mechanical device as a jolley. They cannot be regarded as the sign of an early paste.

On specimens made before 1730, incised symbols can quite frequently be seen. These are often found on the base, and sometimes on the inside of the foot-ring. Many are in the form of incised dots and lines, and in combinations of these two, but they can sometimes be a little more elaborate, asterisks for example. Numerals which have been *incised* are usually of this nature, whereas the *impressed* numerals on service-ware, and on figures, were first introduced about 1763 or a little later.

The purpose of these incised marks cannot be determined with certainty. They may have been used to identify workmen, a particular body, a particular batch of wares, or something of this kind. The fact that they are so numerous and diverse seems to preclude their use to identify pastes.

Höroldt's engagement led to a number of changes in the form of Meissen porcelain. Until the death of Böttger the influence of the silversmith, represented by Irminger and the metalworkers of Augsburg, was everywhere apparent, and the few thrown shapes were based mainly on Chinese prototypes. This was natural. Böttger's enamel colours were primitive, and applied decoration and elaborate shape to some extent replaced the need for painting. After 1720, however, it became increasingly necessary to provide a surface on which to paint, and applied ornament was allowed to fall into disuse until the awakening rococo style brought it again into favour. Much porcelain during the period of Höroldt's greatest influence was thrown on the wheel and, to some extent, the mould was temporarily discarded. Under the influence of Kändler, however, both applied decoration and moulding once more came into frequent use, and painting suffered in the process. For this reason, the period between 1720 and 1735 was, as I have said, termed the *malerische* or painter's period, and the increasing influence of Kändler after 1735 has given the following years the name of the *plastische* (or plastic) period.

Wares with Kakiemon decoration are usually found in conjunction with characteristic octagonal or fluted Arita shapes. Chinese forms were copied, although there are some major differences to be seen by anyone acquainted with Chinese porcelain. As an example, the profile line of the Chinese baluster vase was changed to one which is flatter at the shoulders, and which has a much longer cylindrical neck than is to be found in the original.

The early forms of European derivation were flattened in shape, as can be seen in the teapot illustrated on Plate 23. The covered cream-pot or *bouillon* bowl (Plate 22b) varied little with the passing years from the first examples in the 1720's to those of the later rococo period, except that the latter had the addition of applied leaves, buds and so forth, and the knop was usually floral, in place of the more formal knop of the early years.

Elaborate handles, with a bird's head spout, belong to the early 1720's (Plate 6b), but are sometimes seen with later decoration by *Hausmaler*. These features were used in a still more elaborate manner at Vienna, and can be seen later in the century at Nymphenburg, Höchst, Frankenthal and elsewhere.

The handle in the form of a script capital "T", on teapots particularly, came into use about 1730 (Plate 13b), and persisted into the Academic period. The earlier handles (when they were not elaborate and based on metal work) were in the form of an "S", and these were popular from about 1725 (Plate 10).[1]

Small vessels such as tea-jars and so forth were not uncommonly made of rectangular section during the 1720's and the early 1730's, although the fashion did not persist after this date. Obviously the flat surfaces offered considerable advantages to the painter, and these things are often seen in conjunction with a coloured ground and painting in panels (Plate 15a).

In the early 1730's Höroldt was responsible for introducing

---

[1] When he was first engaged, Kändler reported that he found not a single properly-made handle, and he therefore revised handles, spouts, knops to lids, and so forth.

a moulded basket-work border-pattern termed the *ordinair-Ozier*. Its first important application was to the service made for Count Sulkowski about 1735. This early version has the oziers in sets of four crossing each other diagonally, and divided at frequent intervals by a moulded radial rib. This pattern is confined to the ledge of the plate. An ozier border is shown on Plate 28b.

The *Altozierrand* (old ozier border) has a more conventional basket-work appearance and is divided by radial ribs in the same way. This, also, does not extend beyond the ledge of the plate.

The *Altbrandensteinmuster* (old Brandenstein pattern) was developed in 1741, and is considerably more elaborate. It has panels divided into sets of three, one narrow and plain, one narrow with dotted squares, and one wide with circumferential moulding, crossed by ribs which are a small segment of a spiral. These ribs, for the first time, encroach on the centre of the plate.

The *Neuozierrand* (new ozier border) was introduced in 1742. This had an outer border of basket-work moulding and a plain inner border confined by a moulded line of scroll form which encroached on the centre of the plate. There were, in addition, four sets of spiralling ribs which gave twelve narrow panels and four wide ones.

The *Neubrandensteinmuster* was similar to the old in having the plain narrow panel, and the panel with dotted squares, but in other respects it resembled the *Neuozier*. Some vessels, such as coffee-pots, were occasionally given surface decoration of moulded basket-work.

The *Gotzkowsky* pattern introduced in 1744 has four narrow panels left plain alternating with four wide panels decorated with moulded flowers, which appear also in the centre of the plate. These were termed *Gotzkowsky erhabene Blumen*, and the pattern was copied elsewhere, notably at Chelsea.

The *Brühlsches Allerlei-Dessin* (" Brühl's various " design) was a complicated pattern of basket-work, flowers, shells, and such things confined by rococo scrolls, no two panels being alike. The moulding was confined to the ledge.

The *Dulongmuster* (made for Jean Dulong) was a relief pattern which had four panels surrounded by rococo scrolls, interspersed with varied moulded ornament which intrudes slightly on to the centre, and the *Marseillemuster* has six plain panels surrounded by narrow bands of rococo ornament which also encroach on to the centre of the plate. The plain panels were used for painting, principally " German flowers " and birds, and all these moulded patterns were later copied, sometimes with slight variations, at other German factories.

The *Vestunservice* (Festoon Service) made for Frederick the Great in 1760 has a border of moulded flower garlands, as well as a band of pierced " chain " ornament around the rim.

The influence of Kändler is to be seen in the gradual develop-ment of the more elaborate moulding and applied decoration. As a modeller he was not interested in providing a surface for Höroldt's painters to display their skill, and this attitude can be seen particularly in the Swan Service where the moulded detail spreads across the entire surface of the plate. The use of colour on figures, and on services of this kind, was dictated by the modeller rather than by the painter, and here we have the cause of at least one of Kändler's quarrels with Höroldt.

A much-prized variety of Meissen porcelain is the small boxes and such things decorated with finely-detailed miniature painting, similar to the box shown in Plate 30a. Many of these were ex-ecuted by the miniaturist Johann Martin Heinrici, who worked at Meissen from 1741 to 1756, and then went to Frankenthal to escape the Seven Years' War. Work of the same kind was done by C. F. Herold and Isaak Jakob Clauce.

Shortly before 1760, the *Mosaikrand* began to be much used. The inspiration for these detailed diaper border patterns, which were carried out over a coloured ground, came from China, and a tentative essay in this direction can be seen in Plate 16a, where an early saucer decorated with *indianische Blumen* has a central medallion of this kind.[1] Related to the *Mosaik* is the scale pattern

---

[1] These diapers were probably first used to hide faults in the ground colour.

which is well seen on the Berlin plate shown in Plate 104a. This has an ancestry rather more difficult to trace. It can be seen on Isnik (Turkish) pottery and on early Italian *maiolica*, and probably arrived at Worcester, where it was extremely popular, by way of Germany. Detailed patterns of this kind were especially popular at Berlin, and their principal exponent was Karl Jacob Christian Klipfel, later inspector of the Berlin factory.

A naturalistic kind of bird painting (Plate 28d) was done in rather strong colours, and belongs to the period just before 1763 and later, as do garlands and festoons, which began to be fashionable about the same time.

The earlier baroque decoration—the gilt lace-work and the *Laub- und Bandelwerk*—developed into the asymmetrical rococo scrolls used to frame the painting. The difference can be seen by comparing Plates 23 and 95c. The rococo style was fully developed by about 1755.

When the Academic period began Dietrich was placed in charge of painting. He encouraged the use of Italian and Dutch paintings in the Dresden Gallery as models, as well as engravings in the Elector's Library. He also ordered plaster models of classical statuary which would not otherwise have been available to the factory artists. Heinrici made a direct copy of a Madonna by Raphael on to porcelain, and at a later date Angelica Kauffmann was similarly copied.

Garlands were much used. At first, these were floral, and sometimes formed initials and monograms, but later became more formal and depicted laurel leaves and ribbons. Mostly they were used for cheaper wares. Flowers and fruit were commonly used, with fruit becoming gradually less popular. Amorous encounters were, on the whole, well painted, but—perhaps as a concession to the *bourgeoisie*—lack the raciness of the earlier handling of the same subject.

Plates with Renaissance style *putti*—*Kinder à la Raphael*—were not much esteemed at the time, and still less today. *Putti* after Boucher, first used about 1755, were still to be seen, and children were used as models, but infrequently. Sheep and cattle are not uncommon.

Hunting and battle scenes, pleasant pastoral scenes and miniature portraits can be noticed in the early part of this period, but both battle scenes and derivations from Watteau progressively lost favour towards the end of the century. The black silhouette portrait belongs to the Marcolini period, and a curious decoration of profiles concealed amidst flowers testifies to the paucity of the imagination of the time.

During the Academic period landscapes which were more or less exact representations of particular places became fashionable. This can be seen in the service made for the Stadthalter of Holland already mentioned, and a tobacco jar of the period has a picture of the Albrechtsburg, almost the earliest known representation of it.[1] These landscapes gradually became purely topographical. Views of Saxon castles fall into this category, and the prevailing romantic mood may be noticed in the use of ruins. We can, in fact, trace a gradual change from painted decoration as an integral part of the porcelain to the use of porcelain as a foundation on which to paint a picture, much in the same way as an artist uses a canvas, the white porcelain gradually disappearing under a spate of colour.

Mosaik borders, much in use during the Academic period, disappear thereafter. *Fondporzellan* has some innovations to show—a pink, and a new green, as well as a strong iron-red of distinct orange tone which was used occasionally. The imitation of the *bleu de Roi* of Sèvres never quite succeeded in attaining the colour of the original, despite various larcenous attempts on the secret. Gold stripes were used as a ground, either on white porcelain or over the *bleu de Roi*, generally on vases of a classical form.

Colouring was considerably more powerful. Often two colours only were used—for instance, a combination of iron-red and gold. Sepia and gold was particularly popular at the time.

From 1774 painting was under the direction of Schönau

---

[1] An exception is a vase mentioned by Honey which depicts Augustus the Strong as the Chinese Emperor in a landscape containing a view of the Albrechtsburg.

(Zeissig). He was replaced in 1796 as director by Johann David Schubert who was born in Dresden, and had been at the factory since 1761. Two pupils of Schönau, Richter and Walther, employed as enamellers, were highly regarded, as was Johann Christian August Birnbaum who joined the factory staff in 1743. Karl Gottlieb Grahl was painting instructor from 1780 onwards.

Pastoral scenes, figure painting and miniature portraits were in the hands of Johann Georg Löhnig whose signed work is in existence. Christian Ferdinand Matthäi and Heinrich Gotthelf Schaufuss, who became instructor in 1796, were also figure painters. Cows, landscapes and battle and hunting scenes were done mainly by Kühnel, Ehrlich and Johann Karl Mauksch.

Birds, flowers and fruit were painted by numerous hands, and it is unnecessary to enumerate some of them here since this kind of work is generally unimportant during the period under discussion. They, and some of the other names mentioned, can be traced in greater detail in Zimmermann[1] and Pazaurek.[2]

Meissen Figure Sculpture

Despite the fact that we, today, tend to value eighteenth-century porcelain figures more highly than service-ware, the first two decades of Meissen production showed small enthusiasm for this kind of work.

It is true that during the Böttger period and immediately afterwards figures were made which were both striking and unusual in style and gesture, the vigorous Italian comedy figures in stoneware providing an excellent example, but the early porcelain figures of Chinamen do not show the imaginative quality of the later examples. There were, in fact, no modellers of outstanding merit at Meissen before the advent of Kirchner in 1727, since Georg Fritszche seems to have produced little of importance artistically. The work of von Lücke has not been satisfactorily

[1] *Meissner Porzellan.*
[2] *Meissner Porzellanmalerei des 18ten Jahrhunderts* and *Deutsche Fayence und Porzellan Hausmaler.*

identified, although a number of tentative attributions have been made, including a figure of Augustus, and a bust of the *Hofnarr* (court jester) Fröhlich.

Kirchner was primarily a sculptor, and this much is evident from his surviving work, which tends to abandon the rendering of detail in favour of a broad impression. He found it difficult to work within the limits imposed by the medium, and Kändler's greater gifts as an exponent of *Kleinplastik*, the art of modelling in the smaller size which we recognize as the most typical product of the eighteenth century, was the determining factor which ensured his pre-eminence.

The art of modelling for porcelain first began to make headway when Augustus the Strong conceived the idea of the Japanische Palais. Before becoming Elector he had travelled to various European courts, and had acquired the desire to be known as a patron of the arts. To this end he spent a great deal of money to enrich the Dresden collections, and kept the various artists engaged under his personal control. Undoubtedly he had great influence on the artistic development of the Meissen factory.

Porcelain was the important feature of the Japanische Palais. It was, in fact, its *raison d'être*. Augustus intended something more than a collection. Porcelain was also to be used architecturally. Animals were to be a prominent feature, and for some reason which now escapes us, it was almost an unwritten law to make these as near to life-size as the material would permit. And so we have the series of large animals—many technically imperfect—started towards the end of the 1720's, and on which both Kirchner and Kändler were engaged. These would not take a second firing. Indeed, some barely withstood the first, and enamel colouring had to be rejected as a mode of decoration. Lacquer colours were tried, but were found to spoil the appearance, so the surface was finally left white (Plate 36). The moulds used for making some of these models were broken so that they would be unique.

Although the peculiar exaggerations of Kirchner's style—the almost heraldic appearance of some of his animals—do not seem to support the judgement, many of these were, in fact, modelled from life. Augustus had a collection of animals, indigenous and foreign, which were kept for hunting, and for matching against each other in combat. And at Moritzburg, between Dresden and Meissen, was an aviary to which both Kändler and Kirchner resorted for inspiration.

Kirchner's reputation has been overshadowed by that of Kändler. As an exponent of the baroque his work is, perhaps, the more characteristic of that style. Kändler's animals and birds were modelled directly from nature. The difference is in the approach. Kirchner's style was subjective, and his work is infused with a life of its own. The faces of his animals, in particular, are endowed with a peculiarly life-like expression which is almost anthropomorphic. Kändler's style, on the other hand, is objective and naturalistic. For these reasons the model of the Bolognese dog which is by Kändler might almost better be given to Kirchner (Plate 37b).

Kändler, in the early days, was basically true to his own conception of the baroque, but he founded a new style of figure modelling which was the real beginning of the fashion for this kind of work in Europe.

His early work, particularly that done in association with Kirchner, was for the Japanische Palais. By about 1733 we find him modelling animals in a smaller size, and by 1735 he was also occupied with plastic decoration for services, beginning with that made for Count Sulkowski. The earliest figures which can be said definitely to initiate the fashion for *Kleinplastik* are not much before 1735, and comprise, among other things, the first of a spirited series of Harlequins from the Italian comedy in various poses (Plates 45 and 46).

Before Kirchner's departure a large set of the Apostles had been made for the Japanische Palais, a figure of St. Paul at Leipzig being particularly well known and frequently reproduced.[1] This practice was continued with a series made for Pope Clement

[1] For instance, Schmidt (op. cit.), fig. 107 (English edition).

XII, and for the Empress Wilhelmine Amalia of Austria, and Kändler executed a series in the Louis-Seize style as late as 1772. These works in a religious vein were followed by the Madonna as a symbol of the immaculate conception (1738), a huge Crucifixion intended for Pope Benedictus XIV (1743), and in the latter year was started a series of busts of the Popes in collaboration with Peter Reinicke to the order of Cardinal Albain. Specimens of this kind are shown on Plates 42 and 43.

Porcelain was much used as table decoration. Originally ornaments for the banqueting table had been made in sugar or wax, and porcelain of this kind still belonged to the realm of the confectioner. The *Ehrenpforte*, a Temple of Honour, for Augustus III, was begun in 1748. This was a centre-piece almost eight feet high which consisted of 127 pieces. It is now known only from engravings. Another of 264 pieces was made for von Brühl. A table decoration made in 1774 by Kändler for Catherine the Great of Russia contained all the gods of Olympus, as well as allegories of learning, trade, seafaring and so forth, and personifications of the Russian rivers (Plate 61).

Another large-scale project was a mirror and console table decorated with figures of Apollo and the nine Muses made by Kändler for Augustus III to give to Louis XV. Kändler himself took this to Paris in 1750, but it was destroyed during the French Revolution. This was a superb technical achievement in the full tide of the rococo style.

The desire to achieve heroic proportions for his models seems never to have left Kändler's imagination. He kept returning to it, and his largest and most ambitious work appears to have been maturing in his mind for some years before he actually started work on it. This was the *Reiterdenkmal*, which as the largest porcelain monument ever to be attempted deserves further description.

A model of Augustus III on horseback was made in small size in 1745 and approved by the King. A small-sized version of the *Reiterdenkmal* was made in 1753 by Kändler and Eberlein in association. It appears to have been inspired by a gilded copper equestrian statue cast by an Augsburg maker of artistically-decorated artillery, one Colonel Ludwig Wiedmann,[1] although whether he designed it, or whether the design was by someone else—perhaps even Kändler—is unknown. The copper statue, which was erected finally in 1755 in the market place of Dresden Neustadt, was a portrait of Augustus the Strong, and Kändler took the pose and changed the face to that of Augustus III. The horse, an exceptionally spirited piece of modelling, was a representation of one of the famous Lipizzaner horses—specially trained animals from the Spanish School of Equitation in Vienna.

By 1756 Kändler had scaffolding installed and was paying six sculptors and three joiners from his own pocket. In 1761, 800 pieces of the base had been finished, and Kändler, heavily in debt, asked the State for assistance with the project. This was refused. The State was no longer interested in heroic porcelain statues of its ruler, and Kändler was forced to abandon the project. After his death in 1775 it was said to take up too much room, and was destroyed.

To return to Kändler's *Kleinplastik*, the number of models which can be attributed to him is so large that it would be impossible to do more than indicate a few of the more outstanding trends.

The early figures were painted in strong, rich colouring, sometimes with oriental flowers stylised on a gold or a black ground, and these enamels are characteristic of the baroque period, the later rococo colouring becoming much paler. Thus we find brilliant reds which gradually change to a pale pink, extensive passages of black which eventually is used only for such small details as hats and shoes, a rich buttercup yellow which becomes a pale and delicate primrose, and so forth. Then, too, the simple bases of the early period which had, perhaps, a decoration of

[1] It is amusing to note that this same Ludwig Wiedmann induced William, Duke of Cumberland, to test some cannons he had invented. This was done in 1749 in Windsor Park before many high-ranking officers. The six-pounder burst before completing the test firing, and the others gave an unsatisfactory performance.

flowers and leaves applied, become enriched with scroll-work and gilding as the transition from baroque to rococo proceeds.

The early colours can well be seen in the so-called crinoline figures and groups. This costume, with its huge billowing skirts, was then fashionable, and Kändler was attracted to it as a subject. Most of these were made between 1740 and 1745 (Plate 54b). One group of a gallant with a lady thus attired has often been supposed, erroneously, to represent Augustus the Strong with one of his numerous paramours.

Towards 1740 we find amusing figures of the court fool, Joseph Fröhlich and the postmaster, Schmiedel. These were popular as subjects, and the first example of the use of Fröhlich may be ascribed to the year 1728. This model is often attributed to Kirchner, but it is much more likely to have been the work of von Lücke. Schmiedel was much afraid of mice, and a bust done by Kändler in 1740 shows him holding a mouse by the tail in his mouth.

Another satirical group depicts a tailor riding on the back of a goat replete with the tools of his trade, his pressing iron, for instance, hanging from the saddle. To this, Eberlein added the tailor's wife, similarly accoutred. The story—probably apocryphal—is that von Brühl, in return for a particular service, promised his tailor to grant one request. The request was the embarrassing one of providing a place at a state banquet for the tailor. The figure was modelled and set on the table to extricate von Brühl from the difficulty of having to redeem his promise with the tailor's physical presence. This model was later much copied at Derby, and repeated frequently at Meissen.

In 1745, a series of figures was based on some engravings of the *Cris de Paris* by the Comte de Caylus after drawings by Edmé Bouchardon.[1] Before 1740 Kändler was engaged on the Swan Service in company with Eberlein. The theme—water—was popular at the time, and belongs to the rococo style. Kändler, to

[1] Another series, much more complete, was made by Kändler and Reinicke in association in 1755.

some extent, was indebted to Cellini for part of his shell ornament in the Swan Service.

Mythological figures had considerable vogue, and Kändler made much use of the subject. His handling of the nude figure leaves something to be desired, and both Punct and Meyer were more skilful at this kind of work. Perhaps the least successful of Kändler's conceptions were the groups of figures representing some mythological event. These are rarely satisfying and coherent compositions, although they are frequently technical achievements of a high order.

Classical mythology was particularly studied at the various courts, and allegories based on these legends were made freely at all the principal factories. Such figures were often used to express some abstract idea. The Five Senses, the Four Elements, the Four Seasons, the Twelve Months, Liberty and Matrimony, in fact almost any idea lending itself to personification, was freely modelled. Although, to take the Four Seasons as an example, the figures might be clothed in either antique or contemporary costume, they have attributes by which they can be identified. Most commonly these are flowers (Spring), sheaves of corn (Summer), grapes (Autumn), and furs or a brazier (Winter). The identification of allegories was a popular eighteenth-century parlour game (Plates 80 and 126a).

Hunting of all kinds was popular throughout most of the eighteenth century, and Kändler did many figures and groups bearing on this subject, such things as men and women with the weapons of the chase, stags and similar quarry, and hounds in various poses. In some cases realism was carried to considerable lengths, in depicting the final stages of a stag-hunt for instance. The animal is seen in process of being killed by hounds. Dominicus Auliczek of Nymphenburg did a number of things of this kind, and his work shows an undercurrent of sadism which is missing from similar work by Kändler.

Masquerades were a popular diversion, and it is probably to some such origin that we owe the figures of personages of the court dressed in the guise of miners, which were modelled as a series about 1750. One of the figures is reputed to be Augustus III (Plate 48b).

The theatre was immensely popular and influential throughout the century. First and foremost we have the Italian comedy, incomparably modelled by Franz Anton Bustelli at Nymphenburg (Plate 77b), but with Kändler following closely at his heels. The best known character is undoubtedly Harlequin, but others, such as Pantaloon, Pierrot, Columbine and so forth, are hardly less known—too familiar to need detailed description here. This improvised play had been popular since the sixteenth century. Indeed, Shakespeare refers to the "lean and slippered Pantaloon", and the following lines provide an excellent description of the character, whilst the origin is proclaimed in the opening lines of the speech—"All the world's a stage . . . " Kändler did a number of figures and groups based on this theme, and the theatre was a much more frequent source of inspiration to the porcelain modeller than is generally recognized. His last series, on plain bases, was done in 1771.

Kändler was singularly fortunate in his assistants, Eberlein and Reinicke. Eberlein, who died in 1749, assisted with many important projects, and Reinicke did a vigorous series of Chinese figures in 1743, as well as helping with the *Monkey Band*, the later series of figures from the *Cris de Paris*, and the earlier busts of the Popes. The white bust of Albert II (1397–1439) appearing on Plate 44 belongs to a series of Austrian Emperors modelled by Kändler and Reinicke in association about 1744. These were done to the order of Maria Theresa, and were for a long time in the possession of the Austrian court. Albert was King of Hungary, Duke of Austria, and Emperor of Germany in succession to Sigismund.

Friedrich Elias Meyer has previously been mentioned, and it remains to refer to some of his characteristic work. Some figures of orientals playing musical instruments—the *Malabar* figures—are here represented by a version from Berlin, where he became *Modellmeister* in 1761 (Plate 106). The Meissen examples, whilst somewhat resembling this, are much more grotesque in execution. The other work attributed to him often shows heads which are small in proportion to the body, and limbs which are too long—an idiosyncrasy which is not apparent in the figure illustrated.

Punct belongs to the later rococo period (*die Punkzeit*) and is chiefly noted for mythological figures, and some groups of children.

In 1757 Meissen lost the services of Johann Friedrich Lück, who departed for Frankenthal. J. F. Lück was reputed the son, or the nephew, of Johann Christoph von Lücke, the erstwhile Meissen *Modellmeister*, and his activities are further discussed in the chapters on Höchst and Frankenthal. He is said to have left as the result of a disagreement with Kändler, and returned in 1764 as *Oberbossierer* (chief repairer). Karl Gottlieb Lück, perhaps also related to J. C. von Lücke, was invited to Meissen in 1761 to help with the *Reiterdenkmal*, and may have earlier left the factory in company with J. F. Lück.

In the 1760's Acier was beginning his dreary series of models in the Louis-Seize style which show the malign influence of Greuze in their flavour of *bourgeois* sentimentality. It was at this time that the foundations of the nineteenth-century *Biedermeier* style were being laid. Perhaps the difference can best be expressed by saying that had Acier and Kändler been asked to model a group consisting of a man, a woman and a baby, Acier would have provided a comfortable, self-satisfied, obviously-posed family group, whereas Kändler would have given us a woman confronting her lover with his bastard child. The difference in outlook is fundamental. Kändler depicted the kind of life which went on around him. Acier modelled life as the successful tradesman wanted it to be. He viewed it through a rosy mist, and in the process revealed some soft and overripe spots in his attitude to life (Plate 63c).

Acier's earlier figures and groups are in the Louis-Seize style which accompanied the import of Chardin and Greuze. The bases are often decorated with an openwork design of rococo scrolls which lack the wilder asymmetricality of the earlier use of this style. The later figures have flat oval bases decorated on the edge with such classical motifs as the key-fret.

Acier carried naturalism to extremes, and it was probably due to his influence that the distinctly repellent lace-work, which, in the nineteenth century, developed into elaborately flounced dresses, was introduced. This is a mere technical trick. Lace was dipped into porcelain slip, attached to the figure, and fired. The lace burned away leaving a copy of its mesh in porcelain. The use of such methods is an excellent indication of the bankruptcy of imagination prevalent at the time.

Of the modellers working in the style of Acier, Schönheit took the place of Punct and Reinicke. From Jean Troy nothing can be identified.

After 1780 Schönheit and Jüchtzer together were responsible for much of the modelling, and worked mostly in biscuit, a technique to which the Meissen body was ill-suited. The neo-classical style had by this time taken firm hold, and the lightness of touch to be seen in rococo things entirely disappeared in favour of a sterile severity of line and treatment. The plaster casts of Anton Mengs, principally of Graeco-Roman sculpture, were freely copied and adapted. Wedgwood's influence became noticeable in the frequent attempts to copy his jasper-ware by both Matthäi and Jüchtzer. Another modeller, Johann Daniel Schöne, worked in much the same style. He joined the factory in 1783. Throughout the period little of importance was done, and Meissen modelling degenerated seriously.

The subsequent history of Meissen figure sculpture falls outside the scope of this book. To condemn it would be unfair without a parallel condemnation of the work of other European factories during the same period. The disease suffered by the Meissen factory was contagious. At best some of its work during the nineteenth century is competent and amusing, and a revival of its previous reputation took place in the 1920's and later in the work of Max Esser, Paul Scheurich, Paul Börner and others.

2

THE VIENNA FACTORY

THE second porcelain factory to be established in Europe had its beginnings in Vienna in 1717. Experiments in the manufacture of porcelain had been carried out by Claudius Innocentius du Paquier for some time before this date without success, but in October 1717, Christoph Konrad Hunger was persuaded to desert from Meissen to Vienna by the Graf von Virmont, representative of the Austrian court at Dresden. Hunger claimed to have received the secret of porcelain manufacture from Böttger, with whom he was on terms of friendship, and in 1719 *Inspektor* Steinbrück of Meissen wrote to *Hofkammerat* Michael Nehmitz, asserting that the secret had been imparted by Böttger in one of his frequent bouts of intoxication.

The first attempt at manufacture made by Hunger utilized clay from Passau in Bavaria, near the Austrian frontier, and he mentions these newly-discovered deposits in a letter in which he presses Johann Georg Mehlhorn to follow him to Vienna.

Whether or not Hunger was a competent arcanist is a point which has caused some controversy in the past. Certainly he made porcelain of good quality for the Vezzi factory when he arrived in Venice, but here he used clay from Aue which was imported for the purpose. It has been said that his failure to make porcelain at Vienna was due to the nature of the Passau clay. This may have been so, although Passau supported a flourishing porcelain industry during the nineteenth century.

It is likely that some of the trouble was due to Hunger's deficient knowledge of the firing process, and this receives confirmation from the approaches made to Böttger's kiln-master, Samuel Stölzel, already discussed. Stölzel arrived in Vienna accompanied by du Paquier at the beginning of 1719. Production of porcelain began almost immediately after his arrival, but the clay came from Aue and not from Passau.

The founder of the factory did not enjoy royal patronage. Charles VI was not sufficiently interested in the possession of a porcelain factory to give it financial support. Du Paquier apparently gained his information from a series of letters on porcelain making which were current in Europe at the time. These were written from China by a missionary, Père d'Entrecolles, and described the Chinese processes somewhat inexactly. There are, however, no sources of information still remaining which would enable us to estimate what experiments had been made before the arrival of Hunger.

Du Paquier was a court official of Flemish origin who held the position of *Hofkriegsratagent*, which appears to have been connected with the army commissariat, and was probably equivalent to a commissary-general. He had three partners, Peter Heinrich Zerder, *Hofkriegsrat und Königl. Böhmisch Hofagent*,[1] C. K. Hunger, *Kunstarbeiter* (art-worker), and Martin Becker, merchant, and together they obtained a patent, or monopoly, for twenty-five years. This gave them exclusive rights to make porcelain in the Austrian territories.

But the factory received an early setback. Stölzel returned to Meissen in 1720, taking with him the young enameller, Johann Gregor Höroldt, with whose ability he bought his immunity from the prescribed punishment, and the newly-born factory was at once plunged into a financial crisis. Finances must have been

---

[1] Approximately " Member of the War Council and Minister of the Interior ".

precarious before this, because it seems that Stölzel's second defection was primarily caused by the non-payment of the promised salary of 1,000 thalers. Possibly in a fit of vindictiveness, or perhaps at the behest of the Meissen directorate, his last act before leaving was to spoil the raw materials accumulated for stock. To add to the troubles which were accumulating, Becker, already heavily in debt, was forced to withdraw, and for a time it seemed as though the enterprise would fail almost before it had begun.

At this point the Emperor stepped in and appointed a commission of investigation, and du Paquier found a new financial backer in the person of a merchant of Frankfurt-am-Main, named Balde. A new source of clay was found in Hungary, and the factory remained in existence.

By 1723 matters were on a much sounder footing, and du Paquier attempted to sell the factory as a going concern to the Nürnberg City Council. Nothing came of the negotiations, and in 1727 the financial position had again deteriorated so seriously that du Paquier once more petitioned the Emperor for assistance. This was provided by the City Council of Vienna as a first mortgage on the premises and future production of the factory. The terms were strict. They included divulgence of the secret to the Emperor, and to other persons as directed, and a weekly inspection of books of account by municipal officials![1]

These, however, were but temporary expedients and the financial pressure continued unabated. Another crisis occurred in 1737, when several of the factory's most important artists left to seek their fortunes in more fertile fields, and the factory was taken over finally by the Empress Maria Theresa in 1744, du Paquier being retained in a managerial capacity.

The porcelain of this period, in the beginning, somewhat resembled that of Böttger. The colour is usually that which has been well described by Honey as "smoky", and it has been said that the minute bubbles which often appear suspended in the glaze of Böttger's porcelain are absent from the Vienna glaze, a

[1] J. F. Hayward, *Viennese Porcelain of the du Paquier Period* (Rockliff, 1952).

suggestion which accords with my own observations. The earliest known dated example is a tall chocolate-cup in the Hamburg Museum für Kunst und Gewerbe,[1] which has the incised inscription: *Gott allein die Ehr' und sonst keinem mehr 3 May* [?] *1719*.[2]

The decoration and plastic work are later described in their places, and much Vienna porcelain was decorated by the *Hausmaler*,[3] particularly by Ignaz Bottengruber of Breslau, more fully discussed in the chapter on *Hausmalerei*.

A number of artists of note worked at Vienna at this time. Hunger has already been discussed at some length in the chapter on Meissen porcelain (see p. 35). Johann Karl Wendelin Anreiter von Zirnfeld was born at Schemnitz in Hungary in 1702, and joined the factory in 1725. His principal work on Vienna porcelain was the painting of landscapes and similar themes, mostly in *Schwarzlot*, which was a common technique at Vienna, and in red monochrome. A number of signed examples have been recorded. He was at Doccia in 1737 for a short while, and helped to found the factory there. He died in 1747. His two sons, Heinrich Johann and Anton (Plate 72b) were both porcelain painters. Neither is recorded as having worked at the factory, although Joseph Anreiter appears in the factory list later in the century. Anton did some very distinctive figure subjects for the factory of the Marchese Ginori at Doccia about 1740, one of which I have illustrated elsewhere.[4]

Joseph Philipp Danhöffer (or Dannhofer) worked successively at Vienna, Bayreuth, Höchst, Fulda (the early *faïence* factory) and Ludwigsburg. He was born in 1712 and had left Vienna by 1737, so that his stay may have been relatively short. His work at Vienna cannot be identified with certainty, but it seems reasonably safe to attribute to his hand some landscapes, Biblical subjects, and perhaps *chinoiseries*, often in purple monochrome.

[1] Art and Industry Museum.
[2] Literally " To God alone and to none other be the honour." The date is not clear.
[3] The unlicensed painter, or *Hausmaler*, was termed, at Vienna, *Winkelmann*. The word is not easy to translate, but is derogatory, and carries the implication that the painter in question was of a low class.
[4] *Porcelain through the Ages*, Plate 36b.

Jakob Helchis, also referred to as Helkis or Helchs, is an artist of some importance. He was born at Trieste, but the date is uncertain. He functioned also as a *Hausmaler*, and was an arcanist at Neudeck-Nymphenburg from about 1747 until 1749, after which he disappears from view. His work somewhat resembles that of Bottengruber, whose pupil he may have been, and much of the existing work attributed to him is in *Schwarzlot* (Plate 71).

The earliest production of the du Paquier period was principally of forms derived from silver, and these were markedly baroque in design, the style taking a somewhat more exaggerated form than at Meissen.

A fashion for teapot spouts in the form of animal heads may be noticed, together with handles in the form of the upper part of a panther, the hindquarters merging into scroll-work. The use of human figures as knops to the covers of tureens was a frequent practice, and a mug illustrated by Hayward has a figure of this kind as a handle (Plate 67b).[1] Vases illustrated by the same authority have dragons writhing round the necks.[2]

Most of the early wares are moulded, specimens which have been turned on the wheel being fewer, and considerable use was made of forms with a rectangular section which gave a flat instead of a curved surface for painting—something of an advantage.

Much use was made of moulded details in the making of vases, tureens and things of this kind, and plates and dishes frequently have an exaggeratedly cut edge (Plates 65 and 69b).

Unlike Meissen, very little use was made of far eastern shapes. Hayward[3] illustrates a pair of square bottles derived from *saké* bottles of Arita with, curiously enough, European decoration, and the flask[4] has a very indirect relationship to the Chinese pilgrim flask. We do not see the octagonal and fluted forms of Arita, although the Kakiemon and Imari styles both appear in decoration, and the large trumpet-shaped vases which Meissen

[1] J. F. Hayward, op. cit., Plate 44.   [2] ibid.   [3] ibid., Plate 21.
[4] ibid., Plate 22.

decorated with *indianische Blumen* copied from the *famille rose* are entirely missing.

Vienna, in fact, developed what was an almost completely individual style in its more important things, and despite the fact that it was started with the aid of Meissen workmen, the Saxon factory had little influence on its artistic development.

For the most part Vienna porcelain is prized for its decoration rather than for its form, and the painting is usually of exceptional quality. In particular the *Laub- und Bandelwerk* is extremely fine, and this kind of decoration was much more popular here than elsewhere (Plate 68b). Always meticulously drawn, it often becomes extremely elaborate, and is not confined to the border, frequently covering the entire surface. It was often used as the sole ornamentation, instead of being regarded as subordinate to the main decorative theme as at Meissen, where it was principally used to frame *chinoiseries* and landscapes. The origin of these patterns has been traced by Hayward in some detail, and they owe much to the earlier engravers of Augsburg and Nürnberg.

Surprisingly, too, we have the occasional use of scale patterns which, as Hayward points out, certainly precedes the generally accepted date (*c.* 1755) for the introduction of such patterns. Vienna, however, is much farther south than either Meissen or Berlin, where this decoration was first used extensively, and it was well established on Italian *maiolica* shortly after 1500. Moreover, many of the Viennese decorative themes undoubtedly foreshadow the later *Mosaik*, and it would seem that the source of this kind of work on porcelain is not far to seek.

Chinoiseries do not assume the same importance as at Meissen. Neither was Vienna influenced by Meissen to a great extent. Hayward suggests their derivation from Japanese lacquer, and whilst this seems to be true of most, a few suggest a Chinese origin, and Plate 17c,[1] which seems to me to belong to this type, has a dragon in the sky which is reminiscent of the flying dragons

[1] ibid.

of Höroldt, although it somewhat inclines towards the generally accepted notion of a gryphon (Plate 67b).[1]

This leads me to a digression on the nature of the dragon. It is obvious that the European conception of this animal as shown in the *chinoiseries* of both Meissen and Vienna was completely wrong. This is due to an inexact translation of the Chinese word. By rendering it as "dragon", the animal is thereby endowed with all the habits and attributes of the dragon of western legend, but the Chinese dragon is a harmless and beneficent animal which represents the principle of fecundity in nature. It demands no tribute of virgins; certainly it breathes neither fire nor noxious vapour, and its habits are directly contrary to those of the western dragon. However, the mistake has been made, and the Chinese *lung* must, perforce, remain a dragon. It is amusing to see that, in so many of the earlier *chinoiseries*, it is endowed with a ferocity of aspect which has no relation whatever to its real nature.

The earliest dated *chinoiserie* appears on a clock case of 1725 in the Museo Civico, Turin. Some of the Vienna examples of the use of this motif are so similar to those done by Bayreuth *Hausmaler* as to suggest that they were the work of Dannhofer who worked at both places, but this is by no means certain.

Indianische Blumen appear on the earlier porcelain (Plate 66a), and *deutsche Blumen*, often of comparatively large size, replaced them about 1730, a trifle earlier than at Meissen.

Some experiments were made with *Fond-porzellan* around 1725, but coloured grounds were not much used, nor were they very successful. Porcelain with pierced and reticulated walls can be seen occasionally.

Much work was done in *Schwarzlot* with a little gilding, of which animal and hunting scenes are the most effective (Plate 68a). These were continued for a while during the following state period. Other monochromes include puce, and a fine iron-red (Plate 70). Landscapes, topographical scenes, Biblical scenes,

---

[1] The European conception of the dragon frequently has one pair of feet, and a pair of wings. The Chinese dragon is always a quadruped.

mythological scenes, hunting scenes, and *putti*, are all to be seen. The technique in many cases is reminiscent of the engravings from which they were taken.[1] Battle scenes were drawn from the work of Georg Philipp Rugendas, engraved by G. C. Bodenehr, and used at other factories also. Hunting scenes came from Johann Elias Riedinger, later the source of some of Auliczek's models of animals at Nymphenburg. The most important of the hunting subjects is the *Jagd-service* ordered for the court in 1730.

Figure modelling at Vienna during this period can be seen as ornament to vessels and candlesticks—as knops to the covers of tureens, for instance. Free-standing figures are extremely rare, so much so that examples have only been identified within recent years, and these are limited to a very few. Known examples are not of great importance artistically. It has been suggested that du Paquier employed confectioners as modellers. Their extremely high value, in terms of money, is due to their scarcity rather than to their aesthetic worth.

Du Paquier porcelain is unmarked. The first factory mark was introduced in 1744. Incised figures are to be seen occasionally; these vary from 1 to 4, 1 and 2 being the most common. They may be paste-marks. One or two dated pieces exist, apart from those mentioned. Several pieces signed by artists known to have worked at the factory are in existence, although since most of them also functioned as *Hausmaler*, the circumstances in which such things were signed cannot always be regarded as certain.

All porcelain of this period is scarce, and much sought. Vienna porcelain does not, in fact, become at all common until the following period which commenced in 1744.

The State Period (1744–1784)

When the state took over management of the factory in 1744 it was put under the general direction of the President of the Finance Ministry, Gundaker, Graf Stahremberg. He died in the following

---

[1] The fashion for monochrome painting can be traced to the use of engravings as inspiration, which were not, of course, coloured.

year and his place was taken by his successor at the Ministry, Philipp, Graf Kinsky.

Sales were difficult to make. One reason, perhaps, is that the Viennese *bourgeoisie* had not yet acquired a taste for porcelain. They were accustomed to *faïence* and had little practice in distinguishing the finer points of each. Because they were apt to regard porcelain as a luxury beyond their means, a lottery was held in 1745 to remedy this state of affairs, but it was unsuccessful.

Some new artists were engaged, notably Christian Daniel Busch and Johann Gottfried Klinger from Meissen who arrived in 1746. Busch went to Neudeck in 1749, together with Helkis and other Viennese workmen (see chapter 3). Klinger remained until his death in 1781. He was made *Obermaler* in 1750, and later arcanist.

Mention must be made, too, of Josef Jakob Ringler, who was at Vienna from about 1744 until approximately 1748. His activities are discussed at greater length elsewhere in this volume, but he deserves notice at this point because his knowledge as a painter and a porcelain arcanist was acquired at the state factory.

Born in Vienna in 1730, the son of a schoolmaster, he was apprenticed to the factory at the age of fourteen. He was quick to learn, and soon acquired an astonishing knowledge of its secrets. His precocity, however, was not necessarily a matter of ability. His acquaintance with these closely guarded secrets came to him by reason of a " strong friendship " (*starke Freundschaft*) with the daughter of the factory's director.

He was later connected with another Vienna potter and arcanist, Johann Benckgraff, a much older man (b. 1708) who was partly a charlatan. Benckgraff undoubtedly acquired much of his knowledge from Ringler, and proceeded to sell it to other German factories as recorded elsewhere in this volume. Benckgraff and Ringler were together at Höchst, after which they parted company.

The year 1747 saw the advent of the *Modellmeister*, Johann Josef Niedermayer. He was responsible for the distinctive style of the figurework during the state period until his death in 1784, when his place was taken by Anton Grassi.

Kinsky died in 1749, and was replaced by Rudolf, Graf Chotek. The new President of the Finance Ministry was more liberal with materials, which led in turn to some improvement in the work, but the factory was still struggling to keep going.

It was decided to try to improve the body, and various searches were made for better quality kaolin. This was found, finally, in Hungary, and the resulting wares were much better in quality. An order was therefore made that the impressed shield (the *Bindenschild*) used as a mark hitherto should be discontinued, and an underglaze blue shield used instead. Whilst this is a point to remember in dating Vienna porcelain, the impressed shield was used again from 1827 to 1850.

The Dresden Ambassador, Otto von Brühl, was asked to send reports to Meissen on progress at Vienna. He thought that the factory was concentrating more on artistically decorative pieces than on useful wares. He remarked that it still had large debts, and needed additional artists and workers from abroad.

The factory undertook a certain amount of enlargement at this time, and Maria Theresa allowed them to acquire a house next door for the nominal sum of 1,000 florins, provided two apprenticeships were kept open for her nominees.

During this period, and until 1757, the directorship was in the hands of Karl Franz Xavier Mayerhofer von Grünbühel, but he was frequently ill, and the organization suffered in consequence. In 1755 Andreas Altomonte was appointed co-administrator, but he proved unsatisfactory, and in 1757 was replaced by Johann Michael Peyerl. The latter was also unsatisfactory, and it was decided to organize things on a proper basis. No doubt the decision was influenced by the fact that Meissen was more or less out of the running owing to the Seven Years' War.

The administration was now placed in the hands of the *Hofrat* Quiex von Bodenthal. He reported on the situation, listing his points of complaint which included such things as lack of a good body, carelessness of turners and firers, too many "wasters", casualness in the glazing-shop, and the sulkiness and obstinacy of painters and repairers. He commented that "one of the worst aspects was the atmosphere in the workshops, where people gather together, wives and friends, to drink and gossip".

He suggested that Mayerhofer be relieved of his post, that books of account be kept by the state accountant, and that directorship of the factory be vested in him. This was done, and the factory's fortunes began to improve.

By 1761 porcelain was becoming popular in Vienna. Much of it was made exclusively for the court, and this probably accounts for occasional pieces marked with a crown as well as the shield. It is possible that such porcelain was on loan to the court, and was thus marked to identify it.

In 1762 a great many experiments and enlargements were made, a fact which did not escape notice at Meissen, who sent a man to report on the position.

About 1764 Franz Josef Wolf von Rosenfeld became director of the factory. At this time there were about 200 workers, and a general air of prosperity prevailed. This state of affairs, however, was not to last. In 1767 Josef Ferdinand Kestler, Edler von Rosenheim,[1] who concerned himself with technical direction, was experimenting in the factory's laboratory to try to improve the body. The object, apparently, was to produce porcelain comparable with that of Sèvres. Kestler had a certain amount of knowledge of chemistry and physics, but he suffered from an excessive optimism which prevented him from learning by experience. He wasted large sums of money and much valuable time in abortive experiments. The workers grumbled incessantly about the difficulties of working with the bodies he devised, and Wolf made an adverse report to Quiex von Bodenthal on the position.

Finally the whole matter was brought to a head in December 1767, as the result of a violent quarrel between the foreman-painter, Anreiter, and another painter named Maxwald. Anreiter

---

[1] Knight of Rosenheim.

wrested a dagger from Maxwald and had his wig pulled off in doing it. The directors discharged Maxwald, and he left the factory surrounded by many of the painters to prevent him from being arrested.

The situation was obviously a difficult one, and the following day Quiex von Bodenthal tried to calm the storm by making a speech to the assembled work-people. This made them even more angry. They demanded an inquiry, and when this was refused, walked out in a body.

They petitioned the court, complaining that the porcelain body was improperly mixed, and that the losses caused by the consequent high proportion of " wasters " could only be made up by reductions in wages. Once more they demanded an inquiry.

The matter was settled temporarily by the punishment of the ringleaders, but it was impossible to deny that the quality of the body left something to be desired. Kestler was now involved, but he knew how to defend himself. The President of the Finance Ministry was on his side, and although Wolf opposed him, he survived the storm. The workers' opposition was driven underground, no doubt because they were threatened with discharge, and knew that the factory could soon get other and cheaper hands.

The accounts for 1772 certainly justified the complaints. Although 116 more firings had taken place, the value of porcelain actually produced for sale was less by 12,534 florins, due to breakage and " wasters ". Second quality porcelain was sold for decoration by *Hausmaler*, but this, in turn, caused trouble, since their work was sold by them as Vienna porcelain at cut prices, thus harming the factory's sales. The factory tried to overcome this by marking " wasters " with a cross, and when this proved ineffective, ordered white porcelain to be sold at the same price as coloured. Whilst this had the desired effect, it also killed the market for white porcelain.

Some of the disaffected workers built a kiln in the garden of the Hungarian, Graf Batthyány. This was discovered, the men responsible imprisoned, and Batthyány reprimanded.

PLATE 65

Perfume vase.
Vienna. *c.* 1725.

PLATE 66

(a) Bowl with applied acanthus leaves.
Vienna. c. 1725.

(b) Cup and saucer with the portrait of an Abbot and an Abbey.
Vienna. c. 1725.

PLATE 67

(a) Bowl and cover in *Schwarzlot*.
Vienna. *c.* 1730.

(b) Barrel-shaped mug with mask handle.
Vienna. *c.* 1725.

PLATE 68

(*a*) Tureen and stand probably by Helchis.
Vienna. *c.* 1725.

(*b*) Oval dish.
Vienna. *c.* 1730.

PLATE 69

(a) Inkstand.
Vienna. c. 1730.

(b) Dish with mythological figure.
Vienna. c. 1730.

PLATE 70

Bowl and cover in puce monochrome.
Vienna. *c.* 1730.

PLATE 71

Bowl painted by Helchis.
Vienna. c. 1735.

PLATE 72

(a) Cover of bowl illustrated in Plate 71.

(b) Plaque from centre of dish, by Anton Anreiter.
Vienna. Dated 1755.

PLATE 73

(a) Figure of a Lady, by Dannhauser.
Vienna. 1745–50.

(b) *Neptune and Amphitrite*, by J. J. Niedermayer.
Vienna. *c.* 1760.

(c) *Lady with a fan*, by J. J. Niedermayer.
Vienna. *c.* 1750.

(d) *Mother and Son.*
Vienna. *c.* 1765.

PLATE 74

Group by Anton Grassi.
Vienna. c. 1785.

PLATE 75

Figure of a goose, by Ponhauser.
Nymphenburg. *c.* 1753.

PLATE 76

Crinoline figure attributed to
J. R. P. Härtl.
Nymphenburg. c. 1755.

PLATE 77

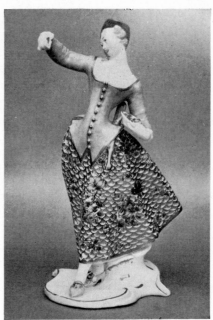

(a) *Tartar Horseman attacked by a Lion*, by F. A. Bustelli. Nymphenburg. *c.* 1760.

(b) *Lalage*, by F. A. Bustelli. Nymphenburg. *c.* 1760.

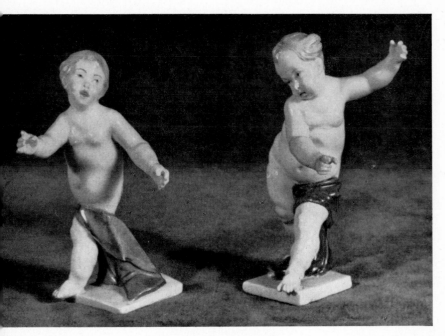

(c) Pair of *putti*, by F. A. Bustelli. Nymphenburg. *c.* 1760.

PLATE 78

Bust of Sigismund, Graf von Haimhausen, by F. A. Bustelli.
Nymphenburg. 1763.

PLATE 79

The Sleeper Awakened, by F. A. Bustelli.
Nymphenburg. *c.* 1760.

PLATE 80

Set of the *Seasons*, by F. A. Bustelli.
Nymphenburg. *c.* 1760.

Finally, the factory went back to the old body, and Kestler gave up experimenting. He also took less interest in the factory, and immediately its affairs began to improve.

Vienna tried hard to keep up with all the modern trends abroad. In 1770 the Ambassador in Paris was asked to get some specimens of Sèvres porcelain which, after some difficulty, he was able to do. A modeller, Christian Adelmann, son of a goldsmith, was commissioned to travel to Rome and Venice to study ancient and modern art, with the object of being the future *Modellmeister* at Vienna. He stayed a long time in these cities, and also at Florence and Lyons, coming finally to Paris. Here he was offered employment in the workshops of the famous goldsmith Germain, and Vienna was forgotten. Attempts were made to copy the *bleu de Roi* of Sèvres, as well as the *rose Pompadour*, and the green ground, but the colours were affected by the hard porcelain glaze, and were often applied in swirls and stripes to give a softer effect.

About 1780 an Englishman attempted to sell his invention of porcelain with a coloured body. This was probably a kind of jasper-ware similar to that of Wedgwood. The factory later made a coloured biscuit porcelain from which they produced medallions and such things inspired by Wedgwood.

Throughout this period the factory was protected by an excise duty on the import of *faïence* or porcelain. Exports were encouraged in every possible way, and attempts made, with varying success, to stop smuggling from Saxony. Porcelain was sold to travelling merchants who took it to fairs throughout Germany, Hungary and Italy. Maria Theresa, however, thought this a trifle undignified, and depots were opened in several cities.

In the export field, Turkey was the biggest single customer. In 1749 Graf Chotek made contact with Chassaud et Cie., merchants of Istanbul, and the trade eventually reached 120,000 pieces annually. Expensive decorated porcelain was presented to the nobility and other suitable persons in Europe with the object of promoting trade.

The baroque style held its own in Vienna for much longer than can be seen elsewhere, and in porcelain longer than in anything else. Christian Daniel Busch brought some new colours from Meissen in 1746 and was commissioned by Graf Kinsky to make a *dejeuner* with his new palette in the rococo style. Busch, however, left in 1748 to go to Nymphenburg in company with other Vienna workmen.

Johann Gottfried Klinger proved to be more stable, and remained for many years. He was responsible for discontinuing the use of heavy gilding, an economy which made him popular with the directorate.

At first, decoration in *Schwarzlot* with gilding in the du Paquier style was continued, but the earlier *Laub- und Bandelwerk* was slowly dropped. The fashion for *deutsche Blumen* was slowly giving place to more naturalistic treatment, and flowers strewn about the surface were popular. At the beginning of the 'seventies flower painting became even more realistic under Johann Drechsler. *Chinoiseries* were used, particularly in conjunction with Mosaik patterns, and the Imari decorations of Arita were copied. Landscapes and figure painting in purple monochrome and in colours had a surround of rococo scrolls.

In 1750 Philipp Ernst Schindler, son of a Meissen painter of boxes, arrived in Vienna from Meissen where he had been a painter and chemist. He was responsible for much of the finer Vienna painting. In 1770 he was made *Obermaler* and arcanist in return for his improvements to the gold and the purple. He functioned occasionally as a *Hausmaler*, a signed example being illustrated by Pazaurek.[1] His most important work includes battle scenes after Rugendas and Watteau subjects.

Of the remaining painters, Joseph Anreiter, who took the dagger from the erring Maxwald, was at the factory from 1753 to 1801, but the record for long service must surely be held by the flower painter, Franz Wollein, who was employed by the factory for seventy years, and awarded a gold medal in consequence.

[1] *Deutsche Fayence und Porzellan Hausmaler.*

Engravings were much used as sources of inspiration, particularly those of Martin Engelbrecht of Augsburg and Preisler.

From 1760 onwards three artists, one of whom rejoiced in the name of Pfnotsch, were specially required to invent new forms of decoration and patterns. The moulded ozier borders of Meissen were used, together with twig handles, and other things of the kind. Many decorative themes were annexed from Sèvres after about 1765.

Figure models, rarely done in the days of du Paquier, became part of the factory's production. Niedermayer was appointed *Modellmeister* in 1747, and Johann Christoph Ludwig von Lücke (self-styled), the erstwhile Meissen *Modellmeister*, was awarded the high-sounding title of "Imperial and Royal Art Chamberlain", and placed on equal terms with Niedermayer. Evidently this arrangement did not work too well, because in 1751 we find Lücke offering his services to Fürstenberg. He left in this year, or the one following. Whilst it is difficult to attribute any particular models to von Lücke, he probably helped to introduce the rococo style. Most of the work of this period is derived from Meissen, and a free adaptation of the Sulkowski Service made at Vienna at this time suggests Lücke's influence. A few signed pieces of somewhat indifferent quality are known.

Niedermayer, himself, was not of the calibre of the great German *Modellmeister*, although his work is always competent, and often very pleasing. He was instructed to analyse every good foreign piece to see how it had been done, and to keep the factory supplied with ideas. He was probably responsible for most of the figures made during this period (Plates 73b and c).

Some Callot figures are awarded on slender evidence to the modeller, Leopold Dannhauser, who was at the factory until his death in 1786. The same man is given some crinoline figures and groups, and may have collaborated with Niedermayer in a particularly charming series done in the 'sixties and 'seventies.

Dannhauser appears to have been responsible for a fantastically large centre-piece done for the Monastery of Zwettl, which was

four yards long and half a yard wide and contained many figures
of mythological personages, *putti*, genre figures, and so forth
(Plate 73a).

In 1778 Anton Grassi was appointed *Modellmeister* in succession
to Niedermayer. He is probably the most important German
exponent of the Louis-Seize style, and his early work is definitely
the better. He was a pupil of J. W. C. Beyer, one-time modeller
at Ludwigsburg and later court sculptor at Vienna, who was
responsible for some statues in the park at Schönbrunn in collaboration with Josef Weinmüller. Grassi's work was influenced
both by Beyer and by the French school. Many of his groups are
scenes from fashionable life of the period. Most of his work falls
in the following period (Plate 74).

The Sorgenthal Period (1784–1805)

Considering its generally unsatisfactory nature, the Wolf-
Kestler régime lasted longer than might have been anticipated, but
unrest among the workers and bad planning of production eventually made its continuance impossible.

A period of financial crisis in 1784, however, caused the state to
offer the factory for sale. No one would buy it, and its direction
was placed in the hands of a woollen merchant, the Freiherr
Konrad von Sorgenthal.

Von Sorgenthal, who brought the factory to its greatest period
of prosperity, was born in Nürnberg in 1735. His father was a
merchant who trained his son to follow in his footsteps. To this
end, young von Sorgenthal was sent on long journeys to Holland,
England, Italy and France. After some experience in a metal
factory, he took over a decrepit woollen factory at Linz, which he
quickly brought to a flourishing business. In 1773 he was made
Hofrat.

Von Sorgenthal was a good organizer, and Kestler was promptly
removed and replaced by the Freiherr von Degelmann as soon as
he took over the directorship of the factory. In a report on the

situation he stated that there was a large amount of outdated porcelain at the factory and in its various depots which he reckoned to be valued at many times its actual worth. He proposed reductions in staff and various alterations in organization, both at the factory and the depôts. The latter, he suggested, should be reduced to a single large shop in the centre of Vienna where all products were to be sold.

Nevertheless, the Kaiser Josef decided that he wanted to be rid of the factory, and after the experience of the previous decades, he is hardly to be blamed. The factory made an appeal to him suggesting that it was an honour for the state to be connected with it. Unfortunately the Kaiser was insensitive to questions of honour in this form, and rejected the proposal. This attitude was, in part, due to Josef's distrust of von Sorgenthal, who was removed and told to devote himself to his woollen factory at Linz.

In the meantime von Sorgenthal had instituted two reforms, the first that all porcelain made after 1st November, 1783 should bear a mark consisting of the last two or three numerals of the year, and that all porcelain sold in white as " wasters " should be marked with incised crossed lines so that it could be distinguished from factory work.

On 9th December a sale of outmoded porcelain was held at the " Golden Rose " in the old meat market. This was successful, and porcelain valued in the books at 5,809 florins actually realized 10,554. Most of the gilded porcelain was bought by two Greeks for the Turkish market.

An attempt was made to sell the factory in May 1784, but no bids were received. Josef promptly did a volte-face, and decided to take von Sorgenthal's advice. The factory was thereupon freed from state interference, and the latter installed as director.

At first von Sorgenthal spent six weeks in Linz and six weeks at Vienna. Wolf was for a time under-director, and in 1786 Josef Rolling was added as controller. A commission was then established consisting of Wolf, Rolling, and Matthias Niedermayer, son of the deceased *Modellmeister*. A new and more practical system of accountancy was devised, and special effort adequately rewarded. The workers of the factory were contented, and headway was made once more.

In the same year six kilns were brought back into operation, and many new orders were received, particularly from Turkey. In 1791 more buildings were added, and the number employed rose steadily.

The dislike of the court for von Sorgenthal was once more in evidence in 1792 when the original agreement setting forth his remuneration was abrogated arbitrarily. Despite protests from von Sorgenthal, and from the Freiherr von Degelmann, he was awarded a lower salary.

In April 1797 the more valuable porcelain was packed ready to be shipped down the Danube to Hungary should Napoleon enter the city. Despite the general trade depression of the time, however, von Sorgenthal managed to keep the factory going without loss. Its reputation had spread widely, and it received many famous visitors, among them being Admiral Lord Nelson and Lady Hamilton.

Von Sorgenthal died in 1805 leaving the factory in a flourishing condition. He was succeeded by Matthias Niedermayer. Throughout this period trade was increasing steadily, and the Turkish market was especially profitable. In 1785 a service was commissioned for the Russian court, and porcelain exported to France, Italy and Russia. The war with Turkey in 1788 temporarily interrupted trade with this market, but a good deal of it was regained, although some was lost to the Thuringian factories. A fine dessert service was made for the Count von Puschkin, a relative of the Russian poet, and another for Countess Tolstoi in St. Petersburg.

Von Sorgenthal tried to raise the artistic level of the work by close co-ordination with the Academy of Arts, and the factory refused to take apprentices who had not first successfully passed the drawing school. He encouraged the established painters to experiment and to do original work. Yearly competitions took place at which the winners were presented with a piece of white porcelain which they were at liberty to decorate and *sign*. Signatures normally were not allowed, and this was a great honour. Matthias Niedermayer's work during this period is also important, since he was responsible for much of the production.

The neo-classical style was adopted and followed at Vienna much more strictly than elsewhere.

Particularly fruitful was the collaboration between Philipp Ernst Schindler and Josef Leithner. The latter had attended lectures in chemistry at the university, and had acquired knowledge of colour chemistry. In 1792 he discovered how to simulate bronze in porcelain, and devised a new blue of fine quality, the *Leithner-blau*. He followed this in 1793 with a more economical way of preparing gold, and in 1796 produced a first-class biscuit body, a black pigment, and a light orange yellow. In 1812 he was awarded a gold medal for his work.

The colours at this time were sometimes over-decorated with relief gilding by a method invented by Georg Perl, and elaborate raised gilding forms a distinct, but not always pleasing, class of Vienna porcelain towards the end of the century.

Much carefully detailed painting of figure subjects was undertaken. This work was of the highest quality, and some of it was copied from such artists as van Dyck, Titian, Rubens, and Raphael, who were represented in the Viennese galleries. Angelica Kauffmann, and the engravings of Bartolozzi, were used, and other English artists to be noticed include George Morland. (Plate 32b).

Probably the most important single feature of the decoration of this period is the superb craftsmanship, which has rarely been equalled, although the disappearance of the white porcelain surface under a spate of enamel colouring is hardly pleasing.

Most of the figures of the period were in biscuit porcelain, of which many were copied from Sèvres. The principal artists were Anton Grassi, and his pupils, Johann Schaller and Elias Hütter.

In 1792 Grassi made a journey to Italy to collect material to develop the neo-classical style. A new work on excavations at

Herculaneum was sent back to Vienna and much used thereafter. Grassi also collected a large number of casts, engravings and drawings which were used for the same purpose. In 1797 he designed a table set for the wedding of the Archduchess Clementina to the Crown Prince of Naples.

The nineteenth century saw a slow decline in the fortunes of the factory, which closed finally in 1864. Some of the more elaborate paintings of the Sorgenthal period were copied on old Vienna porcelain after the close of the factory by Ludwig Riedl and others. These are not uncommon, but can always be recognized by the quality of the workmanship, which falls far below eighteenth-century standards.

3

NYMPHENBURG

NYMPHENBURG is a factory which, for the quality of its service-ware, ranks, perhaps, a little below Meissen, Berlin and Vienna, but its *Kleinplastik* is always of fine quality and in Franz Anton Bustelli Nymphenburg boasted a modeller who could, at his best, outshine Kändler himself.

Nymphenburg is a suburb of Munich, and the first attempts to make porcelain here were undertaken in 1729 when a Bohemian glass-worker, Elias Vater, arrived from Dresden promising the secret. The Elector, Karl Albert, set aside 150 florins for a test, and gave Vater, in addition, a weekly sum and free living quarters. This man had been one of the glass-workers called to Meissen by Böttger to decorate red stoneware, but whether he had ever worked on the manufacturing side is another matter. He appears to have known little, the attempts were unsuccessful, and Vater reappears in Copenhagen in 1731. He had no further connection with the Munich undertaking.

At this time the court at Munich was buying heavily from Meissen, and the search went on during the ensuing years.

Nothing of value appears to have been achieved until the Elector married Maria Anna Sophia, a grand-daughter of Augustus the Strong, in 1747. Somewhat naturally, she was extremely interested in porcelain, and did much to encourage its successful manufacture whilst she was living in Munich. The Hall of Mirrors in the royal Residence was completely decorated with porcelain, and later, many of the rooms were filled with European and oriental ceramics.

In 1747 Johann Lippisch came from Vienna with the secret, but after a few weeks at Munich either fell, or threw himself, into the River Isar, whilst on a journey. In the same year an attempt at manufacture was made by a merchant named Niedermayer. There were several Niedermayers involved in the project, the two principal being, apparently, Franz Ignaz and Augustin. Both were potters, probably engaged in experimental work, and in 1763 records show that Augustin requested permission to buy clay from Passau.

Probably the man chiefly concerned with the experimental work was Franz Ignaz Niedermayer, who bought a house and kilns belonging to the court potter, Georg Strasser. He is said to have had considerable knowledge of chemistry, to have worked at various *faïence* factories, and to have bought the secret of porcelain manufacture from a Meissen workman at an inn. This was not the true secret, which, doubtless, the Meissen workman did not know, but a thriving and lucrative trade was sometimes done by workmen in such scraps of half-knowledge as their position enabled them to pick up.

Niedermayer was financed by the Baron von Zech, who was a favourite of the Elector, Maximilian III Joseph, and he made from porcelain clay some service-ware with gold ornament which has since disappeared.

Maximilian III Joseph was a patron of the arts, and interested in commercial expansion. Rosenfeld, the Bavarian Ambassador to the Court of Vienna, tried to get workers for the Munich project, and engaged Johann Karl Wendelin Anreiter, who died before he could take up the proferred position. Among several others thus engaged was Jakob Helkis, the Vienna painter and arcanist, who arrived in the autumn of 1747, and the whole organization was placed under the administration of Johann Kaspar Kreuttner, who received a salary of thirty florins a month until such time as the factory became prosperous. The costs were limited to 4,764 florins a year, and Niedermayer was excluded from the undertaking, probably because of professional jealousy on the part of the Viennese workers.

Johann Lippisch, already mentioned, was kiln-master, and his unfortunate accident took place in course of a journey to Passau to buy clay. The report on the incident rather heartlessly adds that 150 florins were lost with the body.

The news of the projected undertaking appears to have spread widely because quite a number of porcelain workers, among them Johann Benckgraff (Bengraf, in contemporary records), arrived at Munich, but they were all sacked in a body on the advice of Helkis.

The need for buildings was filled by a castle at Neudeck-ob-der-Au. This had been built in the early part of the seventeenth century, passed for a time from the Electors to a religious order, and back again to the Electors. Ultimately it fell into disuse, only an occasional court festivity being held there, but it had a good water supply capable of driving the factory machinery, and was surrounded by forests which provided the necessary fuel. It was, therefore, the logical choice as the site for the new factory, which was established here in 1747. The castle was demolished in 1903.

The 11th November, 1747 can perhaps be regarded as the date of foundation because it was then that the director of the factory received the first payment. The initial production was poor, and it continued thus until 1749. By 1749 all the Viennese workers had left, and Niedermayer was brought back to reconstruct what remained. He re-engaged Helkis, but the Elector began to tire of the project and withdrew his support. Niedermayer thereupon asked permission to continue alone in the buildings at Neudeck, and suggested that he should have the use of them free of cost under contract to return them to the court at the end of twelve years, and to work exclusively for the court's Department of

Commerce in the meantime. Nothing definite was decided. Niedermayer stayed on as a private citizen, without official support but with official tolerance.

In 1751 the position changed for the better with the advent of the Graf Sigismund von Haimhausen, the moving spirit behind this great factory whose incomparable portrait by Bustelli appears on Plate 78.

Von Haimhausen was then about forty-three years of age, and had travelled extensively throughout Europe, spending some years in Paris. He was interested in porcelain manufacture and got into touch with Niedermayer, financing him and promising him the position of director of the factory if he could make porcelain successfully. Nothing much emerged from this arrangement, but, luckily, in 1753, Joseph Jakob Ringler appeared in Munich, obviously drawn there by the numerous failures to make porcelain.

Ringler was born at Vienna in 1730, and had acquired his knowledge of manufacture at that factory. In 1752 he was at Höchst as adviser on kiln-design, after which he went to Strasbourg in 1753, and worked with von Löwenfinck and Hannong, who had just succeeded in making true porcelain there.

Von Haimhausen received him with open arms, and it was finally due to Ringler that the undertaking emerged from the doldrums in 1754. As technical director he carried the secrets of his work around with him in a great case which contained details of kiln-designs, the preparation of the body, and the secret of mixing colours. These, unfortunately, were lost after his death. Von Haimhausen, somewhat naturally, did his best to persuade Ringler to reveal the secret, but he proved obdurate. His porcelain was bad, and he was finally discharged in 1757 with twenty-four florins to set him on his way. In 1759 he became director at Ludwigsburg (see chapter 8).

His place was taken by Johann Paul Rupert Härtl, a chemist, who had come to Neudeck in the first place under the aegis of von Haimhausen, and who had previously been one of the executives under Ringler.

Härtl had been an attentive pupil of Ringler's, and wily in extracting information. He wrote a book about porcelain with the unwieldy title of *A description of all knowledge appertaining to a porcelain factory, in which by means of unceasing industry and many experiments it was brought to fruition at the Elector's Bavarian Porcelain Factory*. Härtl at first refused to give up the secret and the book was not published until 1761, by which time he had given a copy of the secret to the Elector, Maximilian III Joseph. It deals with porcelain manufacture under two headings—the art of making porcelain, and the art of painting it.

Härtl was a chemist who had studied mining and geology, and, in addition to his directorship of the factory to which he was appointed in 1754, had earlier been made an administrator to the Department of Mines.

In 1754, von Haimhausen persuaded the Elector to give the porcelain undertaking official status, and in November of the same year, Franz Anton Bustelli first appears.

Bustelli was born in Locarno in 1723, the son of a bell-maker. He appears in the archives in a note made by Härtl in 1754, and thenceforth his name occurs year by year. His antecedents are completely unknown, although it has been suggested that he was at one time employed at the factory founded at Doccia, near Florence, by the Marchese Carlo Ginori in 1737. He probably knew something about the manufacture of porcelain, and left a number of " *chymischen Buecher* " among his effects. His distinctive style was strongly influenced by the Munich sculptor, Franz Ignaz Günther (Plate 82a).

His name had no fixed spelling—Bustelli, Pustelli, Bastelli, Pastelli and Pastalli have all been noted. Although the name Pustelli has been regarded as erroneous, it is probably no more than the South German dialect which has substituted the initial " P " for the original "B", and the remainder the kind of phonetic orthography common in the eighteenth century when the forms of words had not become so fixed as they are today.

His work is discussed in greater detail later, and for a note on the suggestion that he worked at Ludwigsburg, see the chapter on that factory's work.

The years following 1754 saw considerable increase in production. Neudeck porcelain became widely known, and there were visits from various noblemen, among them being the Archbishop of Cologne who was uncle to Maximilian III Joseph. A shop was opened in the Rindermarkt in 1757 for the sale of the factory's wares.

Von Haimhausen was made *Geheimrat*, and a special medal of commemoration was struck for him. Despite this, he was not paid for his original investments, and had to content himself with taking whatever porcelain pleased him.

The Elector decided to hand the buildings at Neudeck over to a religious order, the Paulauerkloster, with the proviso that ". . . the newly-erected porcelain factory is to be allowed to continue working without hindrance upon paying an annual rent". The monks promptly demanded 100 ducats for the tiny piece of ground occupied by the factory. The directors ignored this exorbitant demand. The monks pestered the Elector to enforce payment, and also said the monastery was in constant danger from fire because of the porcelain kilns. The factory also needed more space, so, harried by the monks, the directors decided to remove to Nymphenburg near to the castle of the Elector.

The removal took place on 8th April, 1761 to the great annoyance of the monks who saw a source of income slip from their grasp. In 1761 the new buildings were visited by the Elector, accompanied by his cousin, Karl Theodor of the Palatinate, who was at this time negotiating with Hannong for the purchase of the existing factory at Frankenthal.

Von Haimhausen was now the sole director and administrator of the factory. In order to avoid being at the mercy of temperamental arcanists, the Elector ordered all secrets and technical plans to be handed over to von Haimhausen, who was also director of the College of the Mint and Mines. This was aimed at Härtl, who shortly before had been given the title of " Consultant to the

Mint and Mines ". Härtl was obstinate, and pursued a policy of passive resistance. He refused to work at the new factory, and on 13th June, 1761 was ordered by decree to attend at least once a week. When he did not, he was discharged, and his efforts to manœuvre a way back were frustrated.

For two years von Haimhausen ran the factory alone, and in 1763 appointed Joseph Karl von Linprun to the post of director. Linprun was a young man, but his technical skill was undoubted. 1764 saw the premature death of Bustelli which left vacant the post of *Modellmeister*. This was filled almost immediately by Dominikus Auliczek, who took over in January 1765.

Auliczek was born in 1734 at Policka in Bohemia. It was at first intended that he should become a monk, but a physical disability prevented it. At eighteen he made his way to Vienna and studied under Johann Georg Leutner, and also at the Academy of Sculpture, probably at the same time as Franz Ignaz Günther. In 1754 he was in Paris, and a year later in London, where he studied art and practised modelling after nature. 1756 saw him in Rome, by way of Paris, where he took a three-year course in anatomy at the Hospital of the Holy Ghost, a fact which may account for the macabre nature of some of his later work.

In 1759 he received the prize of the Academy of Santa Luca for sculpture, and the Golden Spur for artists from Pope Clement XIII. He joined the studio of the architect, Gaetano Chiaveri, and stayed for three years. He was then persuaded by a self-styled bishop to travel with him to Germany by promises of a high position at one of the princely courts. On the journey his patron ran out of money, and Auliczek had to sell his possessions. In 1762 they arrived in Munich, where the pseudo-bishop was exposed, and by chance von Haimhausen met Auliczek at a time when he was looking for a *Modellmeister* to replace Bustelli.

Whilst much of the work of Auliczek is technically skilful, there is no doubt from his subsequent history that, despite his considerable gifts, his character suffered from grave defects. As much is apparent from his models of animals fighting, of which he did a long series, in which gross injuries are depicted with careful realism. Whilst other artists used such subjects on occasion, it was never with the coldly calculated and unrelieved ferocity displayed in the work of Auliczek. He created great difficulties for the factory, and for his patron, von Haimhausen, by a consistently unco-operative and intransigent attitude, and eventually brought it almost to the brink of ruin, as will later be recorded.

By 1765 Nymphenburg's fame became widespread, and contemporary opinion, at this period, gave it second place only to Meissen. The latter factory, in sending a modeller on a journey to gain technical information in 1764, laid great stress on the importance of a visit to Nymphenburg. Considerable trade was done with the rest of Germany and abroad. In 1761 an agent was appointed in Venice who sent porcelain to the Levantine countries, and large quantities were sent to Brussels, Vienna and Amsterdam. Perhaps this was due in part to the effect on Meissen of the Seven Years' War, but it enabled the factory to establish itself firmly.

At first, sales did not cover the cost of production, and they were stimulated by price reductions which led to increased sales. These merely increased the losses. The tide turned in 1761, however, and because the cost of the new buildings was borne by the state, the factory had some profitable years. The year 1766, however, saw the beginning of a trade slump which was widespread throughout Germany, and the optimistic methods of financing the factory gave much trouble. The book-keeping, and the stock valuation in particular, was singularly unrealistic, and it became essential to reduce costs immediately. Sales were arranged, and concessions to workers cancelled. These measures, however, were not sufficient, and the Elector had to provide a weekly subsidy. Linprun tried to safeguard his future by negotiating with Sèvres, and went so far as to send them a specimen of Nymphenburg porcelain. Sèvres had already acquired the secret from Hannong, which was similar to porcelain already being made at Frankenthal, and since there was then no known source of porcelain clay in France, the offer was rejected.

PLATE 81

Fisherman, by F. A. Bustelli.
Nymphenburg. *c.* 1760.

PLATE 82

(b) Figure in classical costume by Dominikus Auliczek.
Nymphenburg. c. 1770.

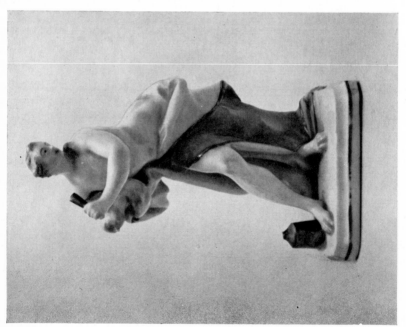

(a) Figure of a Sculptor, attributed to Franz Ignaz Günther.
Nymphenburg. 1755–60.

PLATE 83

(b) Group: *Asia*, by Dominikus Auliczek. Nymphenburg. c. 1765.

(a) Group: *Africa*, by Dominikus Auliczek. Nymphenburg. c. 1765.

PLATE *84*

(*a*) Cup and saucer.
Nymphenburg. *c.* 1760.

(*b*) Rococo ewer.
Nymphenburg. *c.* 1765.

(*c*) Interior of cup illustrated on Plate 84a.
Nymphenburg. *c.* 1760.

(*d*) Pipe-bowl by F. A. Bustelli.
Nymphenburg. *c.* 1755.

PLATE 85

Réchaud (or *veilleuse*) with figures in a landscape.
Nymphenburg. 1755–60.

PLATE 86

(b) The Medicine-seller.
Höchst. c. 1755.

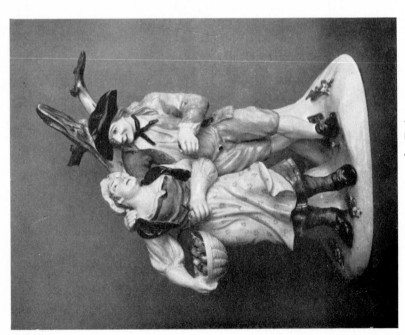

(a) Peasant group after Teniers.
Höchst. c. 1755.

PLATE 87

(c) Gardener.
Höchst. c. 1755.

(b) Scaramouche.
Höchst. c. 1755.

(a) Man playing the Fife and Drum.
Höchst. c. 1755.

PLATE 88

Early group of Gallant and Lady.
Höchst. *c.* 1755.

PLATE 89

(*a*) Arbour Group.
Höchst. *c.* 1755.

(*b*) Group of Lovers.
Höchst. *c.* 1755.

PLATE 90

Chinese Emperor seated on a Throne.
Höchst. *c.* 1765.

PLATE 91

Cobbler throwing a shoe at a stray
dog.

Höchst. *c.* 1765.

PLATE 92

(a) Group of Shepherd and Shepherdess, by J. P. Melchior.
Höchst. c. 1770.

(b, left) Girl with a basket by J. P.
Melchior.
Höchst. 1770.

(c, right) Boy with a bird's nest by
J. P. Melchior.
Höchst. c. 1770.

PLATE 93

(a) *Turk and Companion*, by J. P. Melchior.
Höchst. *c.* 1770.

(b) *Distressed girl and companion*, by J. P. Melchior.
Höchst. *c.* 1770.

PLATE 94

(a) *Putti* in various guises, by J. P. Melchior.
Höchst. *c.* 1770.

(b) *Putti* with a dog, by J. P. Melchior.
Höchst. *c.* 1770.

(c) Family Group, by J. P. Melchior.
Höchst. *c.* 1770.

PLATE 95

(a) Pipe-bowl.
Höchst. c. 1770.

(b) Tankard with Nürnberg silver mounts.
Höchst. c. 1753.

(c) Tea-pot in crimson monochrome.
Höchst. 1755.

PLATE 96

Réchaud (or *veilleuse*) in crimson monochrome.
Höchst. *c.* 1755.

Meantime, the Elector began to withdraw his support, and the factory threatened to collapse completely. To safeguard his interest Linprun offered to run it with some help from the state. His offer was accepted, and von Haimhausen withdrew.

During 1768 and 1769 great difficulty was experienced in paying the workers, and the prevailing economic difficulties in Bavaria made Linprun's task almost impossible. Linprun was released from his position as director, and the Elector brought von Haimhausen back from Italy to make him director with a commission of three to assist him.

Maximilian III Joseph died in 1770 to be succeeded by Karl Theodor of the Palatinate who was already engaged with his factory at Frankenthal. Nymphenburg was relegated to second place, and more difficulties were created in 1778 by the War of Succession.

In 1773 Dominikus Auliczek was made factory inspector because "... he seems to be willing and very sensible". Auliczek did, at first, manage to get the factory on to a self-supporting basis, and in 1782 he was made *Hofkammerrat*. This new appointment seems to have affected him in a distinctly unpleasant manner. He became quarrelsome and secretive and, as the result of a dispute with von Haimhausen, refused to go to the workshops for three years.

By 1780 the demand for figures was lessening, and cheap English earthenware was beginning to flood the continental market. Von Haimhausen had progressively lost interest in the factory after the death of Maximilian III Joseph, and the rest of the commission left the conduct of affairs severely alone. It was not until 1787, therefore, that the muddle created by Auliczek's intrigues was finally uncovered. Even then, he retained his position of factory inspector, although the directorate was changed and the factory placed in charge of Mathias Flurl. Auliczek was the only man who knew the secrets of manufacture, and his salary was, perforce, increased to 1,000 florins, with four florins for every firing, and a free house, heat and light.

"And still the man is not satisfied..." wrote von Haimhausen, and it was proposed to discharge him altogether. For a time he mended his ways, but eventually the position drifted back to its starting point, with von Haimhausen gradually lessening his interest until his death in 1793.

The new director was the Graf Joseph August von Törring, who was an excellent man of business. Auliczek was ordered to disclose his secrets. He replied evasively that it was not a fixed formula, and could only be done from experience. Finally, in May 1797, he was pensioned and ordered to give the secret to his son, also Dominikus Auliczek, who thereupon became his successor.

By 1797 trade had begun to improve, and Johann Peter Melchior was appointed *Modellmeister*. Later in the same year an inquiry was started into certain losses in the kilns which ended by uncovering many irregularities on the part of both the Auliczeks, who were deprived of their offices by royal decree and ordered to leave Bavaria.

In 1798 Bavaria was occupied by Austrian troops, and the Elector, Karl Theodor, died. The Frankenthal factory was closed in 1799, and Mathias Flurl carried out the unification of the two enterprises, removing some of the Frankenthal moulds to Nymphenburg. The Frankenthal recipes also came to Nymphenburg at the same time, by which the latter acquired the results of the work done by Simon Feilner and Bergdoll, as well as the designs of the kilns, much of which had already been published in book form by various authors.

Johann Peter Melchior was born at Lindorf, near Düsseldorf, in 1742. Even as a child his main preoccupation was with drawing, painting and sculpture, although his parents were peasants who knew nothing of art and cared somewhat less. When they died he became a cow-herd, and finally a relative apprenticed him to a sculptor at Düsseldorf. Melchior, however, was dissatisfied with his teaching and tried to get to Paris. Whether or not he got there we do not know, but he arrived in Mainz in 1765 where his work became so well known that he was offered the position of *Modell-meister* at Höchst.

Höchst, however, did not seem particularly promising, and in 1769 we find him negotiating with the Berlin factory by whom he was offered a salary of 500 thalers. Dittmar, the Berlin agent, went to see him to make the offer. Melchior communicated the news of this visit to the director of the Höchst factory, who promptly raised his salary to 800 thalers, and got him the position of court sculptor.

Melchior was in close touch with Goethe and his circle, and did several portraits of the poet. In 1774 Goethe wrote to a friend, " . . . I will send you a newly-done medallion of my nose which is quite successful ".

The friendship does not seem to have been close, since Goethe does not mention Melchior by name in any of his letters, but he was godfather to one of his children, christened, needless to say, Johann Wolfgang !

In 1778 Höchst fell on bad times, and Melchior accepted an offer from Frankenthal. In 1791 he helped to carry many of the valuables from Frankenthal to Mainz to escape from the French and in 1793 left Frankenthal and went to Mannheim. From here he travelled to Nürnberg, where he stayed for three years, apparently in poverty for most of the time. Eventually, he wrote to Karl Theodor asking to be given a job at Nymphenburg because of his existing life-contract with Frankenthal. In 1796 he was summoned to Munich, and probably would have been given a post immediately, but for the necessity of first solving the problem presented by Auliczek.

Finally, he was given the job of *Modellmeister* and chief overseer on level terms with the younger Auliczek who was factory inspector. In 1797 Auliczek *fils* was discharged, and the inspectorate given to Melchior. Misfortune pursued him. He was ill and depressed, his daughter was dangerously ill, his eldest son died, and he did not take up his post until October 1797. For much of 1798 he was too ill to work, and Flurl had to take his place. At the end of the year he wrote a long letter to von Törring on the subject of his troubles, saying that he doubted his ability to continue: " I feel so much the less able to work because I am sickly and hypochondriacal and feel sure that my powers are waning; my eyes are dim, my hearing dulled, and my memory was always weak."

He was lucky enough to be treated with sympathy, and in 1802 he wrote a letter of gratitude to the new Elector asking to be confirmed in the position of inspector at the factory. The Elector replied in April 1802, saying that because of his industry, his conscientiousness, and his exceptionally trustworthy and friendly character he was appointed the real inspector of the porcelain factory. The Elector continued to express the highest satisfaction with his work to date.

The position of inspector was an important one. The duties included the actual mixing of the paste and glaze, the overseeing of the workmen, the control of the kilns and firing, the taking of orders and their execution, and the inventories of stock (made every three years). Moreover the inspector had to see that the whole thing was run on economic lines, and to make from time to time " new and tasteful models, and to teach the young workers drawing and modelling".

The later history of the factory does not fall within the scope of this volume, and Melchior's most important work was done between 1800 and 1810. It is still working and its present production is of the highest quality. The portrait of von Haimhausen reproduced on Plate 78 was sent to me by the factory—the Staatliche Porzellanmanufaktur Nymphenburg.

Neudeck table-wares did not take a particularly original line. The earliest wares were sent to Augsburg for decoration, as witness the coffee-pot appearing on Plate 141b. Porcelain was also sent to Vienna to be painted.

The early influence of Vienna may be deduced from the fact that the painter Helkis sold some Vienna porcelain to Nymphenburg to be used as models, but otherwise he does not seem to have been particularly well regarded. In 1749, as I have recorded, he was discharged because of his continued lack of success. He was re-employed in the same year on less favourable terms, and was also made kiln-master at the same time because, according to his claims, he "understood the firing, preparation of the colours, and the painting itself, indeed everything which was necessary to the art". However, when porcelain was finally produced he was not even entrusted with the kilns, and in Munich he was reckoned only " *als ein mittelmässiger Maler* "—a painter of medium ability —a verdict which Plate 71 goes far to disprove. In June 1750 he left the factory with only thirty florins in his pocket, and nothing more is heard of him.

Although from 1754 onward Bustelli was designing and modelling services for the court, difficulties were still being experienced with enamel colours. Bustelli's contribution lay in the direction of tureens and dishes with moulded decoration in the rococo style, and such things as lemons with leaves as knops to the covers of tureens are characteristic of work of this kind. The court was the chief buyer of porcelain in the eighteenth century, and it took several decades to get the *bourgeoisie* used to the idea of porcelain for daily use. It was expensive, and generally regarded as a luxury. That they turned to it in the nineteenth century was in part due to the lotteries which were held at frequent intervals.

As late as 1755 much work was still being sent outside for decoration, and Aegidius Arenbach who announced that he could prepare *Goldpurpur und Malgold* was discharged because he failed to fulfil his promises. This man is typical of the " arcanists " who arrived in Munich, stayed a couple of weeks, and resumed their travels leaving nothing of value behind.

In 1756 a painter from Vienna named Andreas Oettner (or Ettner), who was later at Frankenthal, Ludwigsburg and Höchst, was employed as *Ordinair Feuermaler*. He was given charge of colour mixing, and appears to have been responsible for the successful development of Nymphenburg enamelling. He re-mained until 1757, and left behind him an apprentice, Johann

Willand, who had come with him from Vienna, and who later (in the 1780's) decorated Nymphenburg coffee-cups for the Turkish market at his studio in Regensburg. Willand received instruction in the art of enamelling from Härtl, and was twice promoted, but he was discharged in August 1758 for "childishly stupid behaviour and bad conduct".

Another painter of the period was Georg Christoph Lindemann, son of C. Philipp Lindemann of Meissen, who painted landscapes, figures and flowers. He later functioned as a *Hausmaler*. Much work was also done by Johann Karl Gerlach, a one-time Meissen painter who probably came from Vienna with Busch, and who was later at Ansbach.

Kajetan Purtscher took the place of Lindemann in 1760. He was still at work in 1800, and died in 1813 at the age of seventy-three. Joseph Zächenberger, who did flowers, historical scenes and landscapes, worked at the factory from 1760 until 1770.

Much of the work of this period had naturalistic flowers as its subject, use being made of engravings by J. D. Preissler and others. *Strohblumen* and bouquets were painted on service-ware, some with rococo relief moulding, with great skill and brilliance of colouring.

The removal to Nymphenburg in 1761 did not cause any considerable reorganization of the painting shops. Ambrosius Hermannsdörfer, painter and designer, was given the task of organizing the work, preparing the drawing and painting of the service-ware, and of overseeing the gilding. Under him were twelve painters and fifty-two apprentices. He remained until March 1764 and died in 1770.

In 1762 we find underglaze blue painting attempted for the first time. Difficulty was probably experienced with this colour, since it was very rarely used. Its introduction has been attributed to a workman named J. C. Kilber.

An apprentices' school was opened by von Haimhausen in 1763, and the sons of the court servants to the number of seventy were taken on. Hermannsdörfer was replaced by Joseph Weiss, a miniature-painter who worked at the factory from 1764 to 1767, dying in 1770. His son, Bartholomäus, was also a miniature-painter and probably functioned as a *Hausmaler*. The elder Weiss specialized in flowers, and did some distinguished work. He became father-in-law to Dominikus Auliczek in 1765, and was discharged in 1767 when the factory personnel was reduced in number. He was not reinstated, although he frequently requested either this or a pension.

Joseph Lerch was employed from 1764 to 1770. He was a skilled painter of flowers and animals, and was a pupil of Franz Anton Winter, a miniature-painter. His work was regarded as outstanding. Johannes Klein worked from 1765 to 1771 as a painter of flowers, fruit, figures and landscapes, and later functioned as a *Hausmaler*, using Nymphenburg porcelain.

The painting of the porcelain surface to represent grained wood, to which is attached a piece of paper painted with a simulated engraving, was copied from Niderviller. Also worth special notice are the coffee-pots decorated with landscapes, flowers and so forth.

Auliczek is not mentioned as a designer of service-ware, but he made some models of tureens in 1772 in the neo-classical style. In 1792 the *Perlservice*, with pearls around the borders, is much in the taste of the time, and was due to Auliczek.

In 1798 Melchior announced that he intended to "improve designs and ideas according to modern taste". He meant the taste prevailing in France, and in this he was helped by Franz Paul Böhngen who had studied in France, possibly at Niderviller.

A speciality of the Nymphenburg factory was the *veilleuse* or *réchaud*—a food-warmer in several parts heated by a small lamp. These were often superbly painted. An example appears on Plate 85. Vases were done, mostly of small size, but some much larger. Auliczek did some with rococo handles and applied flowers. Others from Melchior were in the neo-classical style.

As the century drew to its close, the output of the painting studios progressively lessened, and at one time only five painters were employed. During the early period, Nymphenburg painting is as good as anything to be found in Germany at the time. In some cases signed work makes it possible to hazard tentative attributions to a number of the painters mentioned, but much of it cannot be ascribed to any particular hand.

Nymphenburg was principally noted during the eighteenth century for the quality of its figure modelling—a tradition which persists to the present day.

The work of Johann Theophil Schreiber and Johann Georg Härtl, who worked before 1750, has not been identified, but that of Joseph Ponhauser from Vienna, who worked between 1754 and 1755, is known, and an example appears on Plate 75. Ponhauser seems to have held a position of some influence, and Bustelli was placed under him when he first joined the factory. Johann Paul Rupert Härtl was also a modeller of some groups and single figures around 1755, one of which is illustrated here (Plate 76). Franz Ignaz Günther also modelled for the factory, and is here represented by Plate 82a.

Bustelli is an enigma. His early models show almost the same fully-developed style that can be seen in his later work. Apparently he first carved these things in lime-wood, which has the requisite softness and elasticity, and some of his work certainly gives the impression of having been carved rather than modelled.

The conclusion that he had had some kind of previous experience as a modeller for porcelain seems almost inescapable, since the quality and style of his work hardly varied during the ten years or so he was at the factory, but there is no evidence on the question of where he might have been previously, although Doccia has been suggested without any supporting evidence other than his obvious Italian ancestry.

At first his work was attributed to Auliczek, and the name of Bustelli was first put forward by Herbert Hirth in a posthumously published catalogue of 1901. Brüning, referring to statuary by Auliczek at Nymphenburg, contrasts the two men in a few words of devastating comment:

There can be no more crass contrast than one between these muscle-less broad-shouldered figures standing in rows of organized stupidity, and the spontaneously imagined, enchantingly mobile, slim, highly-bred porcelain figures of Bustelli.

Some are signed " FB " or " B ", and it is probable that he always signed the first model taken from a new mould. Bustelli's figures have been reproduced later, but contemporary examples have a very smooth and creamy-white paste with a slightly greenish-toned glaze.

Probably the most remarkable model to come from Bustelli was the portrait of the Graf von Haimhausen illustrated here (Plate 78). Done just before Bustelli's death, this, too, has been attributed to Auliczek, but with how little foundation can be seen from an examination of it. It has been suggested, too, that this superb portrait was actually done from a mask taken during von Haimhausen's lifetime. After some youthful experience of this kind of work, however, I feel inclined to disagree. Apart from the physical appearance of the thing itself, there is no doubt that Bustelli was fully capable of making it without a life-mask, and von Haimhausen would have been distinctly unwilling to undergo so much discomfort when it was not strictly necessary.

Bustelli's figures are unique. The poses are exaggerated and theatrical, and the mouths frequently open. In lesser hands this would have been a detraction, but Bustelli's skill overcame the drawback. The pose is frozen in the midst of an elegant turn of head and limb, or an expressive gesture. It is movement crystallized at its most significant point (Plate 79).

His bases are at first thin, flat and undecorated, the earliest being without the rococo scroll-work which began presently to appear. By 1760 the scrolls were not only ornamenting the base, making its outline irregular, but were beginning to rise, as in the seated figure of a Chinaman drinking tea, who reclines negligently with an elbow on a wave-like scroll which curves over at the top.

In the case of groups, the scrolls began to rise from the centre of the base often to a considerable height, increasing in elaboration with successive models. A development of it can be seen in the group known as the *Startled Sleeper* of about 1760 in which the male figure is asleep inside the curve of one of the scrolls (Plate 79).

These features were copied elsewhere, even in England, clumsily and without the same elegance. In lesser hands the scrolls were not a coherent and integral part of the design, but degenerated into meaningless additions. An exception possibly is the work attributed to J. F. Lück at Frankenthal, who can approach Bustelli's handling of these details fairly closely. Lück, however, tended to use it as a chance to display his virtuosity as a modeller.

Among Bustelli's better known work must be reckoned a series of sixteen figures from the Italian comedy, which was one of his favourite subjects.

The Italian comedy was an especial favourite with many porcelain modellers from the time of Böttger's stoneware onward. It had become a popular entertainment during the sixteenth century, and existed only in the form of a *scenario*, the dialogue to which was improvised by the players as it proceeded. The comedy was usually acted by troupes of strolling players who moved from place to place throughout Europe.

As porcelain models the designs were taken from a number of sources, including J. E. Nilson,[1] and a series of twelve engravings published in Augsburg in 1729 by J. B. Probst after J. J. Schübler. The seventeen plates by Joullain which illustrated Riccoboni's *Histoire du théâtre italien* of 1730 were also used, as well as the works of Jacopo Callot early in the seventeenth century.

The principal character was usually Harlequin, who wore a coloured patch-work jacket. Other characters included Pantaloon, with black cloak and pointed beard, a merchant of Venice with a young and pretty wife whose *amours* were the subject of numerous

---

[1] Johann Esaias Nilson (1721-1788), an engraver who worked in the rococo style, and whose work was both copied on porcelain and *faïence* and adapted to figure-modelling.

intrigues; Dr. Baloardo, the comic *savant*; the Lawyer, whose part was more or less interchangeable with that of Baloardo; Pulcinella (Punch), sometimes called in Germany Hanswurst, or Jack Sausage, who has a hump; the swashbuckling Captain with a big nose reminiscent of Cyrano de Bergerac; and Scaramouche who is a variant of the Captain. Pedrolino (Pierrot) was a valet, usually in love with a serving maid, and Brighella the villain of the piece—a seducer of women who sometimes serenaded them with guitar and song. Among the minor characters were serving maids whose business it was to be seduced, and a Poet or Lover who languished suitably after his female counterpart, the Inamorata. The serious women characters were often given pretentious names, and are mostly variants of one stock character, Columbine. Mezzetino is a variant of Brighella. Some of these players were masked, the mask being either a special one confined to the particular character, or an ordinary black domino.

Other Bustelli subjects include courtiers and their ladies, hawkers and street vendors, and such things. His cane-handles are often distinguished and amusing pieces of modelling. Snuffboxes, cane-handles, *étuis*, and such things, were made in considerable quantities.

Many of Bustelli's figures are either in white, or have comparatively slight passages of colour, although examples painted more lavishly exist, principally from the early period.

Perhaps because of his earlier training in other mediums, Dominikus Auliczek never seems at home with porcelain modelling. His work is competent but often pedestrian, and he suffers, too, from following someone of the stature of Bustelli. Some of his work was closely copied from Meissen, one or two things being almost identical reproductions. He worked mostly in the Louis-Seize style, and some of his figures which still have traces of rococo influence are pleasing. His single figures of animals are often interesting, but the series of realistic groups of animals in combat, some derived from engravings by Riedinger, are not particularly attractive. They are modelled with careful attention to detail, and such things as protruding entrails emerging from a slash in the muscles of the belly-wall apparently attracted his fancy.

Much of Melchior's work really falls outside the scope of this volume. Most things are in a severe version of the neo-classical style, quite unlike his earlier work. He quite obviously preferred biscuit to glazed porcelain at this time, and did many portrait busts and medallions. Two busts of the children of Maximilian I of Bavaria are distinguished pieces of modelling. He also did figures and groups.

4

HÖCHST

In March 1746, Johann Christoph Göltz, his stepson, Johann Felician Clarus, and Adam Friedrich von Löwenfinck, received a privilege from the Elector of Mayence to organize a porcelain factory at Höchst.

Von Löwenfinck appears to have represented himself to Göltz and Clarus, who were Frankfurt merchants, as a porcelain arcanist, but despite assistance he received from workers whom he engaged from Meissen, he could not make porcelain. In 1749 Göltz and Clarus asked the Elector to release them from their contract with him, and von Löwenfinck then went to Hannong at Strasbourg.

In 1750 it was reported to the Elector that Johann Benckgraff was staying at Künersberg, near Memmingen in Bavaria, and that he had made successful attempts to produce porcelain there. Two authenticated specimens exist, one of which is at Memmingen, and the other in the Bavarian National Museum at Munich.

In 1748 Benckgraff tried unsuccessfully to get the position of arcanist at the Bavarian factory of Neudeck (later transferred to Nymphenburg), and he therefore accepted the invitation to come to Höchst as director and arcanist.

When he arrived at Höchst he found none of the essentials, even for the manufacture of *faïence*. No progress had been made towards the making of porcelain, and even the kilns had to be constructed. This he did on the Viennese model. Numerous experiments towards devising a practicable porcelain body were unsuccessful, and Benckgraff sent for Joseph Jakob Ringler, with whom he had previously been associated. Ringler arrived in 1750 and left in 1751, after which the manufacture of porcelain seems to have been reasonably well established.

Benckgraff toyed with offers of help from many of the charlatans then posing as arcanists, and got his raw materials from all kinds of dubious sources. His own operations seem to have been far from above suspicion. He sent prepared porcelain body to Wegely in Berlin, and arranged for some of the workers to go to Wegely at the same time. He was also in correspondence with a certain Herr Lück in Copenhagen about the founding of a factory in Denmark. Presumably this man can be identified with the erstwhile Meissen *Modellmeister*, Johann Christoph Ludwig von Lücke, who, under the name of Ludwig von Lücke, founded the Schleswig *faïence* factory about 1754. He, too, was an unsuccessful porcelain arcanist in Copenhagen about 1752.

Whether or not von Lücke actually worked at Höchst cannot be determined with certainty, but some connection with the factory is evident. Quite apart from the contact with Benckgraff, his son (or nephew), Johann Friedrich Lück, perhaps worked at Höchst before moving on to Frankenthal.

Late in 1752 Benckgraff communicated with the Fürstenberg director, von Langen, who thought he would be the man to take the place of the charlatan, Glaser. Mutually satisfactory arrangements having been concluded, Benckgraff sent Simon Feilner, then a flower painter, and his son-in-law, Johann Zeschinger, the latter being entrusted with the secret. Then a model of the Höchst kilns disappeared mysteriously. Benckgraff was arrested, and the negotiations with von Langen were discovered. Göltz demanded the secret from him, but Benckgraff, manœuvring astutely, offered it to the Elector. The latter, eager to seize a way of rejecting the claims of Göltz, accepted, and Benckgraff was freed. He left immediately for Fürstenberg, and died a month later.

Göltz ran the factory until 1757, in which year he died leaving it considerably in debt. Höchst was now taken over by the *Pfandamtassessor* Johann Heinrich Maas. Maas was an official whose work was connected with the valuation of property for mortgage purposes, and he was made director on condition that he ran the factory in a business-like way. A privilege was granted to him on 6th March, 1757. The manufacture of *faïence* was discontinued about 1758.

Maas informed the court in 1764 that he no longer felt able to run the factory, and that he would accept the 26,000 florins he had invested in settlement of his claim. This allowed nothing for the value of improvements he had made to the amount of about 19,000 florins.

In 1765 the factory received a patent from the Elector, Emmerich Joseph, and became the *Churfürstliche-Mainzische privilegierte Porzellain-Fabrique*. The director was Peter Clemens Webel, who was followed soon afterwards by Joseph Kauschinger. The latter stayed in this position to the end.

In order to make good some of the losses, lotteries were held, and Laurentius Russinger, who appears in the records as a *Figurer* in 1758, became *Modellmeister* in 1762. This position he held until 1766, although none of the Höchst models can be attributed to him with any certainty. In 1767 he left for Pfalz-Zweibrücken.

Johann Peter Melchior was engaged to replace Russinger as *Modellmeister*, and his best work, mainly in a style which was transitional between rococo and neo-classical, was done at Höchst, between 1767 and his removal to Frankenthal in 1779.

The factory still carried a load of debt, and the Electors were reluctant to spend money to free it. In 1777 a commission was set up to decide whether to continue working, and for a short while the factory ceased work completely. The commission uncovered many misdeeds, such as the payment of a prescribed 10 per cent. dividend out of capital, and the use of porcelain as security for loans. Much angered by this incompetence, the reigning Elector, now Karl Joseph, threatened to close the factory permanently. He relented, and in 1778 he decided to take it over; it was then run by the agents of the Elector whilst a buyer was sought for it.

No one was found, and the factory deteriorated progressively until, in 1798, when the French were in Mainz, it was finally sold for 1,700 florins. Some of the moulds found their way to Daniel Ernst Müller of Damm, near Aschaffenburg, who reproduced them with the addition of the letter "D" to the original wheel mark. Other forgeries in porcelain have been made from the original moulds during the present century.

The earliest Höchst porcelain had a porous body, greyish in colour. This was covered with a glaze having a white appearance. The translucency is poor. There was a distinct tendency to collapse in the kiln during firing, so pieces were made thick and heavy in much the same way as primitive soft-paste porcelains, and for a similar reason. The colours at this period tended to flake off. The skin was tinted a brownish red, in contrast to later painting, which is also much more detailed.

By 1753 improvements had been made, and some rococo scroll-work in the base is to be observed. The bases began to be hollowed, the modelling became much finer, and the colours used in decoration were more in keeping with the rococo style, which was at its height until the time of Russinger. Then the influence of France showed itself in the gradual and increasing change of fashion towards the sentimental which preceded and laid the foundation for what may well be called the *Wertherzeit*. At this time idyllic scenes, shepherdesses and such things, can be seen which are in strong contrast to the early work shown in Plates 86a and 87a.

A later survival from the early period is the *Angry Shoemaker* (Plate 91) which can be dated c. 1765. Another example of this model, illustrated by Röder and Oppenheim,[1] has a replacement dog which is a much less abject animal.

[1] *Das Höchster Porzellan u.s.w.*

Some early figures resemble in style those made later at Frankenthal. From this has been inferred the presence of Johann Friedrich Lück, probably a relative of the von Lücke mentioned earlier in this chapter. Röder, however, advances the opinion that these may have been done by the modeller of the *Apolloleuchter*[1] and related figures at Ludwigsburg, which are perhaps best attributed to a collaboration between Riedel and Göz at this factory. These, also, are similar to work at Frankenthal, and the name of Johann Wilhelm Lanz of this factory has been suggested. Röder was certainly of the opinion that J. F. Lück worked neither at Höchst nor Frankenthal.

This class of figures mostly has trellised rococo arbours of one kind or another, and it is probable that they were all due to the influence of G. F. Riedel, who was at Höchst as well as Ludwigsburg and Frankenthal, and whose work is noticed in more detail in the chapters on these factories (Plate 89a).

The models of Simon Feilner are, to my mind, somewhat doubtfully attributed. His work has been identified with reasonable certainty at Fürstenberg,[2] and two models by his hand at this factory appear on Plates 109 and 110b. Plate 86b shows a model hitherto attributed to Feilner at Höchst which is not the same stylistically as the other two, and it is not certain that he actually functioned as a modeller at Höchst. Plate 87b shows an early Italian comedy figure from Höchst, again often ascribed to Feilner, but which is certainly not by the same hand as the Fürstenberg figures already referred to. These Italian comedy figures, which are sometimes found on plain bases, are distinguished pieces of work, and it has been suggested that they were inspired by the work of Simon Troger, the Munich wood-carver.

The figures of Laurentius Russinger are conjecturally said to resemble the work of Melchior. The *Chinese Emperor* appearing on Plate 90 has been attributed in the past both to Russinger and to Melchior. Russinger seems the more likely. He is also awarded some pastoral groups.

[1] *leuchter*: candlestick.   [2] Ducret, *Unbekannte Porzellane des 18ten. Jahrhunderts.*

Melchior, whose antecedents are noted in greater detail in the chapter on Nymphenburg, did most of the factory's more important figures. His models of children (Plate 94a) are particularly happy, and his work retains many elements of the rococo at first, whilst later moving increasingly towards the neo-classical. Many of his figures have passages of a peculiar rose-pink of which he was very fond. Most have bases in the form of a grassy mound. Striped patterns were much favoured for costumes. His portrait medallion of Goethe is discussed elsewhere, and a similar portrait, signed, of the Elector Emmerich Joseph is in the Sèvres Museum. The departure of Melchior caused Höchst to lose the last artist of any standing. It has been estimated that he was responsible for about 300 models for this factory.

Höchst made a great deal of service-ware. Much of the decoration is derivative, although some subjects after Teniers and the Berlin engraver, Chodowiecki, are worthy of especial notice. Services included those for tea, coffee and chocolate, and snuff-boxes were particularly popular because of a large number of snuff factories in and around Mainz, Höchst being a considerable centre for its manufacture. The *veilleuse* is also to be seen occasionally (Plate 96).

Johannes Zeschinger, who was at first a *faïence* painter, and who went to Fürstenberg with Benckgraff in 1753, has his monogram, "IZ", appearing occasionally on early figures, and is known to have painted flowers. Adam Ludwig was also an early *faïence* painter whose monogram, "AL", appears occasionally on porcelain, and is not to be confused with that of von Löwenfinck. A crimson monochrome is fairly characteristic, and is a very effective type of decoration (Plate 95c). The earlier forms used are sometimes reminiscent of contemporary *faïence*.

Various incised marks and initials on the bases of early figures, in particular, cannot be satisfactorily identified. Probably they are the marks of repairers.

5

FRANKENTHAL

CHARLES-FRANÇOIS HANNONG started a *faïence* factory in Strasbourg about 1709, and was later associated with J. H. Wackenfeld who may have been at Meissen, and who was certainly at one time at the *faïence* factories of Cassel and Ansbach. Wackenfeld had also been making *faïence* in Strasbourg.

In 1724 Hannong opened a branch factory at Haguenau, and in 1732 he conveyed the Strasbourg undertaking to his son—Paul-Anton. The Haguenau factory went to another son, Balthasar.

The exact date on which porcelain was first manufactured at Strasbourg cannot be determined. Mention exists of a porcelain service presented to the City Council in 1726, but this was probably of *faïence*, and no evidence exists of the manufacture of porcelain before about 1752.

Paul-Anton Hannong was of an experimental turn of mind. He introduced enamel colours and the use of gilding in the 1740's, and in 1752 he began to make porcelain with the aid of J. J. Ringler, the arcanist, of Vienna. Ringler is reputed to have learned the art of porcelain making from a friendship with the daughter of the director of the Vienna factory, and later he became a wandering arcanist, arriving in Strasbourg from Höchst.

Louis XV took considerable interest in the factory at Vincennes and in 1754 promulgated an edict forbidding the manufacture of porcelain anywhere in France other than at this factory. This was a serious blow to the aspirations of Hannong. Petitions to the King were in vain, and he decided to move to Germany, leaving the *faïence* factory behind. With the aid of the court physician, Peter Joseph Walk, he came into touch with the Elector-Palatine, Karl Theodor von der Pfalz, and a decree was published in 1755 granting Hannong a privilege for the manufacture of porcelain on exceptionally favourable terms. No other person was allowed to make porcelain in the Palatinate, the sale of foreign porcelain was forbidden, raw materials and finished products were to be free of duty, and certain rights over all the clays to be found within the borders were granted.

Hannong wanted to establish the factory in Mannheim, but was persuaded by the court to choose Frankenthal, which is a Bavarian town about eight miles north of Mannheim, situated on the River Isenach.

When these arrangements had been completed, Paul-Anton went back to Strasbourg, leaving his son, Karl-Franz-Paul, in charge. The buildings were an old barracks, and a mill for glazing and polishing was erected on the site of the riding school. About 200 workers were employed at this time, many coming from Strasbourg and others from Meissen. The new factory got into production very quickly, and seemingly without many of the troubles which beset other factories in their early years. By November 1755, the Elector was able to show successful pieces to the Saxon Ambassador, and Paul-Anton Hannong was awarded the title of *Kurfürstlicher Kammerzienrat*.[1] In June 1756 the Elector and his wife visited the factory and orders to the value of 250,000 gulden were then in hand.

The *Modellmeister* at this time was Johann Wilhelm Lanz who had been chief modeller at Strasbourg from 1748 to 1754. In 1757, as a result of the Seven Years' War, more Meissen workers were engaged, among them Johann Friedrich Lück, probably a

[1] Commercial Counsellor to the Elector.

son of Johann Christoph Ludwig von Lücke, the Meissen *Modell-meister* of the 1720's whose work has already been discussed.

In the middle of 1757 Karl Hannong died, and Paul-Anton sent his second son, twenty-three-year-old Joseph-Adam Hannong, to take his place. In 1759 Joseph-Adam married, and bought the factory for 125,000 livres with his wife's money, the Elector agreeing to the transfer of the privilege from father to son. Joseph-Adam was an excellent business man who did much to improve the factory's markets. Sales increased to such an extent that the kilns had to be enlarged.

In 1760 he published a price-list in the Paris *Journal de Commerce*, and thus threw down the gauntlet to Meissen and Sèvres. Stress was laid on figures particularly, and prices were about one-third less than those charged by either of the two rival factories mentioned. These prices, however, were too low to allow a reasonable margin for profit and operating expenses, and Joseph-Adam pointed out that an important reason for lack of success was the treachery of his young brother, Pierre-Anton, who sold the secrets of manufacture to Sèvres, and who, in turn, was cheated of the wages of sin by the directorate of the royal factory.

For some months prior to 1762 the court Treasury met debts of increasing size on behalf of the factory, and finally, in February of this year, Joseph-Adam was obliged to sell the factory to the Elector, although he retained the factories at Strasbourg and Haguenau which had passed to him on the death of his father. Later, when the edict of Louis XV was allowed to go by default, Strasbourg began to manufacture porcelain once more, but this phase belongs rather more to a history of French porcelain than to the present work.

Under the Elector the management assumed the same bureaucratic character as existed at Meissen and elsewhere. The technical director was Adam Bergdoll, a former thrower, who had been an accountant at Höchst. This man was also paid 3,000 gulden for a secret process he brought with him. Later, he was succeeded by Simon Feilner, who came to Frankenthal by way of Fürstenberg shortly after 1770. Bergdoll was accused of inefficiency, and many disputes took place, but the fact remains that during his term of office most of the finest things were made.

Feilner was appointed inspector in 1770, but it was not until 1775 that he finally replaced Bergdoll as director. The latter was pensioned, and Feilner received, also, the title of court chamberlain. He was a man of considerable resource and experience who introduced a number of novelties and improvements.

The *Modellmeister* from 1762 to 1766 was the court sculptor, Franz Konrad Linck, who had studied at the Vienna Academy, and subsequently at Berlin and Potsdam. He guided the change of the factory's style from rococo to neo-classical, and when he removed to Mannheim in 1766 he continued to provide the factory with designs for some years afterwards.

A certain Pierre Berthevin, who was at the factory in 1769 and 1770, experimented with transfer-printing, hithero a purely English decorative technique. Surviving examples are so rare as to be almost non-existent, but two specimens on which underglaze colour was employed are in the museum at Spires.

In 1779 Johann Peter Melchior, discussed at greater length in the chapter on the Nymphenburg factory, arrived in Frankenthal. His style became increasingly neo-classical, and portrait reliefs occupied a considerable proportion of his time.

Sales were promoted by lotteries, and a price list of 1777 was still insufficient to allow a proper margin over the cost of production. Additionally, there was much political unrest, and competition from other factories became keener. Strasbourg had been making porcelain and selling in competition with Frankenthal for some years past, and figures were becoming increasingly unfashionable. A report from a representative of the Berlin factory mentions that "everything here in comparison with Berlin is rather backward".

By 1790 the number of workers engaged had fallen to seventy, and in 1794 the French occupation of the town of Frankenthal caused work to come to a standstill. During this period most of the porcelain was removed to Mannheim. About 25,000 guldens' worth was bought by Peter van Recum who also leased the factory from the French. In 1797 the left bank of the Rhine passed to France, and the factory with it. It was leased to Johann Nepomuk van Recum, and its production then limited to service-ware. In 1800 van Recum left to start a manufactory of stoneware (*Steinzeug*) at Grünstadt, and the Elector, Maximilian Joseph IV, announced that on account of its financial difficulties, he was not prepared to subsidize the factory any further. It was therefore closed in this year, and the moulds dispersed to Grünstadt and Nymphenburg. The warehouse at Aachen was dismantled, and the remaining porcelain was disposed of in neighbouring towns and at fairs.

Frankenthal is principally noted for its figure work; over 800 different models are on record. The first *Modellmeister*, Lanz, came with Hannong from Strasbourg in 1755, and his work is a continuation of his Strasbourg style. It is, in fact, difficult to separate his work at the two factories, although the Strasbourg examples appear to have been made with a base formed as a grassy mound, whereas the Frankenthal specimens have slight rococo scrolls (Plate 97b). An example of the difference may be found in his well-known group of a huntsman blowing a horn, a dead stag and a dog by his side. This exists with both types of base.

The work of Lanz is powerfully modelled, with more than a hint of the baroque in its conception. His subjects include rustic figures, those taken from daily life, hunting figures and groups, musicians, Italian comedy figures, a series of the gods, and some allegories (Plate 97b).

It is said that Johann Friedrich Lück arrived at Frankenthal from Höchst in 1758, although some opinion is inclined to doubt his presence at the factory at all. The point is discussed in chapter 4. Hofmann awards him the position of *Modellmeister* in succession to Lanz, and he remained, by this theory, until 1764, when he returned to Meissen. His assumed figures stylistically resemble those of Lanz in being somewhat stiffly posed, but they are also elegant. His modelling is not particularly brilliant, but it has a certain sensitivity and competence (Plate 99a).

Lück's work is in the rococo style, but Karl Theodor had leanings towards the neo-classical, and these caused him to engage Linck as *Modellmeister*, and to award him the title of court sculptor. Linck was a modeller of uncommon skill who has been compared to Bustelli. This comparison to my mind is neither justified nor valid. Linck worked in the early neo-classical style which did not translate well into terms of porcelain. Moreover, he was certainly not free from a touch of pomposity, as witness the group entitled *The Apotheosis of Karl Theodor and his wife*. Linck's models have heads which are somewhat smaller than is normal and unusually expressive features. He had a taste for the nude, and for classical draperies. Undoubtedly his work is the most distinguished of any in this style, despite his occasional lapses from grace. He died in Mannheim in 1793 (Plate 101a).

Karl Gottlieb Lück, presumed a cousin of J. F. Lück, did a considerable amount of work of unusually fine quality. He was both " repairer " and modeller from about 1756 to 1775. He must have enjoyed a considerable contemporary reputation because, in 1761, he was asked to go to Meissen to help with the erection of the *Reiterdenkmal*. His son, Simon, was also a " repairer " at Frankenthal from 1782 to 1788. Lück became *Modellmeister* in 1766 when Linck relinquished the position.

K. G. Lück's work was influenced by that of Linck, but he was especially interested in contemporary society, which can be seen from the figure on Plate 97c. His modelling is extremely skilful, and perhaps his best known work is the group called *The Good Mother*, taken from a painting by J. B. Greuze, engraved by Laurent Cars. Chinese figures, and elaborate pagodas with Chinese figures (the *Chinesenhäuser*), as well as hunting groups and such things, can be attributed to him, and he was relatively prolific (Plates 99b and 100).

Adam Bauer, court sculptor to the Duke of Württemberg, was made *Modellmeister* in 1775. He left in 1778. In this time he did a number of figures of gods, and many children as shepherds, shepherdesses, peasants, and the like (Plate 101d).

Johann Peter Melchior's style at Frankenthal became increasingly severe, and unlike his figures in the more sentimental vein, although many of his earlier things were a continuation of his Höchst style. An example of this later work is to be found in a biscuit group representing an *Apotheosis* commemorating the fifty-year jubilee of Karl Theodor. He used biscuit porcelain almost exclusively at this time.

Portrait busts and medallions had more or less superseded figure work by the end of the century when the factory closed.

The body of the early period was made from Passau clay, which varies in colour between a soft white and a yellowish tinge. This is somewhat unusual, since most hard porcelain tends to have a bluish-white tinge, although it is not invariable. In 1774 a new source of clay was exploited. This was cheaper and less satisfactory, and the quality greatly deteriorated in consequence.

Gottlieb Friedrich Riedel, who came to Frankenthal from Höchst, and who is noticed in greater detail in the chapter on Ludwigsburg porcelain, had considerable influence on early designs. The elaborate rococo styles of this period are undoubtedly due to him, and can be well seen in clock-cases, inkstands, and large table-centres. Relief patterns are comparatively common at this time. The ozier pattern and a similar pattern to Meissen's *Gotzkowsky erhabene Blumen* were both in use, and some copying from Meissen in this and other things is evident. An innovation is the rhomboid or lozenge-shaped dish often used as a tray for *cabaret* sets.

Frankenthal table-wares were of extremely good quality with excellent painting. They are especially noted for figure subjects.

Cabaret sets, finely painted, were made in quantity, and many small items of use and ornament, from thimbles and silk-reels to *étuis* and watch-stands, were commonly manufactured. Modelled flowers (*Blümgen*) were a factory specialty. These things are all entered in the 1777 price-list already mentioned.

Flower painting was excellent. *Indianische Blumen* were still used occasionally in the early period, and *deutsche Blumen* were, perhaps, done by Karl Haussman, who was at the factory from 1755 to 1799.

Attributions to individual painters are fairly difficult. There are three of whom we can be reasonably certain. Jakob Osterspei (1730–1782) was at Frankenthal from 1759 until his death. He did "Ovidian", or mythological, figures and landscapes (Plate 102a and c). Winterstein, at the factory from 1758 to 1781, did Ovidian figures and also scenes derived from Teniers. A breakfast service by him, signed and dated 1764, is in the Residence at Munich. Johann Bernhard Magnus, at Höchst in 1758 and at Frankenthal from 1762 to 1782, did battle-scenes, mythological scenes, landscapes and Watteau figures. Occasional early animal painting may be by G. F. Riedel himself.

By 1770, or a little earlier, the influence of Sèvres predominates. The *oeil de perdrix* (literally, partridge eye)—a pattern of dotted circles—was used extensively. Gold stripes, too, were extremely popular. These were used either on the white porcelain, or over a coloured ground.

Feilner did little work as a modeller at this factory, although one or two comparatively minor things are attributable to his hand. The factory modellers were extremely capable, and apparently he was much more occupied with problems of administration and research. He introduced a *bleu de Roi* and a light blue, and also invented an underglaze black, which was used on vases in the Nymphenburg Palace, although as a porcelain ground black was a deplorable innovation. Grained wood was sometimes imitated, and although this, too, is to be deplored, it is not, as has sometimes been supposed, a European invention. I have observed it on Chinese porcelain of the period of K'ang Hsi, which predates its European use by at least fifty years.

I have already mentioned transfer-printing, but the process seems not to have passed beyond the experimental stage.

Vases were commonly made. Many are in an elaborate rococo style which can be traced to the influence of Riedel, and some are finely painted with landscapes and figures by Osterspei and others.

6

BERLIN

w G ʡ ʡ

In the chapter on the Meissen factory I have already commented on the predilection for porcelain displayed by Frederick the Great. He had previously, through his minister von Görne, interested himself in a factory at Plaue-an-der-Havel which produced imitations of Böttger's red stoneware. Attempts were made to engage in porcelain manufacture as early as 1740, and Hunger offered his services, which were not accepted.

In 1751 Frederick received two offers to establish a factory, one from a textile manufacturer, Wilhelm Kaspar Wegely, and the other from two glass-cutters, the Schachert brothers. Wegely was eventually given the monopoly, and the Schacherts established themselves at Basdorf as manufacturers of *Milchglas*—glass made opaque white in colour with oxide of tin so that, superficially, it resembled porcelain.

In 1752 Wegely was in touch with Johann Benckgraff, then about to leave Höchst for Fürstenberg. What the consideration may have been is unknown, but a model kiln and some porcelain earth found its way to Berlin, and manufacture was started with this assistance in the same year. The arcanist, Nikolaus Paul, is doubtfully said to have received the porcelain secret from Wegely's *Modellmeister*, Ernst Heinrich Reichard, and to have been at Fürstenberg between 1757 and 1760. He appears to have been at Fürstenberg in 1758, but there is some slight evidence in favour of his services as an arcanist having been later used at Berlin by Gotzkowsky (see below and page 183). The King at first gave his assistance to Wegely. His raw materials were exempted from customs duty, and his factory site was given free of charge. Reichard was placed in charge of modelling, and the miniature painter, Isaak Jakob Clauce, was brought from Meissen. Wegely obviously hoped for a chance to get at the Meissen secrets during the Seven Years' War, but his porcelain was not good enough for Frederick, who lost interest and occupied himself with the contractor, Karl Heinrich Schimmelmann, to whom he sold the expropriated Meissen factory in 1756. Wegely expected to get both moulds and workmen, and, faced with this new situation, he became discouraged and gave up in 1757.

For some years afterwards Berlin was without a porcelain factory, but since Meissen was then occupied by Frederick, the court did not go short of porcelain. At first Frederick hoped that Schimmelmann would be able to transfer the Meissen factory to Berlin, or to start a new factory there with Meissen artists and workmen to replace Wegely's enterprise, but Schimmelmann was either unwilling or unable to undertake the task, and the King thereupon accepted a proposition made to him by Johann Ernst Gotzkowsky, a financier who had a silk-weaving factory and who manufactured gold and silver plate. The reason for Frederick's selection of Gotzkowsky is a little obscure, since he had neither knowledge nor experience. He had lost money heavily during the Seven Years' War, and was then a speculator of very doubtful pretensions.

The new factory was started in 1761 with the aid of the secret purchased from Reichard. The management was placed in the hands of Johann Georg Grieninger, a *Kommissionrat* of Saxony, who retained his position until his death in 1798. By 1763 a staff of 146 was employed.

When Gotzkowsky started his factory he had little money, and gambled on royal support. This was not forthcoming in sufficient quantity, and he became bankrupt. The King purchased the factory from him in 1763 for 225,000 thalers, and the purchase included a stock of unglazed and undecorated porcelain to the amount of almost 20,000 pieces. Reichard died in 1764, and he was succeeded as arcanist and artistic director by Theodor Gotthilf Manitius. The *Modellmeister* was Friedrich Elias Meyer from Meissen. Painters included Karl Wilhelm Böhme (later *Obermaler*) and Johann Balthasar Borrmann from Meissen. Isaak Jakob Clauce, originally at Meissen and who was Wegely's principal painter, was also included. Second painter, and controller of *Mosaiks*, was Karl Jakob Christian Klipfel.

The new royal factory was given many advantages—free fuel, protection from competition, exemption from customs duty, and so forth. Other schemes which emanated from Frederick's fertile imagination included the so-called "Jew's porcelain", by which his Jewish subjects had to buy and export 300 thalers' worth of porcelain before they were allowed to marry or deal in property. This provision was finally abolished by Frederick William II. In addition, special decrees were aimed at Meissen porcelain which prohibited its sale in Prussian territory, and even its transport across it for trans-shipment elsewhere.

The body at this period was a good colour but inclined to a yellowish grey. In 1765 a new earth was tried from Ströbel in Silesia. This, according to Grieninger, gave a whiter body, but was poor in quality. The experiment of mixing it with clay from Passau was tried, and this proved a useful mixture with but slight yellowing. Porcelain made from this body is probably the finest made at Berlin. In 1771 large deposits of clay were discovered at Brachwitz, near Halle, on the River Saale, which was probably more easily used, but which gave it a cold bluish tinge. This characterizes the greater part of surviving Berlin porcelain, and the beds were still being worked in the twentieth century.

In 1765 attempts were made to copy the work of the Sèvres

factory, and at a slightly later date English influence is to be seen in the form of some plates and dishes particularly. By the 1790's the influence of Wedgwood was marked, and this was also the case elsewhere in Germany, even Meissen making some copies of Wedgwood wares (Wedgwood-*arbeit*).

As *Modellmeister* Meyer was not a conspicuous success. Defects of character led to repeated complaints that he endeavoured to suppress originality of talent among his staff, and that he required them to work in his own style. His younger brother, Wilhelm Christian Meyer, a pupil of François-Gaspard Adam, was a factory modeller, and perhaps it was he who influenced his brother to change the style of his work at Meissen for his less characteristic and rather more mannered work at Berlin. Wilhelm Christian left the factory in 1783, and offers were made to Melchior at Frankenthal and to Auliczek at Nymphenburg which came to nothing. Friedrich Elias continued until his death in 1785, when he was replaced as *Modellmeister* by Johann Georg Müller who retained this position until 1789. Müller had been a modeller at Berlin since 1763, and did mythological and allegorical figures of indifferent quality.

Müller was succeeded as *Modellmeister* by Johann Karl Friedrich Riese who did some excellent work in the neo-classical style, using biscuit porcelain. He collaborated with the court architect, Hans Christian Genelli, who was also a modeller, and Johann Gottfried Schadow who did work of distinction about the turn of the century. Schadow was responsible in 1818 for a table-centre and other appointments which were made for presentation to the Duke of Wellington.

Wegely's porcelain is scarce. His production, however, must have been on a fairly considerable scale, since specimens are not quite so uncommon as circumstances would lead one to think.

Many of the surviving examples are figures. These are usually in white, and the occasional coloured examples tend to show that difficulty was experienced with the enamels since some flaking is usually apparent. Colours were strong, and often applied in unbroken washes. Lacquer colours were sometimes used in place of enamels.

Although some models were imitated from Meissen, most are original and these are probably the work of Reichard. Many are somewhat short in stature with large heads and hands, and can probably be referred to him and mark his characteristic style. Peasants and artisans, gardeners, hunters, and so forth, as well as some well-modelled birds, of which examples appear on Plate 103, are to be seen. Some large vases are particularly to be commended.

In service-ware a few colours were mastered, including a purple which possibly came from Höchst. It is actually recorded that Benckgraff tried to influence some Höchst workmen to go to Berlin. Gilding was good, but underglaze blue was not much in use. Polychrome flowers, and some landscapes, have been noted, the latter perhaps by Clauce. A few examples of moulded patterns survive.

It is difficult to identify the porcelain of Gotzkowsky. It is greyish in colour, usually with a few black specks in the glaze. Specimens are comparatively rare. Because of the large number of uncoloured pieces taken over by the royal factory many examples marked with the "G", which was used by him, may have been decorated later.

The royal period is probably best noted for the size and splendour of its table services. Moulded border patterns were a specialty. Probably these were first introduced by Gotzkowsky, who appears to have liked this kind of thing. The pattern known as the *Gotzkowsky erhabene Blumen* was made for him at Meissen some years earlier. At Berlin the *Reliefzierat mit Spalier* (relief decoration with trellis) was an original moulding used on a service made for the Neues Palais at Potsdam, as was the *Neuzierat* (1763) and the *Antikzierat* (1767). Up till 1790 new relief patterns were continually being introduced, and it is in this that Berlin shows its greatest degree of independence of Meissen.

PLATE 97

(a) *Putto with a Leopard.*
Frankenthal. *c.* 1757.

(b) *The Little Dancer,* by J. W. Lanz.
Frankenthal. *c.* 1760.

(c) *The Knife-grinder,* by K. G. Lück.
Frankenthal. *c.* 1770.

(d) *Europe* from a set of the *Continents.*
Frankenthal. *c.* 1765.

PLATE 98

Ballet Dancer.
Frankenthal. *c.* 1760.

PLATE 99

(a) Group of Musicians, attributed to J. F. Lück.
Frankenthal. c. 1759.

(b) Le Bouquet, by K. G. Lück.
Frankenthal. c. 1770.

PLATE 100

Chinese Pavilion, by K. G. Lück.
Frankenthal. *c.* 1770.

PLATE 101

(a) *Virgins adoring Cupid*, by Konrad Linck.
Frankenthal. *c.* 1770.

(b) *The Music Lesson.* J. F. Lück.
Frankenthal. *c.* 1765.

(c, *above*) *The Three Fates*, by Konrad Linck.
Frankenthal. *c.* 1770.

(d, *right*) *Gardener*, by Adam Bauer.
Frankenthal. *c.* 1780.

PLATE 102

(*a, left*) Tea-pot with figures, perhaps
by Osterspei.

Frankenthal. *c.* 1765.

(*b, right*) Leaf-dish with flower sprays.
Frankenthal. *c.* 1770.

(*c, left*) Tea-pot with peasant figures,
perhaps by Osterspei.

Frankenthal. *c.* 1765.

PLATE 103

(a) Jay, possibly E. H. Reichard.
Berlin. c. 1755.

(b) Cuckoo, possibly E. H. Reichard.
Berlin. c. 1755.

PLATE *104*

(*a*) Plate with pierced border and *Mosaik* ground
Berlin. *c.* 1770.

(*b*) Dish with pierced border with peasants in a landscape.
Berlin. *c.* 1770.

PLATE 105

(*a*) Pair of vases in neo-classical style.
Berlin. *c.* 1770.

(*b*) Tureen from a large service decorated with different landscapes.
Berlin. *c.* 1765.

PLATE 106

Chinese Lute-player, by F. E. Meyer.
Berlin. *c.* 1770.

PLATE 107

Temple of Bacchus. A centre-piece.
Berlin. *c.* 1790.

PLATE 108

Ice-pail from the *Prussian* service.

Berlin. *c.* 1818.

PLATE 109

Pedlar, by Simon Feilner.
Fürstenberg. 1755–60.

PLATE *110*

(*a*) Man with geese.
Fürstenberg. 1755–60.

(*b*) Group of Miners, by Simon Feilner.
Fürstenberg. *c.* 1758.

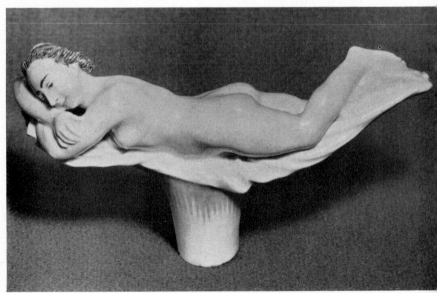

(*c*) Cane-handle by Simon Feilner.
Fürstenberg. *c.* 1755–60.

PLATE 111

(a) *The Lovers*, after a model by Kändler.
A. C. Luplau.
Fürstenberg. *c.* 1770.

(b) *The Lovers*, by Kändler.
Meissen. *c.* 1745.

PLATE 112

(a) Plate with pierced border.
Fürstenberg. Dated 1758.

(b) Porcelain picture in rococo gilt frame. Signed J. G. Eiche.
Fürstenberg. c. 1767.

Mosaik patterns, largely the responsibility of Klipfel, were usually carried out in red, purple, green or gold. Principally these were done at Meissen, Berlin and Ansbach, but Berlin was particularly noted for the meticulous execution and the variety of its *Mosaiks*. They were sometimes used in conjunction with moulded patterns, and sometimes with pierced borders, when they invade the centre of the plate. Ground colours were in use after 1770 (Plate 104a).

Indianische Blumen and oriental figures are not seen, apart from a service made for the Palace of Sans Souci at Potsdam in 1769. Flowers are the kind of *deutsche Blumen* common to the period. Early specimens have pale colouring, but this was later replaced by much stronger colours, in particular a yellow and a brilliant purple. These are after 1770.

Much painting *en camaïeu* is to be seen. This was executed either in one colour, or at the most two. Iron red, purple, overglaze blue, black and green were employed for the purpose.

Underglaze blue was not much used except for the cheapest market. A *Muschel* (shell) pattern, the *Zwiebelmuster*, and some floral patterns imitated from Meissen are the commonest.

Landscape and figure painting was a factory specialty, and the principal artists were Borrmann and Böhme. Böhme executed a series of eighteen landscape engravings for the use of the staff, and insects and birds were copied from various works on the subject, French engravings being the preferred source.

Mostly figure subjects were derived from Watteau (by way of engravings by Le Bas), with some Dutch peasant scenes after Teniers (Plate 104b). Battle scenes, for which Rugendas was the source of inspiration, are to be seen, but some of these *Schlachtenszenen* were, somewhat naturally, taken from the campaigns of Frederick. Boucher provided the *fliegende Kinder*, mostly painted *en camaïeu* in iron red.

Much use was made of engravings, particularly those of J. E. Nilson of Augsburg and Daniel Chodowiecki, a Berlin engraver. From the latter is a representation of scenes from Lessing's *Minna von Barnhelm* on a *solitaire* of 1771, which, from records in his diary, he watched being made.

After 1780 we find some silhouettes done by an artist named Ditmar, and " antique " heads painted *en grisaille* by Franz Tittel-bach. Later still, the influence of Sorgenthal Vienna becomes noticeable in the increasing elaboration of the decoration.

Berlin production of figures was a little uneven in quality. Friedrich Elias Meyer seems to have lost his oft-noted Meissen characteristics of slender proportions, heads which were too small, and exaggerated poses. Some of his early Berlin figures, probably made during the Gotzkowsky period, still show his original style, but the difference between his work at Meissen and at Berlin is in such striking contrast that I am left with the suspicion that some work attributed to him could more accurately be given to his younger brother, Wilhelm Christian. The latter was a much better modeller, and the figure illustrated on Plate 106 may have been an adaptation by him of the *Malabar* figures done by Friedrich Elias at Meissen, despite Robert Schmidt's opinion to the contrary.[1] Other figures attributed to F. E. Meyer include some children, and some rare portrait reliefs, including one of himself and his wife.

The younger Meyer did models of children with allegorical significance, and a series of Muses with Apollo. His finest work can undoubtedly be found in groups with various subjects rather than in single figures, since he had a flair for the harmonious composition of several figures. Most important is the large centre-piece done in association with his brother for a dessert service given to Catherine the Great by Frederick in honour of the alliance with Russia in 1769. The service was painted with scenes from the Russo-Turkish War, and is now in the Hermitage at Leningrad. Some replicas of parts of the service were also made.

A modeller named Pedrozzi did some figures of birds, and reliefs on vases, and some *bourgeois* figures in the costume of the period are due to Johannes Eckstein.

Johann Georg Müller, who replaced F. E. Meyer, did some

[1] *Das Porzellan als Kunstwerk und Kulturspiegel.*

mythological and allegorical figures which are lifeless in appearance and little really good work was done until the biscuit figures of Riese.

A table set was designed in 1793 by Genelli for the wedding of Crown Prince Frederick William and Princess Luise of Mecklenburg-Strelitz, and another was modelled by Gottfried Schadow in 1819 for presentation by Frederick·William III to the Duke of Wellington (Plate 108). The complete service cost 28,452 thalers. Busts of Frederick William II and Frederick William III were modelled by Schadow in biscuit.

Generally it must be said that the best of Berlin figure work had been done by 1772 and that for the most part the later work was negligible. Undoubtedly, with a few notable exceptions, the plastic side was inferior to the service-ware for which the factory was especially noted at the time.

7

FÜRSTENBERG

F F

In 1744 Duke Karl I of Brunswick was approached by Johann Christoph Glaser from Bayreuth who claimed knowledge of the secret of porcelain manufacture. Glaser was a glass and *faïence* painter, but his knowledge of manufacturing technique was so deficient that his claims can safely be regarded as fraudulent. He had previously been associated with a manufactory of *faïence* at Ilmenau about 1740, and was at Bayreuth, presumably as a painter, between 1742 and 1744.

The Duke accepted his offer, however, and attempts at manufacture were made in a castle at Bevern about 1746 under the personal supervision of Johann Georg von Langen, a mining engineer who later functioned in an advisory capacity at Copenhagen.

In 1747 the works were transferred to the western side of the River Weser to an old castle at Fürstenberg, and this can, therefore, be regarded as the year of foundation.

By 1750 an enormous amount of time, money and energy had been spent on experiments, and the first firing took place. It was not porcelain in the true sense of the word, however, since the clay used did not contain kaolin, but von Langen reported that it was very good, and that its translucency was excellent.

The autumn of 1750 saw the production of some experimental

pieces decorated in underglaze blue, and several enamel colours were in use which von Langen considered excellent, except for the gilding, which was not very successful. Soon afterwards, however, he became gloomy about the prospects of his porcelain, complaining that it was not as good as that of Meissen, although it looked like it when broken. In fact, he appeared to be embarrassed because his much advertised porcelain so little resembled the real thing. Moreover, the colours did not sustain his earlier optimistic claims, and the painters who had been engaged were without work.

In January of 1751 Duke Karl noted that the body was not really white, and that neither the glaze nor the colour had the right qualities. The workpeople who had been taken on, including throwers, turners, "repairers", painters and a kiln master, to the number of seventeen, found little work to do.

By 1753 the new enterprise was faced with complete disaster. By a stroke of fortune Johann Benckgraff, then a director of the Höchst factory, was persuaded to come to Fürstenberg by promises of high remuneration, and in May 1753 Benckgraff, his son-in-law Johann Zeschinger, a painter, and Simon Feilner, then a "repairer", started work.

Benckgraff died soon afterwards, but he fulfilled his bargain by first entrusting the secret to von Langen and Zeschinger. Now clay of the correct kind was all they needed, and this was obtained from Passau. It was, however, extremely expensive to transport, but in the same year (1753) a suitable clay was discovered at the village of Lenne, near the city of Oldendorf, which could be used after cleansing.

By the winter of 1753 true porcelain was being made, and the Duke ordered a service for himself. At the same time the factory mark of a script " F " in underglaze blue was adopted.

The year 1754 found Feilner complaining that the body was unsatisfactory and that the green enamel was poor, and "bubbled" when fired. Figures of all kinds were being made even at this early date, the principal modeller being Feilner himself. In 1758 he made some notable figures of Miners (*Bergleute*) (Plate 110b), which are of fine quality, but about which he wrote to von Langen:

> We are very unlucky here. A lot is spoiled in the firing. The miners hold together a bit better; if only they didn't get such big spots on them, and so many holes in their clothes.

Towards the end of the decade the porcelain assumed a less experimental character. In 1758 a purple was successfully introduced. It was somewhat defective, with a bluish tinge, to be distinguished from a much better purple used later. Generally the colours of this period left much to be desired. Some have "bubbled" in the enamelling kiln. Enamels used as ground colours for the rare essays into *Fondporzellan* were prone to flake, and underglaze blue was not satisfactory until 1767.

The Seven Years' War affected the factory seriously, and in 1762 numbers of the workers were sent to the *faïence* factory in Brunswick. Others were allowed to go home, although some painters were retained.

In 1763 von Langen was succeeded by Trabert, whose incompetent administration multiplied the difficulties, and in 1766 an unusual drought brought work to a standstill since the motive power was provided by water-wheels. The driving force which kept the factory in operation during these years was undoubtedly Duke Karl, who, despite these difficulties, always found a way to stave off disaster. It began to flourish after it came under the direction of two court officials, Kaulitz and Kohl, in 1770. Kohl appears to have been the moving spirit, and this happy state of affairs lasted until his death in 1790.

The most important artist to be employed at Fürstenberg was Simon Feilner. Born at Weiden, he was at first a flower-painter at Höchst. At Fürstenberg he was engaged as a "repairer", but later became *Modellmeister*. He left in 1768, and arrived in Frankenthal in 1770. Much of his work was original and important, for example, his figures of Miners already mentioned (Plate 110b), although he did some copying from Meissen originals.

A number of modellers of considerable skill worked at Fürstenberg during the eighteenth century. Johann Christoph Rombrich arrived either in 1758 or 1762, and remained until 1794. Anton Karl Luplau, later arcanist and *Modellmeister* at Copenhagen, was modeller at Fürstenberg from 1765 to 1776. His best-known work is, perhaps, the *Flohsucherin* (*The Flea Search*) which depicts a woman looking for a flea—a concept which can, perhaps, be commended as an antidote to the pseudo-refinement of Acier. A Frenchman, Desoches, was engaged in 1769 and remained until 1774. Karl Gottlieb Schubert arrived in 1775 and remained until 1804. Like Philipp Hendler (1780–1785) his work was competent but undistinguished.

In 1795 Louis Victor Gerverot arrived in Fürstenberg. Born at Lunéville in 1747, he was distinctly a man of parts, being painter, potter and arcanist at some fourteen factories. He studied first at Sèvres, and later at Niderviller. At the latter factory he stole copies of the formulae, and started to travel. He visited Ludwigsburg, Höchst, Frankenthal, Weesp, Schrezheim, Loosdrecht, Wedgwood's factory in Staffordshire,[1] and arrived in Fürstenberg in 1795. Here he was a good administrator, and when, in 1807, the Dukedom of Brunswick became part of Westphalia, he interested Jérôme Bonaparte and his consort in the factory. Their portraits were modelled in biscuit by Karl Heinrich Schwarzkopf, at one time in Berlin. Napoleon was also modelled. For this reason the factory did not suffer from the French occupation, but Gerverot was dismissed after the restoration.

The factory is still in existence, and has reproduced its old models.

Until 1770 when the paste and glaze was much improved, the body was difficult to work. It was yellowish in colour, with a grey glaze which was apt to be specked in firing. For this reason, relief patterns of one kind or another were much used as tending to disguise the defects. The *Reliefzierat* of Meissen and Berlin

[1] It is amusing to note the existence of a slim volume entitled: *An Address to Workmen in the Pottery on the subject of Entering into the Service of Foreign Manufacturers*, by Josiah Wedgwood, printed by J. Smith of Newcastle in 1783.

were copied, and new patterns of the kind devised. Not much *Fondporzellan* was made, only sea-green and underglaze blue being attempted, and examples of these are very rare. The rococo style was much in evidence.

Much use was made of engravings as inspiration for painted decoration. Flowers are often in purple monochrome or iron-red, and were taken from such engravers as Vauquer and Tessier. Dated flower paintings (1767 and 1768 respectively) are known from Johann Friedrich Börger and W. C. Rath. Landscapes are fairly common, as well as derivations from Watteau. The engravings of J. E. Nilson were also used. Poultry and wild birds were painted by C. G. Albert.

A feature of Fürstenberg painting is the *tableaux*, with or without a rococo frame. These have various subjects—mythology, or pastoral or bird life—and were done apparently between 1767 and 1768. One dated 1767 is signed by Georg Heinrich Holzmann. Portraits of the Duke and Duchess of Brunswick done in this way are attributed to the *Hofmaler*, J. A. Oest. The type is represented here by Plate 112b, a pastoral scene signed by Johann G. Eiche in the bottom right-hand corner. Eiche was at the factory between 1760 and 1795. He seems to have been regarded as of some importance at the time, and is mentioned in the list for 1774 as the only painter for figures and landscapes.

The first *Modellmeister* was Simon Feilner. He was discharged in 1768 for laziness. Examples of his work at Fürstenberg appear on Plates 109 and 110b. Some remarks have already been made on the attribution of his work at Höchst and Fürstenberg, and his presence, later, at Frankenthal is discussed in that chapter. A series of Italian comedy figures known to be by his hand differs in several particulars from the early series at Höchst, although some relationship is to be observed. This may be due to both having been derived from the same engravings. The Miners are also an important series. Both these and the comedy figures were reproduced at the factory in a smaller size about 1775. A modeller named Leuenberg did some groups of animals between 1755 and 1758.

The body was difficult to work, and figures tended to collapse in the kiln. For this reason plastic work was virtually discontinued between 1760 and 1770. After 1770 figure modelling was again undertaken on a fairly large scale, the principal modeller being Johann Christoph Rombrich.

A good deal of Rombrich's work was derived either from Meissen or from ivory carvings, and he did in addition some excellent miniatures, as well as portrait medallions in biscuit. Anton Carl Luplau, who arrived in 1765 and left for Copenhagen in 1776, is a little difficult to separate from Rombrich. Apart from the *Flohsucherin* already mentioned, he was probably responsible for the repetition of the Miners. Some Roman and old Teutonic warriors are by his hand, and were taken from engravings (Plates 111a).

The Frenchman, Desoches, was at the factory from 1769 to 1774. His most important work, best known from later reproductions, is that of a family at the coffee table, which shows the influence of Sèvres. His work was probably inspired by Chardin and Greuze.

Karl Gottlieb Schubert copied some Seasons from ivory carvings by Permoser, as well as Artisans from Höchst and Street Vendors, and so forth, from Berlin. He was responsible for two pompous equestrian statuettes of Frederick the Great (*c.* 1779) and the Emperor Joseph II (*c.* 1780). He also did biscuit reliefs in the manner of Wedgwood, no doubt inspired by Gerverot. A model of Leda was taken from a bronze original.

The work of Philipp Hendler, previously at Meissen and Vienna, is almost unknown. A *Metamorphosis of Dryope* is probably by his hand, and is almost the only thing which can be attributed with any certainty.

The factory did a good deal of work in biscuit porcelain, and Wedgwood's jasper- and basaltes-ware were extensively imitated. Forms, also, were borrowed from Wedgwood. The neo-classical style is well marked during the later period. Vases had silhouette portraits in oval medallions, and figures after Angelica Kauffmann are to be seen.

8

LUDWIGSBURG

THE first attempt to make porcelain at this Württemberg factory took place in 1737. This was unsuccessful, but another attempt was made in 1756 by an architect, Bonifacius Christoph Häckher, who also manufactured *faïence*. In 1758 the factory was taken over by the Duke, Charles Eugen, a notable spendthrift who regarded it as "a necessary appanage of lustre and prestige".

The situation, near Stuttgart, was a difficult one. No china clay was to be had locally, and it was brought from Hafnerzell, near Passau. No expense was spared, and in 1759 Josef Jakob Ringler was given the post of director, which he retained for the next forty years.

Gottlieb Friedrich Riedel was brought from Meissen as *Obermaler*. Riedel was born in Dresden in 1724, and was employed at Meissen from 1743 to 1756. In 1757 he visited Paris, and went to Frankenthal in the same year as director of painting. He left in 1759. For a short period before his eventual employment at Ludwigsburg he appears to have been at Höchst. Riedel was not only responsible for painted decoration, but also acted as plastic designer.

The ducal residence was removed to Ludwigsburg in 1766, and this represents the period of the factory's greatest prosperity. It began to decline after 1776 when the court returned to Stuttgart.

In the latter year the Duke visited Sèvres and the Wedgwood factory, and regained his enthusiasm for porcelain, but the competition of the French and English manufacturers was too strong, and after the death of Charles Eugen in 1793, Ludwigsburg declined considerably. The Elector Friedrich tried to revive it by bringing in workmen from France, but it was finally closed in 1824.

The body of Ludwigsburg porcelain was markedly inferior to that used at other German factories in many respects. The glaze was often imperfect, and flowed irregularly. The colour was greyish in tone. To some extent these defects were compensated by its superior plasticity which made it particularly suitable for figure work, and for articles of large size.

Most of the best work from this factory was in the rococo style, fostered by the first director, Johann Gottfried Trothe, who guided the factory until at least 1759. The design of rococo clock-cases has been attributed to him.

The first figures were probably the result of a collaboration between Riedel and Johann Göz, the *Oberbossierer* (chief repairer) from 1759 to 1762. Riedel made engravings of rococo ornament about this time which were later used at other factories. These designs also included sketches for tureens and similar objects, some of which are preserved at Stuttgart.

Attributed to Riedel and Göz are a pair of candlesticks, the *Apolloleuchter* and the *Dianaleuchter*.[1] To these have been added a *Toilet of Venus*, some other mythological figures, and similar things, although doubts have been expressed on the validity of this grouping.

These have a rococo base with scroll-work rising up and branching into candlesticks. The noticeable influence of Frankenthal is no doubt due to Riedel, but a similarity to the work of Johann Wilhelm Lanz, *Modellmeister* at Frankenthal from 1755 to, at least, 1761, has caused speculation on whether or not he might

[1] Hans Christ, *Ludwigsburg Porzellanfiguren.*

possibly have worked at Ludwigsburg also. This, however, is extremely doubtful, and there is little in favour of it.

From 1762 until his death in 1772, Jean-Jacob Louis was *Modellmeister*. Honey[1] refers to a Jean Louis, modeller at Sceaux, Strasbourg and Orleans about 1756 to 1760, and a Jean-Jacques Louis who modelled in Tournai in 1754, suggesting that they might all be one and the same person.

His work at Ludwigsburg, which is extremely good, has been identified by a conveniently scratched " L " in the body under the base. His figures include some rococo dancers, and an excellent *Turk leading a Horse*. Characteristic of his better work are some miniature groups and things of that kind. Plate 120a shows a booth belonging to a series probably inspired by fairs started by the Duke in imitation of the Venetian fairs after his visit to Venice in 1767.

Some Chinese figures, somewhat reminiscent of Bustelli, are probably by the hand of Louis. These have led to the mistaken assertion by Balet[2] that Bustelli actually *worked* at Ludwigsburg. There is solitary record of a modeller named F. A. Pustelli between 1761 and 1763. It is possible that Bustelli was invited to Ludwigsburg, but it is certain that he never worked there.

The record mentioned is in a publication by the Chancellor of the Archives giving the addresses of people working in Württemberg, in which there is reference to " *Ober-Modellmeister* F. A. Pustelli". The only argument it is possible to advance in favour of his absence from Nymphenburg during any part of these two years is that he is first recorded by Härtl in the Nymphenburg archives in 1754—*Franz Anton Bustelli, Figurist is in Arbeit eingestandten den 3ten. November 1754*—and appears every year thereafter until 1761, the date of the transfer of the factory.

It seems probable that Bustelli did, in fact, consider seriously the proposal that he should go to Ludwigsburg, and may have taken steps to join Ringler, since the two men must have been acquainted. It is even possible that he went to that factory, and

---

[1] *Dictionary of European Ceramic Art.*   [2] L. Balet, *Ludwigsburger Porzellan.*

this would account for his appearance in the archives. But, in 1761, his salary at Nymphenburg was raised from six to ten florins a week, and remained at this until his death in 1763. Apparently this low salary was the cause of the trouble.

The journey to Ludwigsburg, therefore, was made, if at all, with the intention of putting pressure on the Nymphenburg directorate. The fact remains that the hand of Bustelli is probably the easiest to recognize of any, and nothing existing from Ludwigsburg does more than suggest his influence. Since his work was well known and much in demand, he did not need to be connected with the factory for this to occur.

A series of figures from the streets, and illustrating the life of the people, is ascribed to the *Modeller der Volkstypen*. The name of the artist is unknown, but the influence of Johann Christian Wilhelm Beyer, *Modellmeister* from 1761 to 1767, is perceptible.

Beyer was an architect, sculptor and painter who had studied at Dresden, Paris, Stuttgart and Rome. In the latter city he made the acquaintance both of Winckelmann, a notable enemy of the rococo style, and the director of the French Academy. Principally, he was a sculptor, and in this capacity entered the service of the House of Württemberg in 1752, taking up his duties at the factory in 1762.

He published several collections of engravings. His *Österreichische Merkwürdigkeiten die Bild und Baukunst betreffend*, 1779, and *Die neue Muse oder der Nationalgarten*, 1784, illustrate not only sculpture, but also some of the porcelain models. His presence in Vienna has already been noted.

Much of Beyer's work exhibits elements both of the rococo and the neo-classical and in this sense is transitional between the two. There is a tendency to somewhat theatrical attitudes which lack the spontaneity shown by Bustelli, and this, superimposed upon the classical models in particular, makes it fairly easy to recognize. There are a number of things in his style which were no doubt influenced by him and may have been modelled by Louis. The models mentioned as appearing in his books can, without doubt, be attributed to his hand (Plate 119).

Domenico Ferretti was court sculptor, and worked at the factory from 1764 to 1767. He decorated the Residence at Stuttgart, and the Ludwigsburg Palace, before passing on to the factory. Some of his porcelain figures can be identified because they are small versions of his work in stone, among them a *River God*, a *Nymph*, *Adonis with the Boar* and *Mars in the Smithy of Vulcan*. Some Chinese figures have been awarded to him on grounds of style (Plate 118).

Pierre-François Lejeune, premier court sculptor, was at the Court of Württemberg from about 1753 onward. His figures have only been doubtfully identified. Balet[1] attributed to him some figures of men and women seated, playing upon instruments, whereas Schnorr von Carolsfeld held the opinion that he did nothing at all. One or two things resemble sculpture in the Residency at Stuttgart, and to this extent his work can probably be recognized. They include some children and some Seasons.

Johann Heinrich Schmidt was *Oberbossierer* from 1774 to 1821. Two white vases with supporting figures, and a pair of memorial columns with wreaths being placed on them by young girls, are by his hand. Adam Bauer (*see Frankenthal*) worked at Ludwigsburg, but his figures cannot be identified.

The work of the latter part of the eighteenth century varied from the " sentimental pseudo-antique to the academic pseudo-antique ", to borrow a concisely descriptive phrase from Hanover, and this period is represented by the work of Philipp Jakob Scheffauer and Johann Heinrich Dannecker, who supplied the factory with models. The former did some biscuit reliefs and medallions of classical subjects, the latter some groups of children as Seasons, and a girl with a dead bird.

The figures of Ludwigsburg can be dated approximately from the colouring. Before 1770 the colours are soft and large parts of the figure left in white, flesh tones being slightly indicated with pink. The hair was sharply delineated. Stronger colours were used in the Beyer period, and later these became still darker, with

[1] op. cit.

exaggerated colouring of cheeks and similar parts. The latter colour scheme was also used on early models reissued later.

A factory at Amberg, in Bavaria, which began the manufacture of porcelain in 1790, reproduced Ludwigsburg models in the nineteenth century.

The Duke was particularly fond of figures, and encouraged their manufacture. The body, however, was less suitable for the manufacture of table-wares, and these are often flawed and greyish in colour. Because they were regarded as a secondary consideration, there were no innovations of importance, although the painting is of extremely good quality.

A scale-pattern in relief, with flowers painted over, is not uncommon, and ozier patterns were borrowed from Meissen. These relief patterns to some extent mitigated the defects of the body.

Painting is inclined to be elaborate and colourful, and over-large in relation to the size of the piece. This, again, was to minimize defects of the body, and we see, for this reason, large birds from engravings by Riedel, although these were also used elsewhere, as witness a Nymphenburg coffee-pot in the Hamburg Museum painted with a design from his *Samlung von Feder-Vieh besonders Haus-Geflügel nuzlich Fabriquen* [sic][1] which was published in 1770 at Augsburg, some nine years before he left Ludwigsburg to become an engraver there.

Ludwigsburg painting includes *putti* after Boucher, and subjects derived from Watteau and Rugendas (Plate 120b). J. E. Nilson was also used very frequently. The best work is by Friedrich Kirschner, who was at the factory from about 1770 to 1783. Kirschner was a pupil of Riedel, and excelled as a flower painter. Johann Friedrich Steinkopf, painter to the court of Württemberg, was responsible for animals and landscapes, although the former are rare. His work falls between 1759 and 1775. Landscapes and ruins are likely to be by his hand.

Johann Philipp Dannhofer from Vienna was at Ludwigsburg

[1] *Collection of Fowl, especially Poultry, etc.*

from 1762 onwards. His work has not been identified, but it is obvious that either specimens no longer exist, or its character is very different from his earlier identified work elsewhere.

Franz Joseph Aess specialized in modelled porcelain flowers which were made about 1763. These were also made at Frankenthal, and the innovation may possibly have been due to Riedel who inspired some Ludwigsburg vases in the style of the former factory.

PLATE 113

(a) Tureen in the form of a
grouse.

Fürstenberg. c. 1760.

(b) Tureen in the form of a
woodcock.

Fürstenberg. c. 1760.

(c) Large pair of vases in the
style of Sèvres.

Fürstenberg. c. 1775.

PLATE 114

(a) *Fruit Vendor*.
Ludwigsburg. *c.* 1765.

(b) Dancer.
Ludwigsburg. *c.* 1765.

(c) *Winter*, from a set of the *Seasons*.
Ludwigsburg. *c.* 1765.

(d) *Autumn*, from a set of the *Seasons*.
Ludwigsburg. *c.* 1765.

PLATE 115

(a) *Map-seller.*
Ludwigsburg. *c.* 1765.

(b) *Miller girl.*
Ludwigsburg. *c.* 1765.

(c) *Butcher and his wife.*
Ludwigsburg. *c.* 1765.

PLATE 116

(a) *Bird-sellers.*
Ludwigsburg. *c.* 1765.

(b) *Minuet Dancers.*
Ludwigsburg. *c.* 1765.

PLATE 117

(*a*) Satirical Group: *A Lady's Toilet*.
Ludwigsburg. *c.* 1775.

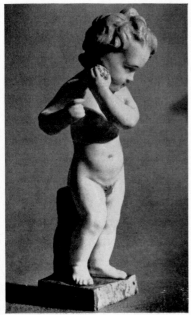

(*b*) *Putto*, from a set of the *Senses*.
Ludwigsburg. *c.* 1765.

(*c*) Beggar with a dog.
Ludwigsburg. *c.* 1780.

PLATE 118

Chinese Prince, probably by Domenico Ferretti.
Ludwigsburg. *c.* 1763.

PLATE 119

Diana and Nymphs, by J. C. W. Beyer.
Ludwigsburg. *c.* 1765.

PLATE 120

(a) Draper's Booth, from a series representing Booths at a Fair.

Ludwigsburg. c. 1765.

(b) Tea-pot of characteristic form with a battle scene.

Ludwigsburg. c. 1765.

PLATE 121

(a) Woman with a Fan.
Ansbach. c. 1765.

(b) Woman dancing.
Ansbach. c. 1765.

PLATE 122

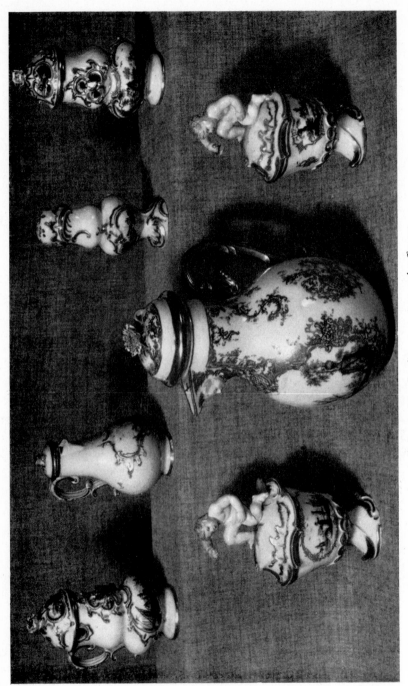

Ansbach porcelain: Condiment set, vases, and coffee-pot.
Ansbach. 1760–65.

PLATE *123*

(*a*) *Soldiers agreeing on a Truce.* Probably
by Vogelmann.

Kelsterbach. *c.* 1765.

(*b*) Covered cup and saucer decorated with
urns and insects.

Fulda. *c.* 1775.

(*c*) *Gardener and Companion.*
Fulda. *c.* 1770.

PLATE 124

Girl with a basket of eggs.
Fulda. *c.* 1770.

PLATE 125

Le panier mystérieux.
Fulda. *c.* 1770.

PLATE 126

(*a*) Set of *putti* symbolic of the *Seasons*.
Fulda. *c.* 1770.

(*b*) Three figures from a set of the *Seasons*. Probably modelled by Xaveri.
Hesse-Cassel. *c.* 1770.

PLATE 127

(a) *Réchaud* decorated with masks and painted floral swags.

Fulda. *c.* 1770.

(b) *Compôtier* with a bluish-green ground, and a view of Gera.

Gera. *c.* 1785.

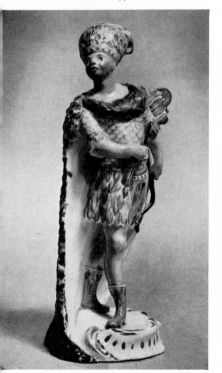

(c) *Europe* from a set of the *Continents*.

Limbach. *c.* 1775.

(d) *Africa* from a set of the *Continents*.

Limbach. *c.* 1775.

PLATE *128*

(*a*) *Mezzetino*, from the Italian Comedy.
Limbach. *c.* 1775.

(*b*) Woman playing a harp.
Limbach. *c.* 1775.

(*c*) *Gardener and Companion.*
Limbach. *c.* 1775.

9

ANSBACH

A FACTORY for the manufacture of *faïence* was founded at Onolz-bach about 1709 with the assistance of the Markgraf, Wilhelm Friedrich von Brandenburg-Onolzbach. The factory was parti-cularly successful, and its products became widely known. "Ans-bach" is the modern version of the earlier name of the town.

In 1757, his grandson, Karl Alexander, began to rule. He had acquired a taste for porcelain during his somewhat extensive travels, but buying from Meissen and Berlin was an expensive business, and he therefore conceived the idea of starting his own factory. This was intended to be an extension of the existing *faïence* factory, and it appears to have been ready by 1758.

Meissen was suffering from the effects of the Seven Years' War and the Markgraf had no difficulty in employing some workmen from the royal factory, including one, Johann Friedrich Kändler, who was related to the Meissen *Modellmeister*, perhaps a nephew. J. F. Kändler was probably responsible for bringing the secrets of manufacture to Ansbach. Closely connected with him was Karl Gottlob Laut, a modeller and woodworker, who—like his associate—remained at Ansbach for the rest of his life.

Two painters who arrived about this time were Johann Chris-tian Pinior, who later went to Ludwigsburg, and Johann Karl Gerlach. The latter had begun his career at Meissen, spent a year or so at Berlin as a miniature painter, a short time at Ansbach in 1758, another year at Nymphenburg, and returned to Ansbach during 1762–1763—a typical example of the *Wanderlust* endemic among early porcelain workers.

Despite the employment of Meissen workmen, the porcelain of Ansbach was influenced rather more by Berlin. The copying of Berlin models and styles was, in fact, so close that some confusion has existed in the past between the work of the two factories. Hofmann,[1] for instance, on one occasion attributed some of Wegely's porcelain to Ansbach on the evidence of the painting, a circumstance which makes the employment of some Berlin workmen at Ansbach a likely supposition, apart from the case of Gerlach instanced above. The palace at Ansbach houses a large collection of Berlin porcelain, particularly in the Mirror Room, whilst a superb chandelier hangs in the Audience Chamber. There is also one of the largest collections of Wegely's porcelain in existence.

The administration of Ansbach was a youthful one. J. F. Kändler was twenty-three years of age, and Laut only fifteen. Nevertheless, by 1762 production was well advanced, and a contemporary announcement refers to "groups; big antique figures, medium and small ones; candelabra; tea and coffee services, white blue and coloured; butter dishes and baskets; chacans;[2] walking-stick handles, etc.".

The porcelain factory was at first housed in the same building as the *faïence* factory, but this led to rivalry between two groups of workmen. An attempt was made to separate the two, but there was insufficient room available and about the end of 1762 the porcelain undertaking was moved to new quarters in an isolated hunting castle at Bruckberg which belonged to the Markgraf.

The isolated situation later had some amusing consequences. The workmen were housed in the castle, and the only form of entertainment available to them was to be found in the local inn,

---

[1] In a Munich exhibition catalogue of 1909.

[2] *Chacans*: walking-stick handles of figures in oriental dress. Apparently the term was derived from the Persian title, *Shah*.

where they adjourned at ever-decreasing intervals to slake thirsts which promised to become legendary. In 1768 it was found that some of the workers were in an almost perpetual state of intoxication and little work was being done. The painters, throwers and modellers spent their nights drinking raw brandy with beer chasers, the apprentices bringing the drinks. This state of affairs culminated in a duel with daggers in which two of the workmen were injured and arrested. The apprentices admitted to fishing in the royal streams without permission, and Kändler complained bitterly that a number of the workmen habitually spoke French together which he could not understand.

Auction sales were started in 1763, when the factory moved to Bruckberg, in order to reduce accumulated stock, and were continued thereafter. Lotteries, in which the winner was paid partly in porcelain and partly in cash, were tried in an attempt to increase sales. The local market was insufficient to sustain the factory profitably and attempts were made to sell it. These were unsuccessful, however, since it was known to be making a loss. Eventually the position was somewhat improved when the factory found export markets in Holland and Vienna.

The Markgraf Karl Alexander came into close contact with Frederick the Great. In 1765 Frederick ordered a table service for the decoration of his new palace at Potsdam, and in 1766 Karl Alexander visited him and liked the service so much that Frederick had one made for him, substituting some light green stripes in the decoration with yellowish-brown. Replacements for this service were made at Ansbach.

Ansbach productions were to some extent influenced by the two mistresses of the Markgraf. The first, a French actress named Hippolyte Clairon, wrote two popular operettas, scenes from which were reproduced. Her successor was Lady Craven, who had a strong predilection for the neo-classical style. Some cups made for her bear her name—*Elisabeth, Gräfin Berkeley*—surrounded by flower garlands.

In 1788 Austria and Russia were in alliance against Turkey,

thus closing a promising export market for porcelain. The Thuringian factories, too, offered increasingly severe competition. The Markgraf had tarried in Italy with Lady Craven and now found himself no more than a suzerain of the Prussians, compelled to accept a Hanoverian, Hardenberg, as his Minister of State.

These difficult trading conditions put the factory into an impossible position. In 1790 an inquiry was started into its affairs, and various reforms were instituted. J. F. Kändler died in 1791.

The finest period of Ansbach production was between about 1767 and 1785 when its porcelain can be said to rank with the best of the German factories for its artistic qualities. Both modelling and painting were exceptional, although examples are of some rarity. Jugs and such things often have masks, usually female, under the spout (Plate 122).

10

KELSTERBACH

HD   HD

THIS factory was situated in Hesse-Darmstadt on the left bank of the River Main between Frankfurt and Mainz. Although, so far as geographical position is concerned, it lies not far from Höchst, the two factories have almost nothing in common.

A *faïence* factory was founded nearby in Königstadt about 1758. This was removed to Kelsterbach in 1761, and the manufacture of *faïence* was almost completely dropped in favour of porcelain.

The arcanist was Christian Daniel Busch, who was at Meissen until 1745 and who arrived in Kelsterbach by a devious route in 1761. Darmstadt had many cultural points of contact with Paris, and Busch arrived in Kelsterbach from Paris after spending a short period at Sèvres. It is certain that he was responsible for organizing the factory.

In 1761 the *faïence* factory was under the control of Kaspar Mayntz and Johann Christian Frede, who were, at the time, in low water financially. Busch offered his services to the Landgrave, Ludwig VIII, who saw in porcelain a good investment for his second son, Wilhelm Georg. The latter already showed some interest in the technical problems of manufacture.

Ludwig purchased the factory from his own purse in order to keep it from the control of his cabinet, and Busch was given the post of *Fürstlicher Direktor*. When he left in 1764 new buildings were erected, and the work put under the control of a court official named Pfaff.

At this time some trouble was experienced with painters. Georg Ignatius Hess, who had been at the factory since its inception, was discharged, leaving only Jakob Heinrich Eger. Eger, however, did not know the secret of making porcelain colours, and for some time these were bought from Höchst ready mixed, which caused technical difficulties since the Höchst glaze was different from that in use at Kelsterbach. This state of affairs was rectified finally in 1765, when new painters were engaged, and fresh materials were bought in Frankfurt.

In 1764 the principal modeller was Karl Vogelmann. It is said that of 131 models then listed, seventy-five were done by Vogelmann, the remainder probably being mostly the work of Peter Antonius Seefried. Jakob and Cornelius Carlstadt were also modellers from 1763 until 1766.

Vogelmann's work is difficult to identify with certainty, but models generally attributed to him are very much in the baroque style, and in this he may have been influenced by the sculptor, Conrad Ferdinand Dietz. It has been said that Vogelmann had not learned the art of duplication, and that a separate mould had to be made for each figure. This is very much open to doubt, since the process of waste-moulding could not be applied to porcelain figure work. Lead copies of the original clay model were taken to facilitate the production of new moulds—a practice not used elsewhere in Germany so far as can be traced, but common in England, particularly at Chelsea. Some lead master-models from the latter factory have survived.

The appearance of some of Vogelmann's models, however, does suggest that much hand-modelling took place, and it is possible that in some cases clothes were added to a basic model (Plate 123a).

Seefried was working with Bustelli at Nymphenburg when he was fourteen years of age, and in 1766 he went as a repairer to Ludwigsburg. He arrived in Kelsterbach on 1st June, 1767.

Seefried's work was influenced both by Vogelmann and by Bustelli, and it was particularly admired by the Landgrave. The latter's death in 1769, however, made the future of the factory uncertain, and Seefried returned to Nymphenburg. Here he remained until 1810 when he was awarded a pension. He died in 1812.

Like Bustelli, his models sometimes have half-open mouths, and this is fairly characteristic.

For most of the time the factory suffered from financial stringencies. The workers were always paid in arrears, and the Prince subsidized it freely. For instance, in July 1768 he provided 975 florins, which eased matters for a while and even provided beer for the workmen, but when the Prince died these subsidies for the most part came to an end. The manufacture of porcelain ceased entirely for a while, although the production of *faïence* was continued. In 1789 an attempt was made to resuscitate the porcelain factory, but this failed because of military operations between 1792 and 1797.

11

FULDA

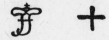

FULDA is the capital of the province of Hesse-Nassau in Prussia, and is situated on the river of the same name. It owes its origin to a Benedictine Abbey which was founded in 744: The abbacy was converted into a bishopric in 1752, and the factory was under the patronage of the Prince-Bishops.

The first factory to be started at Fulda was for the manufacture of *faïence*. It was founded by Amadeus von Buseck with the aid of Adam Friedrich von Löwenfinck and his brother, Karl Heinrich. Von Löwenfinck arrived in Fulda from Chantilly and Ansbach towards the end of 1741. There remains the possibility that he experimented with a soft-paste porcelain of the kind manufactured at Chantilly. In the same year we find mention of Christian Rupprecht as a *Porzellanmacher*, and of Heinrich Eberhardt who received the same designation. I have, however, already commented on the occasional confusion between *faïence* and porcelain. The manufacture of porcelain may have been attempted during this period, but no definite information exists.

The *faïence* factory lasted until 1758 when it fell victim to the conditions prevailing as the result of the Seven Years' War.

About 1757 an attempt was made to manufacture porcelain. The court chamberlain, Johann Philipp Schick, sent Adalbert II von Wallendorf a present of Strasbourg porcelain made by

Hannong. Schick, who had been a painter, had a daughter—Maria Seraphia—who married A. F. von Löwenfinck.

Nothing appears to have been done at the time, but in 1764 Schick returned to the matter and engaged the arcanist, Nikolaus Paul, who arrived in 1764 and stayed until April of the following year. The factory was then under the patronage of the Prince-Bishop, Heinrich von Bibra.

The work of the factory can be divided into two distinct periods—from 1764 to 1767, when it was burned down, and from its rebuilding in 1768 to its closure in 1790. Little is known of the work done during the first period. A number of things have been attributed to a Fulda-born sculptor, Johann Valentin Schaum. Honey[1] mentions figures of little boys symbolic of the Elements and the Seasons which have been identified with fragments of moulds in the Hamburg Museum. To these, perhaps, may be added Italian comedy figures of Harlequin and Scapino, and some Gardeners. A Harlequin is a close copy of one by Johann Wilhelm Lanz, *Modellmeister* at Strasbourg and Frankenthal, who modelled a suite of figures of this kind. The *putti* resemble in style some carved in alabaster by Schaum on the tomb of Amadeus von Buseck about 1744. The figures of this period, however, seem mostly to have been copied from those of Strasbourg without much attempt at adaptation.

When Nikolaus Paul left Fulda, he gave his formula to Schick, but in 1767 the factory was completely burned down, and Schick died during the rebuilding. Johann Abraham Ripp, who had been apprenticed to the *faïence* factory as a blue painter, was appointed arcanist, and spent much time making tests of Paul's recipe. Months passed before a workable body could be devised.

About 1768 the modelling appears to have been in the hands of Wenzel Neu, who first worked in the *faïence* factory in 1744 with A. F. von Löwenfinck, and who died in 1774. Schaum died in 1771. The presence of the Höchst *Modellmeister*, Laurentius Russinger, has been inferred to account for the close resemblance

[1] *Dictionary of European Ceramic Art.*

of some of the factory's figures and groups to those of Höchst. Nothing can be established, but Russinger's movements are not definitely known from 1768 until he arrived in Paris in 1744.

Georg Friedrich Hess is mentioned by Honey[1] as perhaps modelling for Fulda from 1751 to 1757, before the manufacture of porcelain commenced. There appears to have been a family of this name connected with the factory. Schmidt[2] refers to Franz Joachim Hess, certainly later at Cassel, as modelling for Fulda in porcelain. Johann Lorenz Hess, another member of the family, was a painter during the *faïence* period.

Georg Ludwig Bartholomae is mentioned in the church registers as marrying in 1775. He was at first a repairer, but later appears to have functioned as a modeller. He died in 1788 at the age of forty-four.

The finest figures belong to the period between 1768 and *c.* 1775. Work was of exceptional merit, the porcelain being of fine quality, and the painting delicate. The predominant style was rococo, although later examples were not uninfluenced by the Louis-Seize style (Plates 123 et seq.).

Table-wares were of good quality, and, for the most part, copied from Meissen. Some landscapes in iron-red are probably the commonest.

The factory closed finally in 1790.

[1] ibid.   [2] *Das Porzellan als Kunstwerk und Kulturspiegel.*

12

SOME MINOR FACTORIES

A NUMBER of small factories sprang up from time to time and closed again after a few years of life. Mostly they were associated with existing *faïence* factories, and their products are rarely seen outside German museums. Without the aid of a mark it is usually very difficult, and frequently impossible, to identify their work, and some identifications are conjectural and arrived at by process of elimination.

To discuss the more important first, a factory was established at Cassel in Hesse-Nassau in 1766 with the help of the arcanist Nikolaus Paul. Cassel was the residence of the Landgraves of Hesse-Cassel who had patronized various *faïence* factories in the area since the seventeenth century.

The porcelain factory was subsidized by the Landgrave, Friedrich II, and in 1769 it was announced that " Komplette bunt und blau bemalte, gerippte und glatte, Kaffee und Thé-services . . . zu billigen Preisen . . ."[1] were for sale. Most surviving service-ware is painted with underglaze blue, and the factory is chiefly remembered for its rare surviving examples of plastic work.

Max Sauerlandt[2] illustrates a figure of Autumn in colour by the modeller Johann Baptist Xaveri. This figure is also illustrated in

[1] " Complete colour and blue painted, reeded and smooth, coffee and tea services . . . at low prices. . . . "
[2] *Deutsche Porzellan-figuren des XVIIIten. Jahrhunderts*, illustration 99.

an uncoloured version on Plate 126b, together with two others from the same set. A bust of the Landgrave is signed by the painter Eisenträger, and dated 1781. Other names known are the modellers Franz Josef Hess and Friedrich Künckler. Their work has not been identified.

The colour of the body is either a chalky white, to be seen in those illustrated here, or a greyish tone.

The factory closed in 1788.

In 1768 a factory was established in the Duchy of Pfalz-Zweibrücken at the town of the same name. This was under the patronage of Duke Christian IV. The arcanist was named Stahl, and Honey suggested that he may have been identical with Stadelmayer, an associate of C. D. Busch at Sèvres, as well as arcanist at Schönbornlust, the products of which have not been identified.

The *Hofrat* Pauli first attempted to manufacture porcelain here in 1747, but failed. The second attempt was successful, and the factory was established in the Castle of Gutenbrunn. The factory is known either as Gutenbrunn or Pfalz-Zweibrücken, since the former is close to the town.

Laurentius Russinger from Höchst was artistic and technical director until 1768, when he was succeeded by Jakob Melchior Höckel, painter, modeller and arcanist of Höchst, who later went to Kelsterbach. The factory closed seven years later.

For ordinary wares, the factory used a local kaolin, but clay was brought from Passau for the finest work. Most surviving examples are decorated with polychrome flowers, and landscapes in purple with gilt rococo scrolls are known. Figures have not been identified, except for a Boy in Spires Historical Museum, which has the largest collection of this porcelain. Etienne-Dominique Pellevé, mentioned below, may have been connected with the factory.

North-west of Zweibrücken, in the Nassau-Saarbrücken, is the town of Ottweiler. Here a factory was started in 1763 under Prince Wilhelm Heinrich of Nassau-Saarbrücken. The arcanist was

Pellevé, a French painter and potter. Porcelain was made here, although this was doubted by Heuser in his work on Pfalz-Zweibrücken. The factory also made *faïence*.

Pellevé left in 1767, and the factory was eventually leased to two Frenchmen who brought workers from France.

A tureen in the Hamburg Museum is painted with figures after J. E. Nilson, and is signed *Wolfart Prinxit* [*sic*]. This probably refers to Friedrich Karl Wohlfart who was working in Frankenthal in 1766, and was at Pfalz-Zweibrücken in 1767-68, going on to Höchst in 1771. There is also a dated figure (1766) at Hamburg.

Polychrome painting with mythological and Italian comedy scenes after Nilson, as well as decoration in underglaze blue and purple monochrome, have been noted.

A factory at Würzburg in Franconia was started in 1775 by Johann Kaspar Geyger. It seems to have ceased about five years later. A few examples of service-ware are known and some figures have, from time to time, been ascribed to this factory on slight evidence.

Apart from being a source of china clay used at a number of German factories, an attempt was made to establish a factory at Passau, in Bavaria, in 1766, the arcanist being Nikolaus Paul. He sought permission from the Prince-Bishop which was not granted. Ten years or so later a factory was actually started by a painter and dealer, Karl Hagen, who decorated Nymphenburg and Thuringian porcelain for the Turkish market.

The factories of Schney and Tettau in Bavaria were founded late in the century. They are unimportant, and their products during the period under review were few in number. They are represented by specimens in the Bayerisches Nationalmuseum.

Ringler and Benckgraff were at Künersberg about 1747, and some porcelain was probably made here. Specimens are in the same Museum.

Porcelain may have been made at Ellwangen in Württemberg by Ringler about 1758. A few specimens have been conjecturally awarded to this factory. Höxter in Westphalia was the home of

Franz Josef Weber, who was at Höchst, Frankenthal and Ilmenau. Although it was at one time thought that porcelain was made here, this is now considered doubtful.

Ringler was also at Schrezheim in Württemberg, not far from Ellwangen, for a short time in 1757, and some porcelain has been tentatively attributed. There is no definite evidence for manufacture here.

The question of the making of porcelain at Bayreuth is discussed in chapter 14 in connection with the *Hausmaler* Metzsch.

A factory making porcelain and *faïence* was started at Baden-Baden in 1770 by Zacharias Pfalzer which lasted until about 1780. Figures and service-ware were made.

Nothing is yet known of a factory at Ulm in Württemberg except for two interesting figures, both the same model, one of which is in the Victoria and Albert Museum, and the other in the collection of Mr. K. A. L. Rhodes. The latter, which is illustrated on Plate 134b, bears the word *Ulm* incised under the base, together with some workmen's marks. It appears to have been made about 1780.

13

THURINGIAN PORCELAIN

GOTHA

R R·g G

THE factories of the Thüringerwald were small, and their work provincial in inspiration and execution. For the most part they were not dependent on princely patronage, but were owned by ambitious tradesmen. Some, from time to time, received royal support, and in one or two the local princes held large shareholdings. The forests provided a ready source of fuel, and Passau clay was conveniently to hand. The wares produced were plain and simple, the body and glaze often defective and in some cases the decoration was of negligible artistic value, but they formed the basis for a great modern industry which still flourishes. As will later be seen, an important part was taken by the Greiners, a family of painters and potters who were extensively connected with almost all of the Thuringian undertakings in one way or another.

The earliest of the Thuringian factories was that of Gotha which was founded about 1757 by Wilhelm von Rotberg with the aid of the arcanist, Nikolaus Paul, who is mentioned elsewhere in this book. Although Gotha did not receive royal patronage, von Rotberg was *Oberhofmeister*, and was obviously in touch with the court.

The origin of the factory is lost in obscurity, but a letter from von Rotberg to Nikolaus Paul at Fürstenberg in 1758 suggests that the factory was already in operation. It is obvious that trouble was being experienced, since Paul was offered the post of arcanist. A letter from Gotzkowsky in Berlin to Helbig at Meissen in 1761 says that he (Gotzkowsky) had started his factory with the help of an arcanist who was then about to go to Gotha, but nothing certain is known about Paul's movements during this period, and they can only be surmised (p. 148).

The earliest existing specimen of Gotha porcelain which can be dated exactly is a cup in the Leipzig Museum which is marked with an "R", and bears the date *1763*.

By 1767 the factory was in a much better position and von Rotberg was able to enlarge it. He bought some property near the Sundhäusergate with a house, stables, kilns and a garden, to which the factory was transferred in the same year. Until 1772 there was much trouble with the body, which was extremely primitive and little more than a kind of stoneware, but in this year arrived Christian Schultz, a modeller and a painter of flowers, Johann Georg Gabel, a painter, and Johann Adam Brehm, a modeller. Schultz was responsible for the introduction of a new body of much better quality, and, largely as the result of the work of these three men, the factory began to prosper.

Von Rotberg died in 1795, and his wife was granted a monopoly for a limited period of twenty years. In 1802 she sold the under-taking to Prince August von Gotha who put his Chamberlain, Egidius Henneberg, in charge, and in 1805 the factory was removed to Sieberlehn Allee, where it remained. Gabel and Brehm were given new contracts, but Schultz resigned after bitter quarrels. The money due for his inventions was withheld, and his share-holding expropriated by Henneberg. Schultz eventually went to Gera.

By 1780 Gotha was producing porcelain of much better quality, both as regards glaze and body, than the other Thuringian fac-tories, and, at the time, it was even considered to be comparable

PLATE 129

Virgin and Child.
Limbach. *c.* 1775.

PLATE 130

(a) Covered cup and saucer with a view of Gera and an inscription.
Gera. c. 1785.

(b) Cup and saucer with ground imitating wood, and reserved panels. Signed *Rühlig fecit*.
Gera. c. 1785.

PLATE 131

(c) *Pierrot*, from the Italian Comedy.
Kloster Veilsdorf. *c.* 1770.

(b) Italian Comedy figure.
Kloster Veilsdorf. *c.* 1770.

PLATE 132

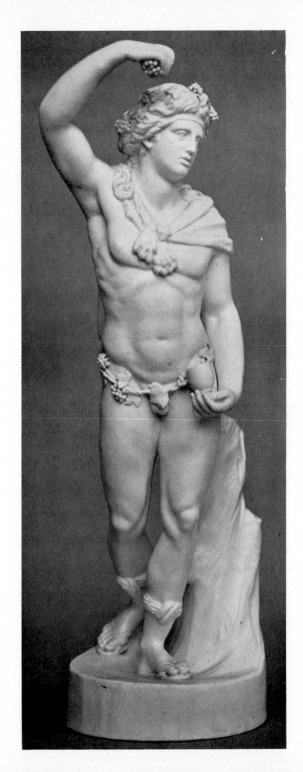

Bacchus. Biscuit porcelain.
Gotha. *c.* 1785.

PLATE 133

Two portrait busts.
Kloster Veilsdorf. c. 1770.

PLATE 134

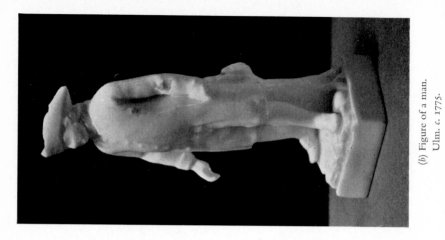

(b) Figure of a man.
Ulm. c. 1775.

(a) Bird-nesting Group.
Volkstedt. c. 1775.

PLATE 135

(*a*) Cup and saucer decorated in iron-red, lilac and gold.
Painted by Aufenwerth about 1725.

(*b*) Cup and saucer of Meissen porcelain decorated in raised and tooled gilding and enamels, by
C. K. Hunger.
c. 1715.

PLATE *136*

(*a*) Vienna porcelain, du Paquier period: mug decorated by Ignaz Preissler.

c. 1730.

(*b*) Vienna porcelain: cream-pot decorated by Ignaz Preissler.

c. 1725.

(*c*) Dresden Hausmalerei: cup and saucer painted in Höroldt style. Marked *Lauche fecit Dresden*.

c. 1725.

PLATE 137

Tea-pot of Meissen porcelain
decorated by Ignaz Preissler
in linear *Schwarzlot*.

c. 1725.

PLATE 138

Cup and saucer, initialled.
Ignaz Bottengruber. 1726.

PLATE 139

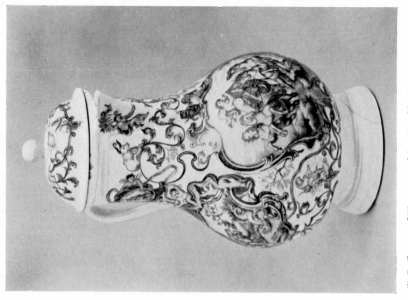

(b) Coffee-pot of Vienna porcelain painted by Ignaz Bottengruber.
c. 1725.

(a) Mounted tankard decorated with characteristic strap-work, by
H. G. von Bressler.
c. 1735.

PLATE *140*

Coffee-pot painted with a hunting scene in *Schwarzlot* and richly gilt.
Bartholomäus Seuter. *c.* 1735.

PLATE 141

(a) Meissen *déjeuner* set in travelling case decorated with *chinoiseries* in gold. Bartholomäus Seuter.
c. 1730.

(b) Coffee-pot of Nymphenburg porcelain painted with gilt *chinoiseries* in the Seuter workshop.
c. 1755.

(c) Tea-pot painted by Bartholomäus Seuter.
c. 1730.

PLATE *142*

(*a*) Meissen cup and saucer with *Kapuzinerbraun* glaze and gilt *chinoiseries*.
c. 1730.

(*b*) Vienna *Hausmalerei*: saucer with a battle scene, and an unrelated cup with a hunting scene.
c. 1730.

PLATE 143

Tankard painted with a landscape, by C. W. E. Dietrich.
Inscribed: CWED in 1730.

PLATE *144*

(*a*) Bayreuth: cup and saucer pencilled with shipping scenes, by J. F. Metzsch.

c. 1750.

(*b*) Cup and saucer attributed to R. C. von Drechsel.

c. 1740.

(*c*) Vienna cup painted with purple monochrome and gilt. Signed: *Bayreuth fec. Jucht.*

c. 1750.

(*d*) Cup painted with scenes by Metzsch from engravings by Kysell after Baur.

1748.

with such factories as Fürstenberg. The body had a characteristic yellowish colour.

The rococo style was little used except for the earliest things, and the general trend quickly changed to neo-classical. Early Italian red-figure vases were copied in 1789, and referred to as " painting *à l'étrusque* ". These may have been taken from the catalogue of Sir William Hamilton's collection of Pompeian antiquities.

The work of many of the larger factories was freely copied, especially figure models from Fürstenberg. No coloured figures seem to have been made at the time, but biscuit figures appear in 1770 (Plate 132).

Table-services were not manufactured in quantity, but many richly-decorated coffee-sets, and small sets of cups and saucers *à deux*, with mottoes and silhouettes, were produced. Much decoration was done in gold, as well as gold-framed medallions with painting *en grisaille*.

Gabel was a pupil of Tischbein, and painted landscapes, historical scenes and flowers; Rüger painted landscapes and flowers, and Frey was responsible for flowers and arabesques. Another painter, one Rothman, left to become a *Hausmaler* in Gotha.

WALLENDORF

w   X

This factory was founded by Johann Wolfgang Hamman at an undetermined date. With some previous experience in the manufacture of *faïence*, he attempted, about 1751, to make porcelain. Although he had little success, he tried to stop Macheleid's attempts to gain a privilege for the Volkstedt factory (q.v.). The Prince, however, denied that his test pieces were any better than those provided by Macheleid, and gave the privilege to the latter.

Eventually Hamman formed an association with Johann

EGP—O

Gottfried Greiner and Gotthelf Greiner, and after many experiments they evolved a body from which they could make pipes. Still in trouble with glazing, they enlisted the help of a glassworker from Coburg, named Dümmler, and finally evolved a suitable glaze between them.

The partners were far from being amicably disposed towards each other, and Gotthelf Greiner got permission from the Prince to build a factory at Limbach without Hamman. But it remained unbuilt at that time, and in 1762 a workable hard-paste porcelain was produced which they sought permission to make at Katzhütte. This permission was refused, and in 1763 they bought the estate of Wallendorf in Coburg-Saalfeld.

In 1764 a privilege was granted to a company consisting of Hamman and his sons, and Ferdinand Friedrich, Johann Georg, Johann Gottfried and Gotthelf Greiner. Most of the money was provided by Hamman, and the necessary knowledge by the last two Greiners.

In 1772 Gotthelf Greiner became displeased with the arrangement and left to found a factory at Limbach (q.v.).

Only the commoner wares were produced at Wallendorf, as well as a few naïvely modelled figures reminiscent of those of Limbach. The humbler Meissen wares were freely imitated.

VOLKSTEDT

Volkstedt was founded by Georg Heinrich Macheleid, who solved the problem of making porcelain without the aid of an arcanist.

Macheleid was born at Cursdorf in 1723. He was the son of a laboratory worker, with theological leanings, and studied at the University of Jena. Later, he abandoned his religious studies to become a porcelain maker, and succeeded finally in making a workable soft porcelain body with sand found by chance.

Macheleid found a patron in Prince Johann Friedrich zu Schwarzburg-Rudolstadt, and asked him for a monopoly of wood and raw materials, as well as special treatment for his workmen. There was another claimant in the field, the Johann Wolfgang Hamman referred to above, but Macheleid was finally given what he asked for in October, 1760, with the condition attached that the monopoly should last only so long as nobody could make better porcelain.

The factory was first established at Sitzendorf, and was moved to Volkstedt in 1762. The mark adopted was that of the hayfork, from the arms of the Schwarzburg family, and the factory is referred to occasionally as Rudolstadt.

Macheleid eventually progressed from the initial soft paste to a hard paste body, and in 1767 the factory was taken over quite suddenly by a merchant dealing in raw materials, by name Christian Nonne. The reason for the change is obscure, but Macheleid had been borrowing money from the Prince. The factory was reorganized and Macheleid was given a share and a life pension. Prince Johann Friedrich died in this year, and his shareholding was taken over by the succeeding Prince, Ludwig Günther, who took great interest in the factory to the extent of cancelling half its indebtedness. It appears to have become increasingly prosperous for some years thereafter.

Relations between the officials of the factory were often strained, and in 1780 the *Hofmaler*, Johann Andreas Greiner, member of the large family of artists and arcanists who were much interested in the Thuringian factories, left Volkstedt for Gera. In this venture he was accompanied by his brother, Johann Georg Wilhelm Greiner. Eventually he consented to return to Volkstedt at a higher salary with a share of the profits, the Gera factory being operated as a branch establishment.

In 1781 Greiner for a short time held the lease of the factory instead of Nonne, but in 1782 he was dismissed and joined his brother at Gera. Nonne resumed his position in the same year, remaining until 1800.

In 1787 Nonne became involved in a quarrel with Meissen over the deceptive mark of the crossed hayforks used at Volkstedt, but at the Michaelmas fair in Leipzig finally settled his differences by contracting not to copy the crossed swords, nor to use a deceptive substitute in future. Nonne worked continuously to expand the factory and to sell its products, and to this end travelled to various fairs and arranged auction sales of the factory's porcelain.

By 1793 Volkstedt was in trouble, and once more the Prince purchased a large shareholding. In 1797 it was sold to Prince Ernst Constantin von Hessen-Philippsthal, and Nonne was dismissed. Furiously he demanded compensation for his removal. He was (he said) entitled to stay until 1800, and in the end was retained until the expiry of his term.[1]

In 1799 the Prince of Hesse disposed of the factory to Wilhelm Heinrich Greiner and Carl Holzapfel of Rudolstadt. Nonne immediately made new demands and threatened to damage the factory if payment was refused. The Prince intervened, and Nonne was finally paid out. The firm then became Holzapfel und Greiner, and later, the Älteste Volkstedter Porzellan-Fabrik.

Only a small number of pieces of the soft paste made by Macheleid have been identified. A few cups decorated in polychrome after the *famille rose* are known marked with the hayforks, and a white portrait bust. The paste is primitive in the extreme, and unusually soft.

The hard porcelain has a greyish colour, and a dirty-looking glaze which is freely covered with fine black specks, probably due to charcoal firing. Firecracks are common, and these, and similar minor defects, were concealed whenever possible by painted flowers. Plates often warped in firing. These defects persisted for a considerable time, and had not been completely rectified even as late as 1800.

Volkstedt porcelain never quite lost its peasant appearance, and the factory was conservative, too, in its approach to fashion,

[1] In 1797 he took over the Bohemian factory of Klosterle and established another at Gieszhübl in 1803.

retaining the rococo style long after the other factories had moved into the ambit of the Louis-Seize.

As may be deduced from the fraudulent use of the hayforks already mentioned, and even the use of the Meissen mark itself, much work was done in the Meissen style. We notice, for instance, the use of the *Altbrandensteinmuster*, as well as of such things as " shadowed " flowers and insects.

Flowers and fruit were fairly common themes. Landscapes and figure subjects, including Watteau scenes, are less frequent, and these were executed in polychrome or in purple monochrome. The prints of Daniel Chodowiecki, the Berlin engraver, were copied, and Prince Johann Friedrich sent engravings to the factory on several occasions, ordering, in 1765, " two broth pots to be painted with the engravings sent herewith " and continuing, " the painter can add something of his own invention as he may think fit ".[1]

A price list of 1795 offers coffee-services from six to eighty thalers, but suggests that "much finer ones can be made to order ". The cheapest of all were painted in underglaze blue.

Nothing painted by the *Hofmaler*, Johann Andreas Greiner, can be identified with certainty.

Figure sculpture, for the most part, was good in quality, although it is somewhat spoiled by the defective material. Relief portraits in rococo frames, painted in colours, were done by Franz Kotta, a modeller and painter who came to the factory from Kloster-Veilsdorf in 1783, and later became *Hofmaler*. Kotta's position was such that at one point in the factory's career he almost replaced Nonne, and in 1797 the Prince took him to Philippsthal as a witness to the negotiations for the sale of the factory. Some vases of rather naïve form, with figures standing on the handles, may properly be attributable to Kotta.

Another modeller, Friedrich Künckler, came originally from Fürstenberg, and later was at Cassel and Berlin for a short while, as well as spending a few months at Kloster-Veilsdorf. His work

[1] Schmidt (op. cit.).

was so popular at the time that the Prince regarded him as indispensable, but it cannot now be identified with certainty, and it is very much a case of one guess being as good as another (Plate 134a).

A curious departure, which I think is unique, was the making of maps in relief.

KLOSTER-VEILSDORF

Kloster-Veilsdorf, one of the principal Thuringian factories, was founded by Prince Friedrich Wilhelm Eugen von Hildburghausen about 1760. The arcanist was Johann Hermann Meyer, who used clay from Passau fired in small kilns similar to those used at Vienna. Meyer had the assistance of a turner, or thrower, named Nürnberger, and it is possible that they had some information from Vienna. Although the factory buildings were being erected as early as 1760, it was not until 1765 that a privilege was granted in the familiar manner. The director of the factory was Friedrich Döll, the court sculptor, and Johann Ernst Bayer was responsible for production.

Because it was a potential source of prestige and income to the court, Kloster-Veilsdorf was assisted to expand, although it was not a profitable undertaking. To help its progress the Prince more or less compelled his Jewish subjects to take porcelain in exchange for money, in the same way as Frederick solved similar problems at Berlin. Despite this expedient, the Prince ran steadily into debt and tried to sell the factory to his brother, Ernst Friedrich II, without success. Finding himself committed to the undertaking, he became its unofficial art director, influencing the designs in favour of the Louis-Seize style, as well as studying colour chemistry.

In 1766, Nikolaus Paul, the wandering arcanist, arrived at the factory. It would seem from a letter written by the Prince which refers to the " young and the old Pauli " that he was accompanied by a son. His position does not, however, seem to have been of great importance, since four other arcanists were already employed —Meyer, Ripp, Dellatorre and Ley.

By 1786 the factory was sufficiently well established for it to be "sold" to two merchants of Minden, Johann Valentin Basson and Jakob Eckhard, and a letter from Princess Caroline to the Prince written in 1786 shows the sense of relief with which the court received the arrangement: "The news of the sale of the porcelain undertaking made me almost cry with joy, that you will at last be able to help yourself a little." But the details of this sale are veiled in obscurity, and succeeding events throw considerable doubt on its validity.

The factory still was not making a profit, and in 1789 Wilhelm Heinrich Immanuel Greiner was employed to try to improve sales. In this task he had small success, and in 1790 the *Hofkommissar* Greiner of Rauenstein offered to lease the factory. It is certain that, when Prince Eugen died in 1795, he left the factory to his nephew, Friedrich, which would not have been possible had the earlier sale to Basson and Eckhard been effective.

A ducal commission decided that this legacy was a doubtful piece of nepotism, and decided to sell it to the sons of Gotthelf Greiner in Limbach, or to the Greiners of Rauenstein, for a mere 15,000 florins—a coin worth approximately eight shillings (or one dollar) in modern currency.[1] But these negotiations were fruitless, and Johann Adam Hofmann and Wilhelm Offney, the latter a relative of the Greiners by marriage, became directors in 1798. The Greiner family operated the factory until 1822, when it was reorganized on a proper commercial basis.

The first productions were of useful wares—tea, coffee and chocolate services, and the like, as well as table decorations, and such humble domestic things as knife-handles and thimbles. These were mainly in the rococo style, and were considerably influenced by the silversmiths of Augsburg.

[1] 1958.

In the decoration much use was made of engravings by Röttier and Nilson with which the Prince kept his factory well supplied. Nilson's engravings were also frequently used at Frankenthal and Berlin, and he was principally an engraver of figure subjects.

Chinoiseries, landscapes with nuns (!), and *Amoretti* after Boucher were all extremely well-painted, the quality often approaching that of the work of Meissen, which was in fact a frequent source of inspiration, the earlier services being taken more or less directly from Meissen prototypes. This may be seen in the occasional use of the *Neubrandensteinmuster*. Painting *en camaïeu* was undertaken in several colours.

Döll was probably the chief painter, and specimens are in existence initialled with the letter "D". Another painter, named Stockmar, copied engravings and did naturalistic paintings. Stockmar was distinctly a man of parts, since he also painted in oils, did miniatures on ivory and parchment, valeted the Prince and cut his hair.

The neo-classical style was adopted progressively after 1780, and by 1790 work is almost entirely of this kind.

Nothing definite is known of the factory's plastic work until after about 1777. In 1767 some figures were sent to a merchant in Mannheim on sale or return terms, but these were returned as unsaleable. In 1779 the Fürst von Kirchberg ordered a table decoration, two altars, and eight pairs of dancing shepherds and shepherdesses. The Prince himself painted the two shields on the altars.

By 1785 the production of figures and similar articles was fairly large (Plates 131 and 133). The best known modeller was Franz Kotta who came to Kloster-Veilsdorf sometime before 1777, perhaps as an apprentice. The Prince recognized his ability and took a paternal interest in his welfare, and Kotta modelled a bust of the Prince from a portrait by the court sculptor, Döll. But Kotta was also frivolous, and when the news that he wanted to marry came to the ear of the Prince, the latter wrote to Bayer:

About Kotta, I think that if he wants to marry, and the girl is presentable and not without means, he could perhaps improve himself, but we must point out to him that he is young and might rue the day. As far as the factory is concerned, I think it would be almost better if he had a wife

—which provides an amusing side-glance at relations between the Prince and his workpeople.

In 1777 Kotta executed relief portraits of Princess Caroline, as well as miniatures of the Prince of Coburg and the Princess Frederica. He deserted shortly afterwards to Groszbreitenbach where he modelled a portrait of the founder, Anton Friedrich von Hopfgarten. In 1778 he left this factory, and went as a modeller to a confectioner in Gotha, presumably to model figures in sugar which were a popular table decoration at the time. In 1779 he returned to Kloster-Veilsdorf, staying until 1783, and then went on to Volkstedt where he became court painter, since he was skilled in both painting and modelling.

The Prince was a little annoyed by these manœuvres, as may be well seen from his correspondence with Bayer, and in 1783 the latter wrote to the Prince that " there is no longer a single modeller in the factory from whom we can demand or expect any decent work ".

A number of complaints were received from Meissen that the mark of the royal manufactory was being copied—a charge which Bayer refuted with more indignation than the facts warranted.

LIMBACH

This factory was founded by Gotthelf Greiner, who was also responsible for starting factories at Groszbreitenbach and Ilmenau.

Greiner was the father of five sons who were all more or less prominent in the porcelain industry of Thuringia, and for this reason deserves also to be regarded as the father of Thuringian porcelain ! He was born at Alsbach, the son of a glass-maker, and spent his youth in Limbach. Gotthelf went into his father's business and became a successful glass-maker, and in 1762 extended his activities by extracting an abortive concession from the Prince for the manufacture of porcelain. But it gave him no advantages in the matter of a supply of wood for fuel, and this created difficulties. His two co-workers, Dümmler and Johann Gottfried Greiner, had in the meantime joined with Hamman at Katzhütte (see section on Wallendorf) and for some time the body and glaze appears to have been mixed at Limbach, whilst the actual work of converting it into porcelain was done at Katzhütte.

Gotthelf Greiner finally left Wallendorf in 1772 and returned to Limbach. Here he obtained another concession. At first he used wood-fuel which should have gone to his glass-house, and tended his kilns single-handed, but later he built the factory into a flourishing concern which he bequeathed on his death in 1797 to his sons, the firm becoming Gotthelf Greiner Söhne.

Production at Limbach was principally for use rather than ornament. Its quality fell somewhat short of the best of the Thuringian factories. Blue painting was a speciality from the beginning, and the mark used (crossed L's) was purposely drawn to simulate that of Meissen. In 1787 Greiner adopted the mark of a clover-leaf after protests from Meissen, but much porcelain marked with the L's and the clover-leaf in addition was made at Groszbreitenbach (q.v.).

Monochrome and polychrome flowers were a favourite until 1790, as well as landscapes with figures and ruins rather sketchily painted, often in purple monochrome. The Meissen chrysanthemum pattern was also copied in the same purple. Later, much use was made of gilding. Although, for the most part, painters were locally recruited, some came from such factories as Kloster-Veilsdorf and Ludwigsburg.

Figures were the most important side of this factory's production. Although they are provincial in appearance, they have a character and charm of their own. Large heads are often a distinctive feature. The names of some of the modellers are known, but it is impossible to distinguish their work (Plates 127 and 128).

ILMENAU

This factory was founded by Christian Zacharias Gräbner who first tried to start a factory at Groszbreitenbach. Here he was forestalled by Hopfgarten, so he applied to the Duke Karl August of Weimar for a concession. This he was given in 1777. It permitted him to manufacture porcelain at Ilmenau and to sell his wares in Weimar. In April 1779 he persuaded the Duke to ban the sale of all foreign stoneware and porcelain in the province.

Despite these advantages he experienced considerable financial difficulties, and tried to borrow money from Karl August. The latter, however, seems to have learned from the experience of other members of the nobility who had become involved with porcelain factories, and the loan was refused. Gräbner tried to mortgage the factory, but the position did not improve and finally, on the pretext of opening new markets, he left hurriedly for Russia, whereupon, in 1782, the Duke took over the factory. In 1783 we find the Duke saying that the Government were prepared to continue in charge until the debts were paid, in the meantime granting to Gräbner a monthly salary provided he was prepared to work. This he would not do, and finally went to Reval, whence he bombarded the Duke with discourteous answers to letters asking him to return. Later he brought a complaint against the Weimar court, but lost his case.

Johann Wolfgang von Goethe, the poet, was a friend of Duke Karl August, and held the position of *Geheimrat* (Privy Councillor), as well as that of President of the Chamber of Finance. In this capacity he opposed the outright sale of the factory, and in 1786 it was leased to Gotthelf Greiner for six years. Greiner freed it of

debt, but gave up the lease at its expiry because the Court wanted
to increase the rent or reduce the wood concession.

In 1792 his place was taken by Christian Nonne who ran the
factory from Volkstedt, and in 1808 it was purchased by Nonne
outright.

There are almost no marked specimens existing before the time
of Nonne, but from a letter which passed between Krafft and
Goethe, we can assume that the quality was poor: " the porcelain
is bad, worse than any in the neighbourhood, and even more
expensive". Krafft urged Goethe not to support Gräbner: " I
told him [Gräbner] that I considered it to be really a poor quality
faïence, and he said he could do better." Goethe sent a cup to Frau
von Stein in 1782, and wrote: "I wish the body was a better one",
and continued that he hoped to send a more acceptable present
when he could get some porcelain from Gotha.

At first the glaze was badly spotted in the muffle kiln, a defect
to be seen sometimes on Volkstedt wares, but the body and glaze
was later improved by Franz Josef Weber, an arcanist of long
practical experience at Ludwigsburg, Kelsterbach, Frankenthal,
and Höchst. He was the author of a treatise on porcelain-making[1]
and director at Ilmenau from 1784 to 1786. In the latter year he
abandoned porcelain making and returned to Höchst.

Figures and sets of figures in variety were made up till the
advent of Greiner. Many were the work of Johann Lorenz
Rienck, who also designed plastically-decorated services. During
the period of Greiner's lease, however, figure modelling appears
to have been discontinued.

Under Nonne, Wedgwood's blue jasper-ware was freely
imitated, including portrait cameos and medallions. Despite an
extensive production, however, very little made before 1800
survives in identifiable form.

[1] *Die Kunst das ächte Porzellain zu verfertigen.*

GERA

ς

This factory was founded by two *faïence* workers, Johann Gottlob Ehwaldt and Johann Gottlieb Gottbrecht, the former acting as arcanist and the latter taking responsibility for the organization of the factory. There is no record, however, that they succeeded in making porcelain on a commercial scale. In 1779 they asked the Graf Henry XXX of Reuss for permission to start, and were given a place called the Gelbeshaus in Gera. In 1780 Johann Georg Wilhelm Greiner and Johann Andreas Greiner wrote to the Prince's Minister with proof of their success in making porcelain, and asking for permission to buy the factory from its founders. Upon agreeing to take over debts of 625 thalers, and assenting to a yearly payment of between thirty and eighty thalers, to be graduated according to the success of the factory, they were given a concession for four years from 1st April, 1780.

These negotiations at first were secret because the Greiners were still under contract to Volkstedt, but on 3rd April Johann Andreas Greiner finally told the Volkstedt administration of his intention. The Rudolstadt officials were much annoyed by the news, and Greiner suggested that they should take an interest in the new factory. Eventually they made an investment of 500 thalers on the understanding that they should have half the profits. Henry XXX was somewhat perturbed by these proceedings, but took no active steps to stop the arrangement. Quarrels with the Volkstedt manager, August Friedrich North, were frequent throughout this period.

In 1782 the agreement between Volkstedt and Gera was allowed to lapse, the Greiners continuing alone. There were, however, occasional disputes with the former until 1788. Until 1782 Gera can be regarded as no more than a branch of Volkstedt; after this date it was a separate concern.

Johann Georg Wilhelm Greiner died in 1792, and the usual

harmony existing between members of the Greiner brood was broken by an attempt by his brother to annex the factory. This was prevented by the court. Johann Andreas Greiner died in 1799. The composition of the directorate at this date was his widow and children and a certain Leutnant von Ridnitz who represented the widow and daughter of J. G. W. Greiner. These ladies were referred to somewhat ungallantly as " die Greiner'schen Relikten ", the Greiner relics.

In 1800 the *Relikten* gained complete control of the factory, but as its debts then stood at about 12,500 thalers this does not seem to have been a particularly astute manœuvre. Quarrelling was, in part, the cause of the money troubles, but competition and lack of capital must take due share of the blame. The financial position was sometimes so difficult that workers were paid in porcelain instead of money.

Throughout this period great difficulty was experienced in producing a satisfactory body and glaze. The body in particular was of an unattractive greyish colour, and the glaze was frequently bluish-green.

Meissen was much copied, and the swords were added freely. The *Zwiebelmuster* and the *Strohblumenmuster* (page 6) appear in a blackish underglaze blue. The form for the most part was neo-classical, although a few figures have rococo bases and these appear to date from about 1785. Some figures are modelled with a certain skill, but the enamel colouring is often poor in quality, and dull. Views of Gera, and a painted imitation of grained wood—the so-called *décor bois*—are both to be found. Occasional use was made of coloured grounds (Plate 130).

GROSZBREITENBACH

Hausmalerei was an established practice here before the factory was founded, and whilst this work cannot be identified, a letter from Krafft to Goethe in 1779 suggests that the painting was superior to that of Ilmenau.

The factory itself was founded by Major Anton Friedrich Wilhelm Ernst von Hopfgarten, who obtained a concession in 1777. Despite good supplies of wood-fuel, it did not flourish, and it was sold to Gotthelf Greiner in Limbach. Thus it became a branch of Limbach, and it remained in the Greiner family until 1869.

Its work is almost indistinguishable from that of Limbach. The crossed "L" mark (see section on Limbach) was discontinued about 1788, and thenceforward only the clover-leaf was used.

RAUENSTEIN

R   *n - n*

This factory was founded in 1783 by Johann Georg, Johann Friedrich and Christian Daniel Greiner. They were granted a privilege in this year by the Duke of Saxe-Meiningen. The factory was housed in a castle which was partially destroyed by fire in 1787.

For the most part production was inferior with a greyish glaze. Meissen was imitated, but the quality was too poor for these wares to be deceptive.

14

HAUSMALEREI

A PROMINENT part in the history and development of German porcelain was taken by the more important of the *Hausmaler*, and the best of this kind of work is often as highly valued as the finest factory work. Something has already been said on this subject in the preceding pages, and these men were regarded by the factories with mixed feelings. In the early period, Meissen gladly sold white porcelain for outside decoration, both in the attempt to make additional sales, and to encourage the craft of enamelling (which still needed much research), hoping to profit by discoveries of the *Hausmaler*.

Whilst Meissen had a monopoly, and could exercise some kind of control over supplies, this policy undoubtedly paid handsomely, but the newer factories were less careful in selling off their white wares for decoration, and not until the *Hausmaler* had manœuvred themselves into an extremely strong position did the factory begin to sense the disadvantages.

It was a frequent practice of some of the *Hausmaler* to sell work done in their own studios as decorated by the factory itself, and whilst this might not have mattered greatly had price levels been maintained, they bought outmoded white ware at low prices, painted it, and sold it at much less than comparable factory prices for new production, thus adding greatly

PLATE 145

Cup and saucer pencilled in black, with baroque scrolls, J. F. Metzsch.
c. 1750.

PLATE 146

(a) Bowl decorated at Bayreuth, by J. F. Metzsch.
c. 1750.

(b) Interior of 146 (a).

PLATE 147

(a) Meissen plate painted with a battle scene, by Mayer of Pressnitz.
c. 1750.

(b) Bowl painted with figures and baroque scrolls, J. F. Metzsch.
c. 1740.

PLATE *148*

Meissen plate painted by Mayer of Pressnitz.
c. 1750.

PLATE 149

(a) Meissen tea-pot decorated in underglaze blue, with later gilt decoration by F. J. Ferner.

c. 1750.

(b) Cup and saucer decorated with pastoral scenes, by F. J. Ferner.

c. 1755.

PLATE 150

(a) Meissen oval tray decorated with incised engraving, by Canon A. O. E. von dem Busch. c. 1755.

(b) Covered sugar-bowl decorated with incised engraving, by Canon A. O. E. von dem Busch.

PLATE 151

Plate painted by J. F. Ferner about 1750 with the birth of one of Jupiter's children—*Nascitur proles Jovis*. Meissen.

PLATE 152

(a) A Meissen cup and saucer made about 1725 overdecorated with gilt *chinoiseries* at Augsburg ten years later.

(b) A small porcelain panel painted with family portraits.
c. 1752.

to the financial difficulties from which all the early factories suffered.

When porcelain was a comparatively new discovery Augsburg, already renowned for its metalwork, took considerable interest in the new material. Some of it was mounted with gold and silver in the same way as *faïence* had been mounted earlier. But also, in Augsburg, were artists who understood the craft of enamelling, and who undertook to decorate porcelain.

In 1711 Böttger sent some porcelain to Tobias Baur, an Augsburg goldsmith, who, lacking in foresight, returned it, but Elias Adam, who married Regina Baur and set up his own goldsmith's shop, looked further ahead and became interested in porcelain. Soon the families of Baur, and of Warnberg and Hosenestel, were all interested. In 1714 Warnberg married Johanna Aufenwerth (Aufem Werth is a variant spelling), and later, in 1731, Hosenestel married Sabina, daughter of Johann Aufenwerth who was one of the earliest outside decorators of Meissen porcelain. The families were thus interconnected.

Our most important consideration, however, is the work of Johann Aufenwerth himself. This must have been of considerable importance in the early days of Meissen porcelain, but controversy now exists on the question of the allocation of certain kinds of decoration between him and Bartholomäus Seuter who also worked in Augsburg.

Certain examples (see Plate 135a) signed "I A W Augsburg" are instantly and certainly referable to Aufenwerth, and a measure of assistance in attribution can be obtained from the style of the baroque scroll-work and of the *Laub- und Bandelwerk* used by him. These were taken from books of designs published about 1710 by J. C. Weigel of Nürnberg which consisted of engravings by Paul Decker, Johann Leonhard Eysler and J. C. Reiff. The books in question were published for engravers and craftsmen generally, and were often used as source material at the German factories for this kind of thing, particularly at Vienna.

There is little doubt that Pazaurek[1] was in error in attributing much work to Aufenwerth which was actually done by Seuter. Three examples which form a useful comparison may be seen on Plates 135a, 140 and 142a. The first is certainly by Aufenwerth, and is also figured by Pazaurek. The signature is undoubted proof. Plate 140, the coffee-pot, is undoubtedly by Seuter. Not only does it bear no resemblance to Aufenwerth's signed work, but underneath the flange supporting the cover will be noticed some " C "-shaped scrolls with a central dot. The same can be noticed on the gilt *chinoiserie* cup and saucer in Plate 142a. These scrolls are said to be a Seuter characteristic, and there seems good reason for so regarding them. If this is correct, however, there is evidence for removing many of Pazaurek's attributions to Aufenwerth into the ambit of Seuter. In particular, scenes after Watteau, consisting of large figures shown in something less than three-quarter length, are the more likely to be by his hand (Plate 141c). There is so much difference between the style of Plate 135a, which is undoubtedly Aufenwerth, and the Watteau scenes figured by Pazaurek, that it is difficult to see how the two could have been confused in the first place, but hind-sight is the easiest approach to any problem.

Aufenwerth did not have the same range of colours at his command as Seuter. A signed example of the gilt *chinoiserie* exists, and some copies of Meissen *chinoiseries* in polychrome were claimed for him by Schnorr von Carolsfeld; attributions should be made cautiously, and with the characteristics of Seuter's work duly borne in mind.

It is probable that, through his connections with Adam and Baur, Aufenwerth had some influence with Meissen, because, in 1728, when he died, the factory stopped sending supplies of white porcelain to Augsburg altogether, so that his daughter, Sabina, was unable to profit by the improvements her father had made.

Bartholomäus Seuter was born in 1678 into a family of engravers and goldsmiths, and he, in turn, continued the tradition,

---

[1] *Deutsche Fayence und Porzellan Hausmaler.*

becoming in addition an enameller and a silk dyer. The latter occupation may have been because he married into a family of silk dyers who had a factory founded in 1676. According to a contemporary record he was "überhaupts in chymischen Künsten und Zubereitungen sehr erfahren" (in all chemical arts and preparation very accomplished) as well as "und zu schönen Erfindungen ungemein ausgelegt" (uncommonly good at inventions).

Much of his work is on the *faïence* of Nürnberg and Bayreuth, but despite difficulties in procuring porcelain, a considerable proportion of the work attributed to him uses this as a medium.

He is the subject of a number of contemporary references which comprise most of the available information about him. J. G. Keysler, an art historian of the period, wrote in 1729:

> Seuter verkauft die schönsten Porzellanwerke, deren er viele noch ganz weiss von Dresden kommen lassen, und durch nette Gemälde und Email noch viel kostbarer gemacht hat. Er besitzt durch über hundert gemalte Schüsseln von Francesco Duranei.

That is to say: "Seuter buys the best porcelain ware, which he has sent mostly in white from Dresden. This he improves enormously by the addition of painting and enamel work. Also he has over 100 painted dishes by Francesco Duranei."

This establishes him as a porcelain painter in 1729.

He became involved with an animal painter of Augsburg, Johann Elias Riedinger, who was later director of the Augsburg Academy of Art, and together they illustrated a book in several volumes written by Dietrich and Bieler entitled *Phytandros Iconographia* or *Eigentliche Darstellung einiger Tausend in allen vier Welt-Theilen gewachsener Bäume, Stauden, Kräuter, Blumen, Früchte und Schwämme u.s.w.*, which can be translated (literally) as *Special representation of several thousand in-all-four-corners-of-the-world-growing trees, shrubs, weeds, flowers, fruits, sponges, and so on.* This book was lavishly illustrated, and its publication was attended *mit grossen Unkosten*.[1] This was used as one of the sources from which the Meissen *deutsche Blumen* were taken.

The work of Seuter has already received some attention in the chapter on Meissen porcelain (page 62) and in the remarks on Aufenwerth immediately preceding. Additionally, some over-gilding of defective Meissen blue and white porcelain may have been done by workers in his studio, as well as by F. J. Ferner later discussed.

It seems likely that Seuter was actually the owner of a workshop in Augsburg where porcelain from various sources was painted, and this may have continued to function after his death. The coffee-pot shown on Plate 141b is very much in his style, although the porcelain bears the Nymphenburg mark, and was probably made after his death in 1754.

Christoph Konrad Hunger has already received notice in the chapters on Meissen and Vienna, but he functioned also as a *Hausmaler*. Particularly he specialized in relief work in enamel and gold, and there is a signed cup and saucer in Vienna of this kind. He is here represented by Plate 135b. He worked also on gold and copper.

The most important of the *Hausmaler* is, without doubt, Ignaz Bottengruber (or Pottengruber) of Breslau. The date of his birth is unknown, but he was married at Breslau in 1720, and at this time was known as a painter of miniatures and small water-colours. He worked for Johann Georg Pauli, a patron who collected pictures and books, and who supported him financially. His early work on Meissen porcelain includes a coffee-service with a Bacchanalian feast which he did for Pauli.

A contemporary historian, Kundmann, wrote of porcelain: "It is painted and refired at Breslau where Herr Preussler has painted with grey on grey, or black, but Herr Pottengruber with all colours, and in such perfection as has not been seen hitherto."[2]

Bottengruber flourished, as a porcelain painter, between 1720

---

[1] "With large debts."
[2] *Sammlung von Natur- und Medizinae-, auch Kunst- und Literaturgeschichten* (1723).

and 1730, and by 1723 was able to use a palette with a considerable range of colour which was at least equal to the Meissen achievement, and his work is undoubtedly superior artistically either to that of the factory at this time, or to contemporary *Hausmaler*. The earliest known signed and dated piece (1726) is illustrated on Plate 138. This is in colours, with rich gilding, and is notable for its vitality and for the decorative *Bandelwerk*. This peculiarly baroque ornament is seen at its best in his work, and he passed on his fondness for it to his pupil, Hans Gottlieb von Bressler (Plate 139a).

Bacchic scenes were a particular favourite with Bottengruber, but his battle and hunting scenes are remarkably fine, and curious fabulous animals are frequent. He was fond of *putti*, and these appear comparatively often in his work.

His simplest painting is carried out in iron-red and violet-purple, together with a little gilding. The gilding is inclined to be reddish in tone, and the figures are usually heavily outlined and well-modelled. The drawing is not always as successful as the colouring.

In 1728, when Höroldt decided to stop supplies of white porcelain to the *Hausmaler*, Bottengruber turned to Vienna, and since Breslau was included in the Kingdom of Austria, his raw material was tax-free.

The resemblance between some early Meissen porcelain and that of Vienna during the du Paquier period has led to some confusion as to the origin of the porcelain on which he worked, although, in general, this is not a matter of any great moment. From the style of some Vienna painting it is obvious that he had great influence on some of the factory's painters, and it has been suggested that he worked there, but no definite evidence can be found to determine the point. Jakob Helchis (Plate 71) was certainly much influenced by Bottengruber's style.

No dated specimens are known after 1730, and he then vanishes completely.

It is difficult to overestimate the importance of Bottengruber's work. Although he painted on Chinese porcelain occasionally, all his known work is completely devoid of oriental influence, and in this sense he is the most German of all the early porcelain painters, as well as being the most baroque. Kundmann writes of him thus: "Perfektion als es sonst niemals allhier geschehen",[1] and his influence on the decorating styles of his time was profound.

Bottengruber had two pupils, Karl Ferdinand von Wolfsburg and Hans Gottlieb von Bressler. Von Wolfsburg was the son of an Imperial counsellor, who was an amateur decorator. There are some signed examples in existence. Plates in the Oesterreichisches Museum are pompously inscribed—*Carolus Ferdinandus de Wolfsbourg et Wallsdorf Eques Silesiae pinxit Viennae Aust. 1731*, from which may be deduced an inordinate pride of achievement which far outran his technical skill. Generally, his work is much inferior to that of Bottengruber, although, in one case where it is considerably better than usual, the suggestion has been made that Bottengruber was, at least, partly responsible. Examples are very rare.

Von Bressler was likewise a noble amateur, distantly related to King Wenzel, who painted principally to amuse himself and his friends. His palette is similar to that of Bottengruber, and he used the same reddish gilding. His style was predominantly that of his master, but his work is considerably better in quality than that of von Wolfsburg. He was extremely fond of German flowers, and used them frequently.

Jakob Helchis, whose career is traced in greater detail in chapters 2 and 3, may also have been a pupil of Bottengruber's, and his work, as already mentioned, shows the influence of the latter's style.

A little before Bottengruber's appearance, we have the enigmatic Preusslers (or Preisslers). Herr Preussler is mentioned by Kundmann, who records him as decorating over one hundred pieces for the collector, Dr. Ernst Benjamin von Löwenstadt und Ronneburg, who had employed him as an interior decorator for seven years.

[1] " Perfection as never before."

The Preusslers worked on Silesian and Bohemian glass, and Chinese, Vienna and Meissen porcelain. Many of the family during the seventeenth century were glass-workers, painters, cutters or polishers, but others were schoolmasters, linen-weavers, and the like. Some were described as *Vagabundus*, or, of the women, *iam notorie corrupta*, followed by a note of their illegitimate children.

It seems that the Preusslers at present under review were Daniel (1636–1733) and his son, Ignaz. The latter was christened in 1676 at Friedrichswalde in Silesia.

Much of their presumed work was done in *Schwarzlot* in particular, and in red and purple monochromes, as well as *en grisaille*, as recorded by Kundmann. *Schwarzlot*, especially, has a Bohemian and Silesian parentage, and is in direct line of descent from the seventeenth-century *Hausmaler*, Johann Schaper, whose work is to be found on *faïence* and glass, by way of Johann Ludwig Faber somewhat later in the century, to the Preusslers.

It is probable that Daniel Preussler's work was nearly all on Chinese porcelain. Ignaz, who worked at Kronstadt in Bohemia for the Graf Franz Karl Liebsteinsky von Kolowrat, also used Chinese porcelain, since the Graf preferred it, but it is likely that whatever work was done by these two on European porcelain came from the hand of Ignaz.

Landscapes, hunting scenes, battle scenes and mythological subjects have been attributed to them, although some may be by others working in a similar style. Some *chinoiseries* can be related to Augsburg engravings. *Laub- und Bandelwerk* was used in the baroque manner (See Plates 136a and 137).

Schwarzlot painting, commonly attributed to Aufenwerth, Seuter and the Preusslers, was common at the du Paquier Vienna factory, and can also be seen in the independent work of J. K. W. Anreiter and Jakob Helchis. Anreiter's signature is to be found on the porcelain of Meissen, Vienna and China. Anton F. J. Schulz also worked in *Schwarzlot* and in colours. He painted first for the Vienna factory, and became an independent decorator in 1741.

Bayreuth, in Bavaria, made a great deal of important *faïence*, and also much brown-glazed ware inspired by Böttger's red stoneware. An example of this appears on Plate 4a. Before proceeding to a discussion of Bayreuth *Hausmalerei*, however, this is an appropriate place to record what little is known of the manufacture of porcelain there. About 1735 some Meissen workmen joined a conspiracy to get away from the factory with the intention of going to Bayreuth to make porcelain. Among them were Adam Friedrich von Löwenfinck, and the sons of Johann Georg Mehlhorn. Their father seems to have been almost continually disaffected, and approaches were made to him from Vienna some sixteen years earlier.

Another attempt to make porcelain coincides with the presence of the swindler-arcanist, Johann Christoph Glaser, between 1742 and 1744, after which he moved on to Fürstenberg. A little porcelain was probably made around 1745 with the aid of Christian Daniel Busch, and more seems to have been made during the 1760's. In 1779, Johann Peter Dümmler, who had been at Wallendorf with the Greiners (see chapter 13), was also engaged in porcelain manufacture.

The work was, at all times, on a very limited scale, and it has even been suggested that it did not pass beyond the experimental stage. Identification of specimens is conjectural.

Bayreuth was, however, an important centre of culture at this time, as it still remains. The building of the Residence of the Markgraf, Friedrich von Brandenberg-Kulmbach, caused steadily mounting debts, and numerous architects and designers, as well as artists of all kinds, came to Bayreuth to work on this and other projects. The *faïence* factory in the suburb of Skt. Georg-am-See was fully equal to the other important factories of Ansbach and Nürnberg, and the Markgraf's consort, Frederike Sophie Wilhelmine, favourite sister of Frederick the Great, set herself to build a smaller version of Versailles. The Opera House and the Hermitage were rebuilt, the University of Erlangen founded, and an Academy of Liberal Arts started. In 1732 Wilhelmine had a cabinet decorated with porcelain, and in 1744 the Graf's room in the Hermitage was decorated with Vienna porcelain.

Johann Friedrich Metsch (or Metzsch) is one of the more important *Hausmaler*, and flourished at Bayreuth between 1735 and 1751. He was a gold-worker and enameller, and is actually recorded in the latter capacity as visiting Dresden in 1731. He announced at this time that he could paint with gold and all colours, but did not want to join the factory's staff. He asked for some white porcelain at " um billigsmassigen preis " (cheaply), but was rewarded contemptuously with one tea-service and the remark that "there are too many bunglers about".

It seems that the resentment Metsch felt at this treatment led to the attempt to suborn the Meissen workmen mentioned above. Of this number the three sons of Mehlhorn, a flower painter named Marcus Thausend, and others, were apprehended and imprisoned at Waldheim, and only Löwenfinck escaped.

It is probable that Metsch founded a painting studio at which a number of known artists worked. Joseph Philipp Dannhofer of Vienna was at Bayreuth, painting mostly on *faïence*, and the *Hofmaler*, Johann Christoph Jucht, a signed example of whose work appears on Plate 144c, is in the records as *Hofcabinetmahler* [sic] in 1751. He was also one of the decorators of Castle Dorndorf.

Jucht lived near the factory and appears in the church register of Skt. Georg-am-See in August 1743 as court painter. He married in 1744, and there are later records of the christening of his children. The register of the city church of Bayreuth shows, in August 1747, the baptism of his illegitimate son by the widow of the court accountant, J. M. Keyser: " in Unehren erzeugt " (born out of wedlock), although such things were common enough in Bayreuth at the time.

Ferdinand Teutscher of Vienna may have worked in the Metsch studio. He specialized in Dutch figures.

In 1751 Metsch went to Fürstenberg since it seems that insufficient white porcelain was forthcoming to keep him in business as an independent decorator, and the *Hausmalerei* of Bayreuth ceases abruptly. At Fürstenberg he tried to get away to the Archbishop-Elector, Klemens August von Köln, and also attempted to assist Zeschinger to leave the factory. He last appears in company with Glaser at the Malerische Akademie in Brunswick, which seems to have been regarded as a house of correction for recalcitrant artists.

The work of Metsch is not uncommon, and his painting is fairly characteristic. *Schwarzlot*, as well as figure painting, landscapes and similar things, can all be seen. He used baroque *cartouches* fairly often to enclose his painting. Allegorical and emblematical devices are frequent, and medallions with coats of arms not uncommon. These can usually be traced to south German families. Inscriptions in Latin, French and German are to be seen. His work is illustrated on Plates 144d and 145.

Rudolf Christoph von Drechsel, a court official, has been suggested as working with Metsch as an amateur on the evidence of a specimen signed *de Drechsel 1744*. This, however, may be an ownership mark and not an artist's signature (see Plate 144b).

Although the penalties were severe, a considerable amount of *Hausmalerei* was actually done in and around Meissen, particularly by the factory's artists. No doubt some of it was on porcelain legitimately acquired from the factory as *Ausschuss*[1] but some was certainly on porcelain which had been purloined. Perfect porcelain was rarely available for purchase by the outside decorator. Moreover, Höroldt would not allow engravings to be used as copies for decoration,[2] and was so conservative that he provoked Kändler to say: "He has no new ideas, but always sticks to the old ones." It is likely, therefore, that the factory's artists tried out their own new ideas in secret and sold the work privately. Most of their work would be in a flat, rather dry palette, in direct contrast to the brilliance of the factory colouring.

One of the local *Hausmaler* was Johann Georg Mehlhorn, who was employed as inspector to the grinding and polishing mill in

---

[1] Wasters, lit. rubbish.
[2] He appears to have made an exception of his own engravings of *chinoiseries*.

1709. In 1712 he was accused of stealing some red stoneware, but managed to regain Böttger's confidence, and was eventually sent to spy on Samuel Kempe at Plaue-an-der-Havel.

His sons were unfavourably regarded. A report on the Mehlhorns says that they were " alles lauter wind und Maulmacherey wie mit Meerheimen "—all hot air and talk like the Meerheims. The latter were father and son who also worked as *Hausmaler* in Dresden, and made themselves a great nuisance to the directorate. The report on Mehlhorn continues: " He can neither read nor write. Even the son has been ruined by the army—a disorderly offspring."

Johann Ernst Mehlhorn was imprisoned after a large consignment of porcelain destined for Bayreuth had gone astray. Johann Gottfried Mehlhorn, the second son, was at the factory as a painter and lacquer worker. He was imprisoned with the painter, Johann Georg Heintze, in the fortress of Königstein, and when they were discharged they led the life of wandering vagabonds for a time.

The elder Mehlhorn died in 1735, at which time his three sons were all in prison at Waldheim, as I have already recorded.

Nothing can be attributed to the Mehlhorns with certainty, and they are chiefly interesting for the sidelights thrown by their careers on the conditions existing at the factory at this time.

Another *Hausmaler* in Dresden was Augustin Dieze, born in 1696 in Rocklitz, who is first mentioned as being arrested for debt. He joined the factory in 1725, and took the oath of loyalty. He rose to be overseer of painters, but he and his wife intrigued against Höroldt and he was discharged. For some time he supported himself as a *Hausmaler*, but after ten years in the wilderness patched up his quarrel with the *Obermaler* and was reinstated, remaining at the factory until 1762. He died in 1769.

There were at the factory a father and son, both named Philipp Ernst Schindler. The father was born in 1695, son of the silversmith to the Elector, and became a painter at Meissen in 1725. He painted miniature portraits and tobacco-boxes. The work of

Schindler *père* as a *Hausmaler* lies between 1730 and 1733 when he temporarily left the factory and joined with Dieze.

His son was apprenticed to the factory as a miniature painter in 1740. In consequence of a *liaison* with an unknown woman he vanished from Meissen in 1744 without even telling his parents. Subsequently, in 1750, he reached Vienna. Here he made a successful career, following J. S. Fischer as director of painting in 1770, becoming assistant arcanist after Anreiter in 1777, and finally arcanist in succession to Klinger in 1781. He died in 1793. Some enamelled boxes are signed *Schindler fec.*

Christian Friedrich Herold, apart from his work as a factory painter, appears in the Meissen records as an unregenerate *Hausmaler*. This work was done at home, and his house was searched on more than one occasion for evidence. His relationship to Johann Gregor Höroldt has never been entirely settled, but if Marcolini can be regarded as an authority, he was a cousin: " C. F. Herold's work resembles that of his famous cousin's in many ways, the palette, harbour scenes, and so on", which suggests that some of the harbour scenes also came from the brush of the *Obermaler*. It would seem that this relationship saved him from the fate which befell others who indulged in like practices. His work on copper boxes, utilizing Meissen patterns, is signed *Herold fecit*.

Hausmalerei in Meissen did not abate, and a long and pompous edict by Augustus III dated 27th August, 1761, threatens prison for any offender who " in spite of our express wish . . . paints white Meissen porcelain with figures and other decorations and fires it in their own kilns ". Johann Balthasar Borrmann's departure for Berlin was due to his discharge from Meissen for his activities as a *Hausmaler* (Plate 136c).

The identification of work done in this way is a little difficult. The factory was always against signed work, so everything bearing a signature, or some similar means of identification such as initials, was probably done outside the factory.

Franz Ferdinand Mayer worked at Pressnitz in Bohemia. Much

of his work was on *Ausschuss* porcelain, marked with the crossed swords. It is not at all uncommon; in fact its frequency has given rise to the supposition that he had a decorating studio at which others were employed. Most of these things are similar in style and variable in quality.

Among a series of plates with Italian comedy and *genre* scenes is one inscribed *F. Mayer Cath. inv. et pinxit Ano 1747*. It is odd that he should have thus recorded his religious affiliations, but this fixes the earliest date of which we have record.

There is a contemporary note which says: " . . . das Haus des Malers Mayer in Pressnitz nebst drei Nachbarhäusen in folge eines Blitzstrahls am 27 Juni 1776 abbrante ". That is to say: " . . . the painter Mayer's house was burned down along with three of his neighbours', after being struck by lightning ".

This is the latest date, and he has, therefore, a known working life of about twenty years. His first appearance in Pressnitz seems to have been about 1752.

A great deal of his work is on outmoded porcelain of the 1720's, and his subjects were extremely varied. Much of the decorative ornament shows Augsburg influence, and there is little rococo ornament to be noticed. Flowers, such as roses, narcissi, tulips and the like, frequently appear as border decoration on plates. In his later work the colouring deteriorates, but the execution is much more painstaking. The colours are often dirty, particularly the light greens, and insects are used to cover up faults. His colours are usually dry in appearance and lacking in brilliance (Plates 147a and 148).

Little is known of F. J. Ferner. Even the whereabouts of his studio is unknown, but he used Meissen, Berlin and Vienna porcelain, as well as some from Thuringia. It is possible that he was located somewhere in the Thüringerwald. Signed specimens are known and provide the means for identification. Work in this style is far from uncommon.

Much of his work consists in over-gilding defective Meissen blue and white porcelain by adding clumsy gilt traceries with occasional flowers in enamel colours. I have observed one Vienna blue and white piece done in this way by his hand, but there may be more in existence. This kind of work is similar to that done by Dutch enamellers on Chinese blue and white porcelain and termed "clobbering".

Other examples have artlessly drawn primitive figures and flowers in a dry palette. These are usually inserted between the elements of the factory underglaze blue decoration. Apparently, to judge by stylistic variations, Ferner had some helpers, and the porcelain which they were able to obtain was often of a standard which other *Hausmaler* would have rejected as worthless (Plate 149).

Nothing is known of these other artists, although some work of this kind may be referable to a painter named Johann Michael Weiss on the evidence of a cup in the Prague Kunstgewerbe-museum dated 1746. On the other hand, several initialled pieces exist apart from this one, and it is at least as likely that these are ownership marks.

August Otto Ernst von dem Busch (1704–1779), Canon of the Collegiate of the Holy Cross at Hildesheim, did some rather unusual work which consisted of drawing the design on the glaze with a diamond, and filling in the incisions thus made with lamp-black or Indian ink. This, incidentally, will wash off, and the remedy is to renew the design with the same pigments. The Canon, of course, was an amateur decorator, and some of the work was done for the Duke Karl I for the Castle of Salzdahl, near Wolfen-büttel. The porcelain for this was obviously ordered from Meissen by the Duke, since von dem Busch was only able to get *Ausschuss* porcelain. His work also appears on the porcelain of Fürstenberg. Signed examples are in existence.

The subject matter varies very considerably. Human figures are rare, but animals and birds less so. Ruins and urns, as well as plants and flowers, form a greater part of surviving specimens (see Plate 150).

Work of the same kind was done by another Canon of Hilde-sheim, Johann Gottfried Kratzberg, from whom signed examples exist, and Canon C. A. F. Werther of Cologne passed his hours of meditation in the same way. This work appears to have been very much the preserve of the church.

This chapter discusses those of the *Hausmaler* who are important to the collector. The practice went on during the rococo period and later, but this work is not generally regarded as important, and it is not, for the most part, worth troubling about. The earlier work falls within the period when both factory and the *Hausmaler* were experimenting with new materials and processes. The factory, with all its advantages, drew ahead technically, whereas the *Hausmaler*, deprived of regular supplies of porcelain of good quality, fell steadily behind. Until 1760, however, work of this kind was often fully comparable with that of the factory and in consequence is sought after as an important addition to collections of German porcelain of the period.

About 1763 Meissen instituted a system of cancelling the mark on porcelain sold in white to *Hausmaler*. A cut was incised into the glaze, usually across the centre of the crossed swords. This indicates that the decoration was not done at the factory. Two cuts are said to indicate defective porcelain painted at Meissen, but this is not certain. Decoration of porcelain thus marked is generally poor in quality, but there are exceptions. It is nearly always possible to see distinct variations from normal factory work.

15

FORGERIES

FEW marks have been so consistently abused and misused as that of the Meissen crossed swords. Starting in the eighteenth century with the Thuringian factories, the copying of Meissen marks has gone on ever since.

To detect the really competent forgeries of the more important kinds of German porcelain is an excellent test of connoisseurship, since there is comparatively little difference in paste and glaze between the old and the new, and the indications must be sought elsewhere—in the colouring, which is usually the safest test, and in the modelling so far as figures are concerned. Service-ware is not copied so frequently with serious intent to deceive, although reproductions and archaizing patterns are common enough. The drawing is often sufficient to reveal the fraud.

Some of the existing German factories still copy the old models, and whether or not this is done with fraudulent intent can be decided from the marks, which should clearly record the fact that they are modern manufacture in some way or another. During the nineteenth century, as I have recorded elsewhere in this volume, the old moulds were used to reproduce early work, an example being the recasting of some Ludwigsburg figures at Amberg.

Höchst figures have been copied in porcelain, sometimes from the old moulds, which were certainly in existence in the nineteenth century. Some of these emanated from the firm of Dressel, Kister & Co. of Passau, and are fairly dangerous. Earthenware copies from the same original moulds are to be seen, but can easily be identified by the difference in the materials used.

Almost equally misused is the royal monogram of Augustus, "AR". This was used extensively in the nineteenth century by Madame Helena Wolfsohn of Dresden, more particularly on quatrefoil cups and saucers decorated alternately with panels of flowers, usually on a turquoise or a yellow ground, and Watteau figures, copied from a not unusual type of the 1740's. This monogram, originally, was put only on things for royal use, or intended as royal gifts, and certainly not at any time on cups and saucers of this kind. Neither the colouring nor the drawing is in the least deceptive to anyone acquainted with genuine examples, and it is doubtful whether the lady really thought her work could be passed off as belonging to the eighteenth century. After a lawsuit with the factory, she was obliged to change her mark to a crown, with "Dresden" in script underneath, and this is the "Crown Dresden" of the provincial auctioneer. It is of no value to the collector and student.

The copies of Karl Thieme of Potschappel are sometimes dangerous to the less experienced eye, and Edmé Samson et Cie. of the Rue Béranger, Paris, have reproduced Meissen figures as they have reproduced almost everything else. They state that their copies always have an "S" added to the crossed swords, but I have certainly seen Samson figures without it, although the identifying "S" may have been removed subsequently for questionable purposes. Weise of Dresden have made some uncommonly good copies which are only accused by the colouring. Those of the Voigt Brothers of Sitzendorf are tawdry, but are often offered as Dresden. They used a mark consisting of two lines crossed by a third, which has a colourable resemblance to a rarely used factory mark.

It is a good general statement that eighteenth-century figures have brown eyes, whereas blue-eyed figures are later, but like

EGP—Q

most things of its kind, it is an over-simplification, and brown eyes by themselves prove nothing. Brown pigment was certainly not unknown in the nineteenth century, nor is it unknown today. Unless all the other points correspond, therefore, it is not a reliable guide.

It is a good test to look at the painting. Most eighteenth-century work was done painstakingly, and with meticulous attention to detail. The decoration of later copies is usually slovenly, and carelessly carried out, often with inaccurate colours and sketchy drawing. It is also extremely difficult for a forger to keep out of his work the artistic idiom of his time, and although it is not always easy to detect contemporary forgeries, the sugary sentiment of nineteenth-century work is usually evident to twentieth-century eyes. The difference can be well seen by comparing the Wolfsohn panels already mentioned with an eighteenth-century example of the same thing. The difference sticks out like a sore thumb.

Chromium oxide came into use early in the nineteenth century and this substance yields a peculiar opaque green, and a maroon pigment, both of which are comparatively easily recognized. Their presence on something purporting to be eighteenth-century work immediately condemns.

The red stoneware of Meissen was the subject of many contemporary copies, the closest being made at Plaue-an-der-Havel. The brown-glazed ware of Bayreuth and Ansbach, which is certainly inspired by Böttger's stoneware, only resembles it superficially. The Meissen examples are the hardest ever to be made, and very few files will so much as scratch it. Most of the copies are much softer. Copies have been made during the nineteenth and twentieth centuries at various factories.

Forgeries are often given chips and scratches which add to the appearance of age, and they may even have been broken and restored to give an air of verisimilitude. These things should be borne in mind when making an assessment.

Perhaps the greatest single safeguard is to remember that eighteenth-century factories, especially during the early period, had no exact methods of preparing materials in a pure state, nor were they able to control the manufacturing processes with the precision possible later. This led to many minor defects of one kind or another, of which the " firecrack " is the most obvious. Forgeries are usually " slick ", with a glossy glaze and a " machine-finished " appearance.

The *Hausmaler* are a frequent source of embarrassment to the student. Their work often diverges considerably from the more usual styles of factory decoration. Eighteenth-century painting from such outside sources needs to be judged in relation to the standards attained by the factory at the time, and valued accordingly. The work of Bottengruber, for instance, judged by any standards, is at least as important as anything done at the time in the factory workshops. Generally, forgers tend to keep to established factory styles, and do not often venture on to the manifestly unsafe ground of the unusual. The inquiring state of mind aroused by an unusual example is something they wish to avoid.

Fakes are not particularly numerous in German porcelain, and the practice of cleaning off slight decoration with hydrofluoric acid in order to redecorate in more valuable styles is, in my experience, confined to French and English porcelain. Possibly this is due to the nature of the feldspathic glaze used at the German factories. On the other hand, much white German porcelain from all factories has been coloured subsequently.

The only possible way of learning to detect forgeries is to live with genuine examples. The habits of mind thus engendered will enable the student to recognize the often trivial differences which even the cleverest forger cannot avoid or conceal. It is necessary to look at all divergences from what appears to be normal. There may be a perfectly good explanation for them, but they should not go unquestioned. It is equally foolish to regard the unusual as necessarily fraudulent. The correct attitude is one of scepticism, tempered by a willingness to be convinced if observation justifies a change of mind.

A few additional remarks on forgeries and reproductions will also be found elsewhere in this volume in the appropriate chapters.

APPENDIX I

GERMAN porcelain is usually well-marked. Nevertheless, a mark is neither a safe nor satisfactory test of genuineness. At best it can only provide confirmatory evidence. This list includes all the more usual marks to be found, but, for the sake of brevity, it omits workmen's marks, and marks which are self-explanatory, e.g. " Gera ", which is sometimes used in full under topographical paintings of this town. For a more detailed list the reader is referred to Honey (*Dictionary of European Ceramic Art*) or Chaffers (*Marks and Monograms*), where the various ancillary marks are recorded in full.

ℵℙℳ   MEISSEN. 1723–1724. For Königliche Porzellan Manufaktur. Also " K.P.F." (Königliche Porzellan Fabrik) and " M.P.M." (Meissner Porzellan Manufaktur).

    MEISSEN. 1723 onwards. The caduceus (*Merkurstab*) used principally on coffee-cups for the Turkish market.

    MEISSEN. 1725 onwards. Date of cessation doubtful, but prior to 1763. The monogram of

Augustus, for Augustus Rex.   Used generally on pieces intended for royal gifts or for the Elector's personal use.

MEISSEN.   An early version, about 1725. The mark was introduced about 1724. The crossed swords from the Electoral Arms of Saxony.

MEISSEN.   The usual type of mark appearing in the 1740's.

MEISSEN.   1763–1774. The Academic Period (*Die Punktzeit*).

MEISSEN.   1774–1814. The Marcolini Period. The asterisk between the *points* at an earlier period on blue painted ware is a workman's mark.

VIENNA.   Du Paquier Period. 1719–1744.   An imitation Chinese seal-mark. Other imitations of Chinese marks have been recorded.

VIENNA.   1744–1749. Impressed. An early version.

VIENNA.   1749–1820. Painted in blue. The impressed shield was used again after 1820.

NYMPHENBURG.   1754–1765. The early variety.

NYMPHENBURG.   *c.* 1765–1780.

NYMPHENBURG.   Used from 1763 to 1767 on some specimens. The hexagon mark. This was painted in underglaze blue.

HÖCHST.   1750–1796. In crimson or purple. Slight variations from time to time. The mark also occurs (rarely) in an impressed form.

HÖCHST.   Probably between 1765–1774. The wheel surmounted by the Electoral Crown.

PH   FRANKENTHAL.   Impressed. Mark of Paul Hannong. Also to be found on Strasbourg porcelain.

FRANKENTHAL. 1756–1759. Lion from the Arms of the Palatinate. Sometimes found in conjunction with "IH" impressed, for Joseph Hannong, who owned the factory from 1759 to 1762.

 FRANKENTHAL. *c.* 1756. In blue. From the Electoral Arms.

 FRANKENTHAL. With slight variations from 1762 to 1793. The commonest mark. The monogram of the Elector, Carl Theodor.

W BERLIN. Wegely's factory. Impressed and in blue.

G BERLIN. 1761–1763. Gotzkowsky's factory. In blue underglaze.

Ɣ BERLIN. 1765–1770. The sceptre mark.

ǀ BERLIN. 1770–1800.

ℱ FÜRSTENBERG. In blue. This, and the following mark, are early. Later, it was added much more sketchily.

ℱ FÜRSTENBERG. In blue.

 LUDWIGSBURG. 1758–1793. The monogram of Carl Eugen, Duke of Württemberg. Usually in blue.

 LUDWIGSBURG. Another version of the mark listed above. Late marks are often crudely drawn.

 LUDWIGSBURG. Late eighteenth century. Stag's antler from the Arms of Württemberg.

A ANSBACH. The "A" is for the Markgraf, Alexander. In blue.

B ANSBACH. Impressed.

ANSBACH. Sometimes found with the "A" beneath.

HD KELSTERBACH. From 1768 to the end of the century. In blue or manganese. For Hesse-Darmstadt.

HD KELSTERBACH. From 1766, but usually a late mark. In blue or impressed.

F FULDA. From c. 1780. For Fürstlich Fuldaisch. The *Heinrichsmarke*.

+ FULDA. From c. 1765 to 1780. An early mark.

HC HESSE-CASSEL. In blue. It appears on the figures illustrated on Plate 126b.

T. TETTAU. From 1794 onwards.

R GOTHA. From at least 1783.

R.g GOTHA. From 1783 to 1805. For Rotberg (?).

G GOTHA. From the end of the eighteenth century. A late mark.

W WALLENDORF. c. 1778 onwards. This should not be confused with the mark of Wegely's Berlin factory.

W WALLENDORF. An early mark imitating Meissen.

Y VOLKSTEDT. 1760–1799. A pseudo-Meissen mark.

R VOLKSTEDT. 1799 onwards. Period of Greiner and Holzapfel.

C·V· KLOSTER-VEILSDORF. 1760–1797. The commonest mark.

CV KLOSTER–VEILSDORF. Probably before 1765. Rare.

✛ KLOSTER-VEILSDORF. From 1797 onwards. Also used at Limbach, Groszbreitenbach and Ilmenau from about 1788.

ℒ LIMBACH. 1772–1788.

᙭ LIMBACH. An imitation Meissen mark.

φ LIMBACH. After 1788. Clover-leaf. Also used at Kloster-Veilsdorf, Groszbreitenbach and Ilmenau.

i ILMENAU. c. 1792.

G GERA. The name is sometimes inscribed in full.

R RAUENSTEIN. This, and the following mark, from about 1783 onwards.

R - n RAUENSTEIN.

APPENDIX II

SELECTED BIBLIOGRAPHY

BAYER, A. *Ansbacher Porzellan* (Ansbach, 1933).

BERLING, K. *Meissner Porzellan und Seine Geschichte* (Leipzig, 1900).

BERLING, K. *Festschrift der königlichen sächsischen Porzellanmanufaktur Meissen, 1710-1910.* Also an English translation entitled: *Publication to commemorate the 200th Jubilee of the oldest European Porcelain Factory* (very rare).

BRAUN, E. W., AND FOLNESICS, J. *Geschichte der k.k. Wiener Porzellan manufaktur* (Vienna, 1907).

CHRIST, HANS. *Ludwigsburger Porzellanfiguren* (Berlin, 1921).

GRAUL, R., AND KURZWELLY, A. *Alt-Thüringer Porzellan* (Leipzig, 1909).

HANDT AND RAKEBRAND. *Meissner Porzellan des Achtzehnten Jahrhunderts, 1710-1750.* (Dresden, 1957).

HANNOVER, EMIL. *Pottery and Porcelain* (Benn, London, 1925).

HAYWARD, J. F. *Vienna Porcelain of the Du Paquier Period* (Rockliff, London, 1952).

HOFMANN, FRIEDRICH H. *Frankenthaler Porzellan* (F. Bruckmann A.G., Munich, 1911).

HOFMANN, FRIEDRICH H. *Geschichte der bayerischen Porzellan-manufaktur Nymphenburg* (Karl Hiersemann, Leipzig, 1921-3).

HOFMANN, FRIEDRICH H. *Das Porzellan der europäischen Manu-fakturen im 18ten. Jahrhundert* (Propyläenverlag, Berlin, 1932).

HONEY, W. B. *A Dictionary of European Ceramic Art* (Faber, London, 1952).

HONEY, W. B. *Dresden China* (Faber, London, 1947).

HONEY, W. B. *German Porcelain* (Faber, London, 1947).

LENZ, G. *Berliner Porzellan: Die Manufaktur Friedrichs des Grossen, 1763-86* (Berlin, 1913).

MEYER, H. *Böhmisches Porzellan und Steingut* (Leipzig, 1927).

PAZAUREK, GUSTAV E. *Deutsche Fayence- und Porzellan-Hausmaler* (Hiersemann, Leipzig, 1928).

PAZAUREK, GUSTAV E. *Meissner Porzellanmalerei des 18ten. Jahrhunderts* (Stuttgart, 1929).

RÖDER, K., AND OPPENHEIM, M. *Das Höchster Porzellan* (Mainz, 1930).

SAUERLANDT, M. *Deutsche Porzellanfiguren des 18ten. Jahrhunderts* (Cologne, 1923).

SCHERER, C. *Das Fürstenberger Porzellan* (Berlin, 1909).

SCHMIDT, ROBERT. *Das Porzellan als Kunstwerk und Kultur-spiegel* (Munich, 1925).[1]

SCHNORR VON CAROLSFELD, L. *Porzellan der europäischen Fabriken des 18ten. Jahrhunderts* (Berlin, 1912).

SCHÖNBERGER, ARNO. *Meissener Porzellan mit Höroldt-molerei.* (Darmstadt *c.* 1955).

ZIMMERMANN, ERNST. *Die Erfindung und Frühzeit des Meissner Porzellans* (Berlin, 1908).

ZIMMERMANN, ERNST. *Meissner Porzellan* (Leipzig, 1926).

[1] Translated by W. A. Thorpe as *Porcelain as an Art and Mirror of Fashion* (Harrap, London, 1932).

INDEX OF PLACES

229

INDEX OF SUBJECTS

231

INDEX OF PERSONS

236